The Global Hunger Crisis

THE GLOBAL HUNGER CRISIS

Tackling Food Insecurity in Developing Countries

Majda Bne Saad

PlutoPress
www.plutobooks.com

First published 2013 by Pluto Press
345 Archway Road, London N6 5AA

www.plutobooks.com

Distributed in the United States of America exclusively by
Palgrave Macmillan, a division of St. Martin's Press LLC,
175 Fifth Avenue, New York, NY 10010

British Library Cataloguing in Publication Data
A catalogue record for this book is available from the British Library

ISBN   978 0 7453 3068 6   Hardback
ISBN   978 0 7453 3067 9   Paperback
ISBN   978 1 8496 4860 8   PDF eBook
ISBN   978 1 8496 4862 2   Kindle eBook
ISBN   978 1 8496 4861 5   EPUB eBook

Library of Congress Cataloging in Publication Data applied for

This book is printed on paper suitable for recycling and made from fully managed
and sustained forest sources. Logging, pulping and manufacturing processes are
expected to conform to the environmental standards of the country of origin.

10   9   8   7   6   5   4   3   2   1

Designed and produced for Pluto Press by Chase Publishing Services Ltd
Typeset from disk by Stanford DTP Services, Northampton, England
Simultaneously printed digitally by CPI Antony Rowe, Chippenham, UK and
Edwards Bros in the United States of America

To Zaid, Haider, Noah and Jacob

Contents

Illustrations

BOXES

DIAGRAMS

Abbreviations and Acronyms

ADB	Asian Development Bank
AoA	Agreement on Agriculture
AMCEN	African Ministerial Conference on the Environment
AMS	Aggregate Measure of Support
BMI	body mass index
BMR	base metabolic rate
BRAC	Bangladesh Rural Advancement Committee
CAP	Common Agricultural Policy
CGAP	Consultative Group to Assist the Poorest
CIDA	Canadian International Development Agency
CMR	crude mortality rate
CTE	consumer tax equivalent
CUTS	Consumer Unity and Trust Society
DAWN	Development Alternative with Women in a New Era
DNA	deoxyribo nucleic acid
rDNA	recombinant DNA
DPPC	Disaster Prevention and Preparedness Commission
EALA	East African Legislative Assembly
EC	European Commission
ECPUTW	Economic Convention on Protection and use of Transboundary Water Resources and International Lakes
EEC	exchange entitlement collapse
EIP	ecologically integrated paradigm
ESCWA	UN Economic and Social Commission for West Asia
EU	European Union
FAO	Food and Agriculture Organization of the United Nations
FAD	food availability decline
FED	food entitlement decline
EWS	early warning system
G8	Group of Eight
GAD	gender and development
GATT	General Agreement on Tariffs and Trade
GB	Grameen Bank
GDP	gross domestic product

GFC	global financial crisis
GHG	greenhouse gas
GM	gender mainstreaming
GMO	genetically modified organism
GNI	gross national incomes
GP	general practitioner
GR	Green Revolution
HIV/AIDS	human immunodeficiency virus/acquired immune deficiency syndrome
HYV	high yielding variety seeds
IAASTD	International Assessment of Agricultural Knowledge, Science and Technology for Development
IATRC	International Agricultural Trade Research Consortium
IIED	Institute for Environment and Development
ICT	information communication technology
IDA	iron deficiency anemia
IDD	iodine deficiency disorder
IFAD	International Fund for Agricultural Development
IATRC	International Agricultural Trade Research Consortium
IFC	International Financial Corporation
IFIs	international financial institutions
IFPRI	International Food Policy Research Institute
IMF	International Monetary Fund
IPM	integrated pest management
IRBM	integrated river basin management
IWRM	integrated water resources management
LSIP	life sciences integrated paradigm
MC	marketing cooperative
MDGs	Millennium Development Goals
MFI	microfinance institution
MIS	management information systems
MLAR	market-led agrarian reform
MUAC	mid-upper arm circumference
NAFTA	North American Free Trade Agreement
NFIDCs	net food importing developing countries
NGDOs	non-governmental development organisations
NGOs	non-governmental organisations
NPS	non product specific
NRA	nominal rate of assistance
ODA	official development assistance

ODI	Overseas Development Institute
OECD	Organisation of Economic Cooperation and Development
PCM	protein-calorie malnutrition
PEM	protein-energy malnutrition
PP	productionist paradigm
RNA	rural non-farm activities
RRA	relative rate of assistance
SADC	Southern Arica Development Community
SAPs	structural adjustment programmes
SIDA	Swedish International Cooperation Agency
SMEs	small- and medium-sized enterprises
SRI	system of rice intensification
TRQs	tariff-rate quotas
UN	United Nations
UNCED	United Nations Conference on Environment and Development
UNDP	United Nation Development Programme
UNEP	United Nation Environment Programme
UNESCO	United Nation Economic Scientific and Cultural Organisation
UNESCAP	United Nation Economic Scientific and Social Commission for Asia and Pacific
UNFCCC	United Nations Framework Convention on Climate Change
UNICEF	United Nation International Children's Fund
UNSCN	United Nation Standing Committee on Nutrition
UNU	United Nations University
UNWWDR	United Nations World Water Development Report
US	United States of America
USAID	United States Aid Agency
USDA	United States Department of Agriculture
WFS	world food system
WHO	World Health Organisation
WID	women in development
WIDER	World Institute for Development Economic Research
WRM	water resource management
WTO	World Trade Organisation
VAD	vitamin A deficiency

Preface

Globally, we are moving into major and unprecedented food crises. The volatility of world food prices has increased dramatically over the last six years; for example, prices for maize, wheat, and rice have risen by an average of 180 per cent. Among the many reasons for this new trend are: climate change; the increased demand for food (especially milk and meat) in the emerging economies; increasing prices for oil and agricultural inputs; and support and subsidies for the alternative use of food commodities as biofuel. There are declining food stocks and export restrictions on food by traditional exporting countries, plus the impact of stock market speculation. Higher prices are likely to boost supply, but they also affect the purchasing power, and hence the nutritional intake, of the bottom billion people in poorer countries.

Analysts indicate that the number of malnourished people in South East Asia in 2011 was 600 million, and they estimate that the number in Africa could treble to 600 million as the world's population grows by more than a third over the coming decades. A new demographic analysis indicates that there needs to be a 'second Green Revolution' to produce more food as the global population rises from 7 billion in 2011 to an estimated 9.2 billion by 2050.

Two-thirds of the world's malnourished people live in only seven countries, almost all of them in sub-Saharan Africa and South East Asia. Some questions require serious analysis: first, how can low-income, food deficit, agriculture-based countries increase their food production while continuing to improve their production of export crops? In other words, what are the factors constraining these nations from achieving food self-sufficiency and food security. We know that overall national self-sufficiency in food is not a sufficient condition for achieving food security for every individual in the country, so there is a clear need for specific policies that target the poor and vulnerable and that aim to generate income and enhance their entitlement to food.

This book is based on courses I teach at postgraduate level on food security and famines, with special reference to the food-insecure in low-income developing countries. In this subject area, there is a marked lack of course material, at both undergraduate and postgraduate levels, for students from a multidisciplinary academic background. This book attempts to make a contribution to the academic fields of development studies, agriculture, and rural development, and to be relevant to a range of related areas such as international development, globalisation, geography, and environmental studies. It is hoped that its non-technical and practical approach will also appeal to those looking for an introduction or means of refreshing and updating their knowledge on these subjects, including policymakers and development practitioners.

Part I of the book contains four chapters, which address: the causes and consequences of food insecurity; chronic and transitory food insecurity (famine); world food systems and their limitations in relation to combating hunger; and peasants' farming, its limitations, and future prospects. Part II contains a further six chapters on the factors constraining stable and sustainable food production in Net Food Importing Developing Countries (NFIDCs): access to land; determinants of rural labour markets in agriculture-based countries; rural financial services; water for livelihoods; and gender and food security. The final chapter of the book, 'Food Security in Perspective', provides the conclusion.

The content of the book reflects the experiences and research interests of its author and her continuing interest in food security and the food policies of developing countries.

Acknowledgements

Many people supported the idea of writing this book and the work that has gone into its preparation. First of all, I thank my students, who have made valuable contributions throughout the years of teaching agriculture and rural development policies, food security, and famines. With great appreciation I would like to thank John Coakley for his comments on the idea of the book and David Farrell, head of the School of Politics and International Relations in University College Dublin, for reading chapter abstracts. I am grateful to the anonymous reviewers and their valuable insights which helped to shape the book's content and direction. I am grateful to Stephen Devereux, Institute of Development Studies, Sussex University, who read Chapter 2, and to Simon Maxwell, former director of the Overseas Development Institute London, who read Chapter 1, for being generous with their time and for providing their valuable comments and advice, as well as guiding me to the right literature. Special thanks should go to Stephen McGroarty of the World Bank for his help and generosity in providing me with much-needed information on up-to-date sources of books and reports. I extend my sincere gratitude to Wendy Cox for reading the entire manuscript and for making many valuable comments and suggestions. I would like to extend my sincere gratitude and appreciation to the Pluto team, especially Roger, David and Robert for their unfailing, efficient and friendly support throughout the preparations for this book. And for Dan Harding I say thank you for his excellent editorial work, which is greatly appreciated. Thank you to Melanie Patrick for impressive work on the cover design and my great appreciation for their work on the book goes to Dave and Sue Stanford and to Sue Carlton for compiling the book's index. Finally, I am so grateful to all those authors who have put their research in the public realm and whose work I have drawn on extensively. Needless to say, any errors of interpretation or expression remain entirely my own responsibility.

Majda Bne Saad
University College Dublin
April 2012

Introduction

Over the last three decades, the world food situation in terms of food availability and prices has been characterised by dramatically different trends at different times. In the mid-1970s, the world was beset by acute food shortages and high food prices associated with increased oil prices. Then, during the 1980s, the prices of staple foods fell to their lowest levels in real terms since the 1920s, due to the structural overproduction of food in the industrial farming systems of the United States of America (US) and European Union (EU), and the resulting accumulation of surpluses which outstripped domestic and international growth in demand for food. At the same time, the debt crisis of the early 1980s, along with rising food self-sufficiency in key Asian markets, including India, Pakistan, and Indonesia, and falling oil prices, all constrained demand from developing countries for imported food. Then, a shift in policy in the US, designed to stabilise prices, meant that farmers there had to reduce production to consumption level. This was followed by the EU decision to reform the Common Agricultural Policy (CAP) and to end the 'food mountains' created by dumping, export-support subsidies, and food aid.

In the mid-1990s food prices again increased due to high oil prices and further problems with food supply, all of which contributed to the accelerated rate of inflation experienced by consumers in developing countries. In 1996, double-digit increases were reported for grains, vegetable oils, meats, seafood, sugar, bananas and various other commodities that represent the basic staples of human consumption (Trostle 2008: 8).

Soon after the start of the twenty-first century world food commodity prices started to increase steadily and have reached historically high levels, with nominal peaks in mid-2008 (Abbott and de Battisti 2009: 4). In particular, the price of wheat and rice more than tripled in international markets, while maize and soybean prices more than doubled. High energy prices, the declining dollar, biofuels, and patterns of demand that exceeded supply all played a role. In addition, 'starving your neighbour' policies, whereby many countries that were surplus producers closed off or reduced their exports in an effort to ensure food security at home, have proved disruptive (ibid).

1

High and volatile global food prices, along with rising energy prices, are contributing to macroeconomic instability in many countries. For net importers, the average impact on terms-of-trade can be very significant, and can exacerbate high current-account deficits. It is estimated that more than 100 million additional people are falling into poverty. Higher prices may also heighten inequality within countries – the effects of food prices on child malnutrition, and the vulnerability of many children living in conditions of conflict, instability, and drought, are already visible (Lin 2008: 3).

While most experts agree that there is no single reason for the current crisis, many explicitly blame speculation in commodity futures markets for inflating food prices. Evidence shows that there is a growing use of commodity futures as an asset class, and investors who traditionally invested in stocks and bonds have recognised that diversifying their investment portfolios by using commodities reduces the overall risk level and therefore increases returns (Abbott and de Battisti 2009: 11).

Experts in futures markets reject this argument, asserting that price changes must be accompanied by quantity adjustments, so that some end users must be paying the high prices for final uses or stock holding. They further argue that present transaction volumes are not out of line with past high-price events, and suggest that in fact there may be inadequate speculation in the markets (Sanders et al., in Abbott and de Battisti 2009: 11).

A dependence on the markets for food is dangerous if markets are unreliable, so that 'response failure' during a food crisis is possible. Markets can fail to function well either intertemporally or spatially. ÓGráda (2009: 144) points out: 'most populist critiques of how markets worked during famines focused on the intertemporal aspect. They held that traders often, if not always, tended to underestimate the size of the harvest in poor years, and thus engage in "excessive" storage'. Moreover, 'hoarding food, whether for precautionary or speculative reasons, can magnify food shortages and price rises, exaggerated fears of future shortages result in panic hoarding beyond what is justified in reality' (Devereux 1993: 187).

Developing countries' responses to the current situation vary from one country to another, but reactions include: altering trade and domestic agricultural policies in an attempt to stabilise the domestic market; reducing tariffs and taxes on imports; increasing food subsidies; imposing export taxes to protect domestic users;

and in some extreme cases banning exports (Abbott and de Battisti 2009: 2).

Some countries, as a result of the collapse of confidence in the international grain market and out of fear of future trends, are opting to achieve self-sufficiency in food and to rebuild their own public reserves. Lin (2008: 6) argues that: 'no doubt this will have its own implications for the world food trade system'.

Many writers agree that combating hunger and promoting food security in low-income food deficit countries requires long-term strategies involving promoting efficient growth in the food and agriculture sectors through:

- Accelerated agricultural output growth via technological, institutional, and price incentive changes designed to raise the productivity of small farmers;
- Rising domestic demand for agricultural output, derived from an employment-oriented urban development strategy; and
- Diversified, non-agricultural, labour-intensive rural development activities that directly and indirectly support, and are supported by, the farming community (see for example, Mellor 1986; Tovar et al. 1987; Ellis 1992).

Thus, an agriculture- and employment-based strategy for economic development requires, as a minimum, three basic and complementary elements:

- Improving income distribution, and enhancing the purchasing power of the poor by increasing productivity and employment;
- Achieving a satisfactory nutritional status for the entire population through the provision of a minimum-subsistence 'floor' which meets basic needs; and
- Establishing adequate food availability to insure against bad harvests, natural disasters, or uncertain food supplies and high prices (Tovar et al. 1987; Mellor 1990; World Bank 2007).

Henceforth, what is the best way to get agriculture moving in low-income food deficit countries? Historical evidence shows that success stories abound about agriculture as the basis for growth at the beginning of the development process. Agricultural growth was the precursor of the industrial revolutions that spread across the temperate regions of the world, from England in the mid-eighteenth century to Japan in the late nineteenth century (see Stevens and

Jabara 1988; Eicher and Staatz 1990). More recently, in China, India, Vietnam and Ghana, rapid agricultural growth was the precursor of the rise of industry and of poverty alleviation (World Bank 2007: 44–7).

Estimates from many countries show that GDP growth originating from agriculture is at least twice as effective in reducing poverty as GDP growth originating from industry and services (World Bank 2007: 46). China's institutional innovations, which included assigning user rights for individual plots of land to rural households, the use of 'high yielding variety' (HYV) seeds, and partial price-liberalisation, were accompanied by major declines in rural poverty: from 76 per cent in the early 1970s to 12 per cent in 2001. In India, technological innovations, including the adoption of HYV crops, the use of fertilisers, stabilisation of the water supply, and provision of credit to farmers, led to a 34 per cent reduction in both rural and urban poverty. Ghana's agricultural growth, due to better economic policies, an improved investment climate, high commodity prices, and particularly the expansion of the area under cultivation, alongside increased use of fertilisers, led to a decrease in poverty levels from about 52 per cent in 1999 to 24 per cent in 2006 (ibid.).

Thus, Part I of this book raises the following questions: Will these new trends of high and increasing volatility in world food prices continue into the future and what kind of impact will they have on the rest of the world, and specifically on the food insecure in low-income food deficit countries? Part II discusses the agricultural development challenges and options in low-income food deficit countries, and asks why some nations have been successful in increasing farm productivity and agricultural production per capita, while other nations have achieved little growth.

There are ten chapters in this book, including the conclusion; a brief description of each is as follows:

Chapter 1 explores the concepts of food security and insecurity and the costs of food insecurity to individuals and nations. It provides discussions on how the current food-security situation is more complicated than 'scarcity amidst plenty', and shows that the current crisis is somewhat different from the crises of 1973–1975.

Chapter 2 examines famine as a sequence of 'entitlement failures' and explores how famine has been explained in the literature. Starting with the pre-modern view of famine in terms of 'food availability decline' (FAD), it goes on to examine the modern view of famine which emphasises failure of access to food that is 'food entitlement decline' (FED), and then to a postmodern explanation which focuses on failures of accountability and of national and international responses.

Chapter 3 examines the world food system and a number of key drivers for change in terms of the paradigms used in food production worldwide. It goes on to discuss these changes, elaborating on the 'productionist' approach (that is, Green Revolution/industrial agriculture); the life sciences and the ecologically integrated approaches highlighting both the advantages and limitations of each. Finally some suggestions are made for using affordable and environmentally sustainable approaches to improve the productivity of small farmers in low-income food deficit regions in developing countries.

Chapter 4 focuses on the question of food supply in low-income food deficit countries. It describes the main characteristics of peasants' farming systems and identifies the constraints facing peasants' societies within the wider changes that have taken place in national as well as world political, economic, and agrarian systems.

Chapter 5 examines the diversity and types of land tenure systems in developing countries, and analyses the wide range of land tenure options available to farmers, which could enable them to respond strategically and effectively to changing market conditions, opportunities, and external environmental constraints. It analyses the successes and failures associated with state-led land and agrarian reforms and elaborates on market-led land reform, and women's access to land.

Chapter 6 deals with the question of the human resources that are available to the agricultural sector. It examines the structure and main characteristics of rural labour markets, elaborating on the factors affecting the supply of and demand for labour in rural areas, including the impacts of population growth and the HIV/AIDS pandemic.

Chapter 7 examines credit institutions, both formal and informal, focusing on micro-credit institutions and the conditions required for their sustainability.

Chapter 8 examines irrigation, water supply, and the existing constraints (legal, political, social, economic, technical, and environmental) hindering low- and middle-income countries in Asia and Africa from providing a stable and sustainable supply of water to their food and agricultural production.

Part I

Food Security and Insecurity: Causes and Consequences

1
Food Security

Food security has been a centrepiece of food and agricultural policy discussion since the food crises of the 1970s, and it has risen to prominence since 2007 among national governments, multilateral and bilateral institutions, and non-governmental organisations following the recent food crisis.

No one really knows how many people are malnourished. The statistics most frequently cited are that of the Food and Agriculture Organization of the United Nations (FAO), which measures 'undernutrition', with the most recent estimate, released on 14 October 2009, indicating that 1.02 billion people are hungry, 15 per cent of the estimated world population in that year of 6.8 billion. This represents a sizeable increase from its 2006 estimate of 854 million people. Almost all of the undernourished are in developing countries, in which about 11 million children under five die each year. Malnutrition and hunger-related diseases cause 60 per cent of these deaths (UNICEF 2007).

This chapter begins by defining food security and insecurity, and goes on to trace the evolution of these concepts since the 1970s. It provides some discussions on the costs of chronic food insecurity and malnutrition to individuals and nations. The chapter then examines the causes of food insecurity, both chronic and transitory, elaborating on the factors behind the repeated occurrences of transitory food insecurity. Finally, it is imperative to examine the key factors that caused the 1972–1973 food crises, and to consider whether the same factors have been operating since then, leading to the most recent crisis of 2007 and beyond.

WHAT IS FOOD SECURITY?

Concern with food insecurity can be traced back to the first-world food crisis of 1972–1974 and beyond that at least to President Franklin D. Roosevelt's 'State of the Union Address' on 6 January 1941, before the US entered the Second World War, in which he spoke of 'four essential freedoms': freedom of speech, freedom of faith, freedom from want, and freedom from fear (Rosenman, in Shaw 2007: 3).

In 1943, the FAO's founding conference was organised to consider the goal of freedom from want in relation to food and agriculture. Freedom from want was defined then as 'a secure, an adequate, and a suitable supply of food for every man' (FAO, in Shaw 2007: 3).

The overall objective of the conference was to promote the idea of ensuring 'an abundant supply of the right kinds of food for all mankind', with a clear emphasis on nutritional standards as a guide for governmental agricultural and economic policies for improving the nutrition and health of the world's population. The conference declaration also recognised the causes of hunger and proposed some solutions (Shaw 2007: 3):

- Poverty is the first cause of malnutrition and hunger;
- Increasing food production will ensure availability but nations have to provide the markets to absorb it, thus, an expansion of the world economy should provide the purchasing power needed to maintain an adequate diet for all. Clear emphasis is put on the need for opportunities to create jobs, enlarged industrial production, and the elimination of labour exploitation;
- With an increasing flow of trade within and between countries, better management of domestic and international investment and currencies, and sustained internal and international economic growth, the food which is produced can be made available to all people.

During 1973, the world witnessed the most publicised food crisis, triggered by rising oil prices and consequently increasing input prices for items such as fertiliser and transport costs, in addition to a bad harvest year in the former Soviet Union, China, and India (Mackie 1974). These combined with the gradually increasing demand to absorb worldwide grain reserves (Leathers and Foster 2004). In the face of this crisis, the FAO held an international conference in 1974 at which the 'Universal Declaration on the Eradication of Hunger and Malnutrition' 'solemnly proclaimed' that 'every man, woman and child has the inalienable right to be free from hunger and malnutrition in order to develop fully and maintain their physical and mental faculties'. The Declaration recognised the role of governments, and urged the participants to work together for increased food production and a more equitable and efficient distribution of food between and within countries. It reiterated that 'all countries, big and small, rich or poor, are equal. All countries have a full right to participate in decisions on the food problem'. It also provided a definition of a world food security system (UN 1975: 2):

> The wellbeing of the peoples of the world largely depends on the adequate production and distribution of food as well as the establishment of a world food security system which would insure adequate availability of, and reasonable prices for, food at all times, irrespective of periodic fluctuations and vagaries of weather conditions, and free of political and economic pressures, and should thus facilitate, amongst other things, the development process of developing countries.

Despite this clear understanding of the complexity of the issue of food insecurity, the policy trends of the 1970s were largely concerned with ensuring national and global food supplies to satisfy the most urgent emergencies and needs in low-income food deficit countries. The annotated bibliography compiled by Maxwell and Frankenberger (1992) contains 200 items, which together trace the evolution of the concept of 'food security' from concern with national food stocks in the 1970s (declining food availability) to a preoccupation with individual entitlements in the 1980s, and to accountability failures, the failure of informal safety nets, food aid failure, and the political and economic priorities of countries in the 1990s (Devereux 2009).

Devereux and Maxwell (2001: 13–21), highlighted three paradigm shifts which followed global and local trends:

1. From global and national to household and the individual – adequate world supplies of basic foodstuffs to offset fluctuations in production and prices and satisfy growing demands (UN 1975) – seeing food supply as the problem.
2. From a 'food first' perspective to a livelihood perspective – food is one part of the jigsaw of secure and sustainable livelihoods; meeting food needs as far as possible given immediate and future livelihood needs – concerns the long-term environmental capacity to supply food and the institutional capacity to enable access to food.

3. From objective indicators (the conditions of deprivation) such as poverty being seen as the main cause of subjective perceptions (feelings of deprivation, lack of self-esteem and self respect) (Kabeer 1988; Chambers et al. 1989) to the 'fear that there will not be enough to eat' (Maxwell 2001: 13–27).

Interest among academics and policymakers in defining and refining the concept of food security is evident from the significant amount of literature devoted to providing definitions, indicators, and conceptual models to measure and determine households' and individuals' food security status. Maxwell and Frankenberger (1992) cited 30 definitions put forward from 1975 to 1991, which have either been influential in the literature or which summarise agency views. Among the most influential are: Siamwalla and Valdes (1980), the FAO (1983), and the World Bank (1985). Most writers agree with the general idea proposed by Reutlinger (1982; 1985), that food security is:

Access by all people at all times to enough food for an active, healthy life. Its essential elements are the availability [Supply] of food and the ability [Demand] to gain it.

The United Nations (UN 1993) added another dimension to the definition: 'a household is food secure when it has access to the food needed for a healthy life for all its members, adequate in terms of quality, quantity, safety and cultural acceptability'. The 1996 World Food Summit adopted a still more complex definition, encompassing regional and global levels, and this definition was adapted by the FAO in 2001:

Food security, at the individual, household, national, regional and global levels [is achieved] when all people, at all times, have physical and economic access to sufficient, safe and nutritious food to meet their dietary needs and food preferences for an active and healthy life.

Maxwell and Frankenberger (1992: 4) identify four core concepts, implicit in the notion of 'secure access to enough food at all times'. These are: (1) sufficiency of food, defined mainly as the calories needed for an active, healthy life; (2) access to food, which is inclusive of both the supply side [availability] and the demand side [purchasing power]; (3) security, defined by the balance between vulnerability, risk, and insurance; and (4) time, since food insecurity can be chronic, transitory, or cyclical.

Hahn (2000: 2) introduced a new definition of 'nutrition security' at the Scientific Academies Summit in 1996: nutrition security is achieved if

> every individual has the physical, economic and environmental access to a balanced diet that includes the necessary macro and micro nutrients and safe drinking water, sanitation, environmental hygiene, primary health care and education so as to lead a healthy and productive life.

The following points sum up the meaning of the term, and the conditions that are essential to the attainment of 'nutrition security' at national and household levels (See Diagram 1.1):

- *Food availability*: refers to overall regional, national or even global food supply and shortfalls in supply compared to requirements (Hahn 2000: 2). It also means sufficient quantities of appropriate types of food from domestic production, commercial imports or food aid, which is consistently available to individuals or is within reasonable proximity to them or is within their reach (USAID 1992; 2006). However, providing a sufficient supply of food for all people at all times has historically been a major challenge. Institutional, technical, and scientific innovations have made important contributions in terms of quantity and economies of scale in the last 50 years but have fallen short of maintaining sustainability of production and access (Koc et al.: 2010).
- *Access to food*: refers to individuals with incomes or other resources that enable them to obtain appropriate levels of consumption of an adequate diet/nutrition level through purchase or barter; accessibility also deals with equality of access to food for every member of a household within and between regions. Inequities have resulted in serious entitlement shortfalls, reflecting class, gender, ethnic, racial, and age differentials, as well as national and regional gaps in development (ibid.).
- *Cultural acceptability*: the food system and practices of food distribution should reflect the social and cultural diversity of people, and this includes the suitability and acceptability of

new scientific innovations to the social and ecological concerns
of the nation in any given country (ibid.).

- *Food utilisation*: has a socioeconomic and biological aspect.
It concerns a household's decision making on the kind of food
needed and how the food is allocated between the members of
the household, in addition to the composition and the balance
of the consumed food (carbohydrate, fat, protein, vitamins, and
minerals). It also includes employing proper food processing,
storage, provision, and the application of an adequate
knowledge of nutrition and child-care techniques, along with
adequate health and sanitation services (USAID 1992).

- *Sustainability*: is defined in terms of the adequacy of relevant
measures to guarantee the sustainability of production,
distribution, consumption, and waste management. A
sustainable food system should help to satisfy current basic
human needs, without compromising the ability of future
generations to meet their needs. It must therefore maintain
the ecological integrity of natural resources such as soil, water,
fish stocks, forests, and overall biodiversity (ibid.).

WHAT IS FOOD INSECURITY?

Food insecurity is the lack of access to enough food; it can be
chronic, and/or transitory and cyclical (World Bank, 1985: 1).

Chronic food insecurity is 'a continuously inadequate diet caused
by the inability to gain food'. It affects households that lack the
ability either to buy enough food or to produce their own. Poverty
is considered the root cause of chronic food insecurity (World Bank
1985: 1). Moreover, a continuously inadequate diet is synonymous
with the term hunger or undernutrition, which is a medical term
describing a situation of 'stunting' or stunted growth, resulting
from food intake that is continuously insufficient to meet dietary
energy requirements (FAO 2005a). This process starts *in utero* if
the mother is malnourished, and continues until approximately
the third year of the child's life, leading to higher infant and child
mortality. Once stunting has occurred, improved nutritional intake
later in life cannot reverse the damage.

There are four types of malnutrition, according to Mayer (in
Leathers and Foster 2004: 25). Firstly, over-nutrition occurs
when a person consumes too many calories, and this is the most
common nutritional problem in high-income countries and among
high-income people in developing countries. The diet of the world's

high-income people usually consists of higher calories, saturated fats, salt, and sugar. Their diet-related illnesses include obesity, diabetes and hypertension.

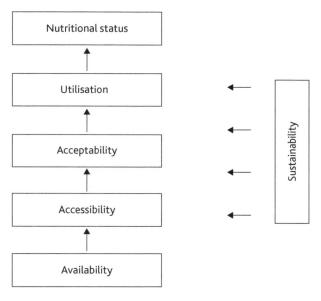

Diagram 1.1 Conditions of food and nutrition security
Sources: Adapted from Gross (1999) and Hahn (2000).

Secondly, when a person has a condition or illness that prevents proper digestion or absorption of food they have secondary malnutrition. Public-health measures such as providing sanitary human-waste disposal and clean water are especially important in reducing secondary malnutrition. Low-income people in developing countries are at risk of undernutrition (insufficient calories), which is commonly exacerbated by secondary malnutrition (for example, a diarrheal infection that robs the body of nutrients). Because of the strong link between the two, undernutrition and secondary malnutrition are commonly grouped together and called simply undernutrition (Leathers and Foster 2004: 25–33).

Thirdly, dietary deficiency or micronutrition is concerned with deficiencies in vitamin A, iodine, and iron. Fourthly, there are two other related types of malnutrition, protein–calorie malnutrition (PCM) and protein–energy malnutrition (PEM). PCM, is concerned with under consumption of protein and PEM is caused by a diet short of the protein and minerals (such as zinc) that are needed for normal growth, health, and activity, and which are essential to the growth of very young children. Vitamin D deficiency causes diseases including rickets (soft bones) and scurvy, and beriberi and pellagra[1] are caused by deficiencies in B vitamins. Kwashiorkor and marasmus represent extreme forms of PCM and are most prevalent in low-income countries where poverty is widespread (ibid).

The causes of chronic food insecurity

One of the key factors affecting all underlying determinants of chronic food insecurity is poverty.[2] A person is considered to be in absolute poverty when he/she is unable to satisfy basic needs such as food, basic health, clean water, basic education, and shelter (UN 1993; World Bank 1993; Frankenberger 1996; Sachs 2005). The effects of poverty on child malnutrition are pervasive. Poor households and individuals have inadequate resources to generate enough income and are unable to utilise food or contribute to enhancing their resources in order to maintain their health and wellbeing and to achieve food security on a sustainable basis (Smith and Haddad 1999; Hahn 2000; Bne Saad 2002).

Measuring chronic food insecurity or nutrition insecurity is important for determining the nature, extent, and causes of food and nutrition insecurity. Most literature begins with an identification of the food insecure, determines their geographic location, and attempts to measure the extent of malnutrition at the individual level.

Table 1.1 shows that, on average, the proportion of undernourished people in the developing world is about 16 per cent of the total population. The vast majority of the world's food insecure people live in Asia (see FAO 2009a: 47–50).

However, the most recent 'Global Hunger Index' published by the IFPRI (2011) indicates large percentage increases of hunger from 1990 to 2011 in 6 countries, with the Democratic Republic of Congo topping the list with 63 per cent, followed by Burundi at 21 per cent, North Korea at 18 per cent, Comoros at 17 per cent, Swaziland at 15 per cent, and Cote d'Ivoire at 8 per cent.

Past nutrition intervention programmes have often been consumption-oriented (FAO 2004), with an emphasis on nutrition education and food production. This was influenced by earlier research and writing by experts such as Reutlinger and Knapp (1980) on the 'minimal level of food consumption'; Siamwalla and Valdes (1980) on the 'target level of consumption'; and the FAO (1983) on 'food adequate intake to meet nutritional needs', and Maxwell and

Table 1.1   Prevalence of undernourishment and daily energy supply (DES) in world regions

World regions	Total population 2001–2006 (millions)	No. of people undernourished 2001–2006* (millions)	Proportion of undernourished in total population 2001–2006 (%)
World	6,483.3	872.9	13
Developed countries	1,269.5	15.2	–
Developing countries	5,213.8	857.7	16
Asia and Pacific	3,518.7	566.2	16
East Asia	1,394.5	136.3	10
Southeast Asia	551.9	84.7	15
South Asia	1,492.0	336.6	23
Central Asia	58.4	5.8	10
Western Asia	15.8	2.1	13
Latin America and the Caribbean	551.1	45.3	8
North East and North Africa	427.7	33.8	8
Sub-Saharan Africa	716.3	212.3	30

Source: Compiled from FAO (2008).

* The FAO estimates that 1.02 billion people were undernourished worldwide in 2009.

Frankenberger (1992) on 'Household food security indicators and measurements'. Such nutrition interventions can temporarily address problems of specific low-income population groups which do not adequately benefit from the national development processes. Thus, nutrition needs to be recognised and addressed within the context of national development policy to enable long-term sustainable improvement in the nutritional status of the whole population (FAO 2004: vii–viii).

In determining the causes of chronic food and nutrition insecurity, there is a need to focus on food security at both the individual and the household level (see, Gross 1999; Hahn 2000; FAO 2004; Leathers and Foster 2004). Two broad concepts of food insecurity represent different views on ways of solving this problem. UNICEF, according to Hahn (2000: 4–7), focuses on the problem of malnutrition among children with due consideration to their health situations. The second concept takes into account more relevant determining factors such as food availability 'supply-side', health, environmental, and social considerations (dietary habits and practices which are influenced by cultural norms and value systems), yet it omits other important factors such as political processes, macroeconomic conditions, and the capacity of both private and public institutions to tackle the problem of chronic food and nutrition insecurity (see Diagram 1.2).

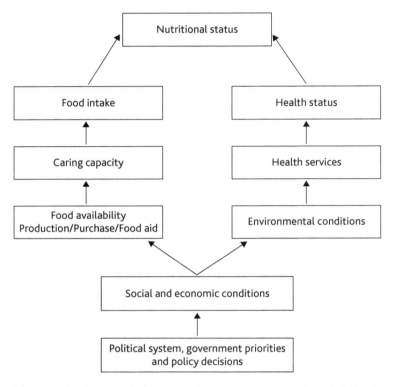

Diagram 1.2   Conceptual frameworks for nutritional status at household level
Source: Adapted from Hahn (2000: 5).

MEASURING CHRONIC FOOD INSECURITY

Various methods are used to assess and measure nutritional status at the individual level, and findings are usually aggregated over community, district, or subregional levels (Hahn 2000: 7). Leathers and Foster (2004: 41) outline four common methods of direct assessment of the nutritional status of an individual. These are: clinical, biochemical, dietary, and anthropometric. Each method has shortcomings and each may result in a somewhat different assessment of the nature and extent of nutritional disorders. Box 1.1 briefly introduces some of the methods used to measure under-nutrition.

Box 1.1 Measuring chronic undernutrition for individuals

Clinical assessment: this relies on the examination of physical signs on the body that are symptomatic of nutritional disorders. Most common are the micro-nutrient deficiencies of vitamin A and iodine (see Leathers and Foster (2004: 41 for details).

Biochemical assessment: this requires examination of bodily fluids such as blood or urine for the complex metabolic changes that accompany nutritional disorders such as anaemia by hemoglobinometry (to detect iron deficiency). Anaemia leads to a reduced degree of physical activity in an individual and increases his/her vulnerability to infection (see, Guillespie 1998; Hahn 2000: 8). The difficulty with these methods is their complexity and cost – for example the effort required to organise blood samples from a large population, and the need to transport these samples to appropriate laboratory apparatus for analysis before they deteriorate, especially in hot climates (Leathers and Foster 2004: 42).

Dietary assessment: surveys are usually carried out to assess nutritional status. Two approaches are used: dietary recall, in which the person is asked to remember what he or she ate, say, during the past 24 hours or the past seven days; and dietary record, in which the amount of food consumed at mealtimes, is recorded, often by weighing it.

Anthropometric assessment: this is the science of measuring the human body and its parts. It serves as the most commonly used measure of nutritional status, based on an understanding of how human physical growth and development respond to nutritional status. Leathers and Foster (2004) provide a full explanation of the impact of undernutrition on physical growth and development and of anthropometric assessment. These measurements include: low height-for-age, or stunting; low weight-for-height, or wasting; low weight-for-age, or underweight; and fat composition of the body from mid-upper arm circumference (MUAC). Body mass index (BMI) is applied with adults and is becoming more and more accepted as an important indicator for the nutritional status of adults, and nature versus nurture (or heredity versus environment).

Another method is used to determine the *base metabolic rate* (BMR) for the population. The BMR shows the number of calories needed for survival when the body is at rest.

Source: Leathers and Foster (2004: 41–7)

Policymakers need information and data about the extent of undernutrition in a continent or subcontinent, in a country, and in a state or region of a country, for the purpose of planning interventions. Leathers and Foster (2004) observed three types of indicators: inferences drawn from a sample; mortality or disease rates; and food balance sheets or food availability measures (see Box 1.2).

Box 1.2   Measuring nutritional status at national level

Inferences from a sample: to determine the extent of malnutrition in a country or among a group, a representative sample is usually selected and anthropometric methods are used to provide evidence of the prevalence of malnutrition among the sample. The evidence then can be aggregated and generalised to the regional and or national level Leathers and Foster (2004).

Mortality and/or disease rates: data on indicators such as low birth weights or high infant-mortality rates in a country or region are assumed to indicate a high rate of undernutrition. Aggregate data such as this can provide a good first approximation of the number and location of undernourished people.

Food balance sheets: this term refers to a comparison of the total supply of each food item against total use or consumption. Indicators such as average per person food intake (calories per capita per day) are used to identify regions or countries with nutritional problems. These should be available on a country-by-country basis in the food balance sheet which is published annually by the FAO. The food balance-sheet shows supply and consumption of over 100 separate food items on an annual basis. Sources of food listed include available stocks (after harvest), production, and imports; uses include stocks (before harvest), exports, animal feed, and human consumption. However, the food balance-sheet method of assessment reflects average per capita production and consumption of food, which can be a misleading measure of the nutritional status of the different income groups and individual members of the population.

Sources: Leathers and Foster (2004: 57); FAO (2002a; 2010)

Cost of chronic food and nutrition insecurity

There are clearly significant relationships between malnutrition, diseases/ illnesses and low performance in schools, low productivity at work and loss of national economic outputs. It is a known fact that the economic growth achieved by developed countries can be attributed to better nutrition and improved health and sanitation. Just as the nutritional well-being of the whole population is a precondition for the development of societies, and a key objective of progress in human development, the cost of malnutrition can be detrimental to many aspects of an individual's and a nation's life. The following are examples of the costs of malnutrition and its impacts on human health and well-being:

• Inadequate diets lead to malnutrition, which affects an individual's mental and physical state, resulting in poor health and poor work performance (WHO 2002);

• A hungry malnourished child may have mild to serious learning disabilities, resulting in poor school performance (ibid.);

• A sick and poorly nourished individual will not respond well to treatment, delaying the speed of recovery and predisposing the patient to infections. This could result in the loss of many working hours, and may continue to drain family and national resources (for example, individuals suffering from malnutrition are more likely to visit the general practitioner (GP)). Their higher vulnerability to different conditions increases their need for health and social care, as well as hospital care (EU Nutrition, January 2010);

• Malnutrition may undermine investment in education, health and other sectors (for example, malnutrition costs the United Kingdom alone up to £7.4 billion per year due to increased vulnerability to disease) (ibid);

• Iodine deficiency disorder (IDD) and iron deficiency anemia (IDA) can reduce gross domestic product (GDP) by 2–4 per cent. According to the FAO, over 2 billion people in the world suffer from micronutrient malnutrition (FAO 2010). IDD can lead to visible goiter and impaired physical and mental development (with 741 million people worldwide affected by goiter). Worldwide, 20 million people are mentally retarded due to iodine deficiency (FAO 2002a);

• Vitamin A deficiency (VAD) principally affects pre-school age children. VAD can lead to xerophthalmia,[3] night blindness and, eventually, total blindness. Every year between 250,000 to 500,000 children lose their sight as a result of VAD and two-thirds of these children are likely to die. An estimated 1 million additional children die each year of infectious diseases because VAD impairs their resistance to infection (FAO 2002a);

- Studies show that IDD can reduce work capacity and productivity by 10–15 per cent, and GDP by 0.5–1.8 per cent (FAO 2002a).

It is a well established fact that chronic food insecurity is caused by poverty, which is the result of lack of access to resources, in addition to lack of opportunities and choices available to enable the poor to lift themselves and their children out of poverty and vulnerability. Sudden internal and or external shocks such as increases in food prices, severe climatic conditions and political instability, undermine their resilience to cope and be free from hunger and insecurity. In fact, those poor households suffering from chronic food insecurity both in rural and urban areas are more vulnerable to the fluctuations and volatility of domestic and world food prices as these are the most important determinants of transitory food insecurity.

TRANSITORY FOOD INSECURITY

The World Bank (1985) defines transitory food insecurity as a 'temporary decline in households' access to enough food'. More precisely, it is a temporary decline in food consumption below acceptable levels. It results from: instability in world food prices (which to some extent impact on domestic prices), instability in food production and lack of food reserves and/or an inability to import food due to weak foreign exchange or a decline in household income. In addition there can be other associated factors such as political and civil unrest and wars. However, famine can be the worst form of transitory food insecurity.

Transitory food insecurity can be further divided into cyclical and temporary food insecurity (Canadian International Development Agency (CIDA), in Maxwell and Frankenberger 1992). Temporary food insecurity can happen for a limited period of time because of unforeseen and unpredictable circumstances, while cyclical or seasonal food insecurity is a regular recurrence of inadequate access to food during the dearth season. This may be due to logistical difficulties or to the high cost of storing food.

Three variables can influence household's consumption and to some extent can predict the vulnerability of households to transitory food insecurity. These are: (1) world food prices, which influence (2) domestic food prices, and (3) household purchasing power (World Bank 1985). The question here is: what causes the instability in world food prices?

Instability in world food prices

The food crisis of 1972–1973

Before discussing the causes of the grain price increases of 2007 and beyond, it is imperative to look back and contrast the causes of price instability during the period from 1972 to 1973 with the causes operating since 2007. It will be important to consider whether the most recent food crisis represents the beginning of a new trend characterised by more volatile, if not higher, commodity prices.

Historical data and studies show the extreme volatility of both agricultural commodity prices and food prices during the 1972–1973 period. Mackie's paper (1974) on the 'international dimension of agricultural prices' provided a perspective on commodity prices from the 1950s to 1973, with the largest increases in the international prices of primary products in 1972 and agricultural products in 1973 – even larger than during the immediate post-Second World War period or during the Korean War commodity price boom.

Between 1972 and 1973 the largest increases were for oilseed cake and meal (140 per cent), wheat (71 per cent), oilseeds (59 per cent), maize (54 per cent), rice, pork and sugar (35 per cent), wool (129 per cent) and cocoa (87 per cent).

Mackie (1974: 14–15) explores four hypotheses to explain the causes of the 1972 and 1973 world food crisis. The first hypothesis focuses on the rapid rise in affluence around the world, which provided incentives for greater growth in demand for food. Watkins (1991: 39–40) confirms that during the 1960s, in both the US and the EU, farm surpluses were absorbed, admittedly amid growing trade frictions between the two major producers of food in their attempt to dominate world food markets and capture the expansion of world agricultural trade.

The most dynamic force behind this trade expansion was the demand for food imports on the part of developing countries, which grew at double the rate of demand from Organisation of Economic Cooperation and Development (OECD) countries. Although acceleration in income growth in industrial countries was certainly a contributory factor in 1972–1973, especially in relation to animal feeds and protein meals, the sharp price increases for agricultural products resulted mainly from supply shortages, which were associated with both an increase in import requirements and a reduction in production and export supplies outside the US (Mackie 1974: 14–15).

A second hypothesis is that the world has lost its ability to feed itself and to increase output relative to demand, because there is limited land and limited production technology that will continue to hold food supplies below world demand for many years to come. However, evidence from the available data shows that food production increases are outstripping the population growth rate from 1961 to 2005 (FAO 2005a), so one can argue that it is not that the world has lost its ability to feed itself, but rather that national interests and government priorities have determined the level of investments (in the form of subsidies and export support) which are available to increase production. The two major factors were the US government's decision to reduce production to consumption level by setting aside land, and the EU imposition of the same measures in addition to the introduction of a production levy and a quota system to curb overproduction of food. These policies played a role in reducing the level of stocks available for export at a time of unusually large surges in world food import demand.

Watkins (1991) explained the shift in US farm policy and how policymakers have grappled with this problem throughout the post-war period. It was envisaged that new legislation aimed at reforming government payments to farmers to remove land from cultivation (land set-aside), coupled with tight controls on imports, would prove sufficient to support farm incomes without excessive budgetary expenditure. However, these price support mechanisms failed. Although land set-aside reduced cultivation acreage, farmers were given incentives to maximise output on their remaining land by increasing the application of chemicals and other inputs. By the 1960s, structural overproduction and corporate grain exporting interests, notably the Cargill Corporation, had forced a shift in policy emphasis away from supply control and towards aggressive export promotion.

However, the explicit aim of the US Public Law 480, passed in 1954, was 'to lay the basis for a permanent expansion of their exports of agricultural products with lasting benefits to themselves and peoples of other lands' (ÓGráda 2009: 226). From the late 1960s the US's domination of world markets came under challenge from the EU, where high guaranteed price supports under the Common Agricultural Policy (CAP), allied to technological advances, promoted huge productivity gains and production surpluses. Moreover, the success of the Green Revolution (GR) in South East Asia led some developing countries such as India to become exporters of food.

A third hypothesis is that the food shortages and high prices of the 1970s were caused primarily by currency instability and subsequent speculation in agricultural commodities. Crop shortfalls and high demands for food put further pressure on total world imports, thereby increasing uncertainty, hoarding and speculation in food commodities. This speculation was aided by the international monetary situation and the dramatic increase in oil prices (Mackie 1974: 18).

The fourth hypothesis maintains that the world food shortages and high prices were directly related to crop shortfalls. One of the major factors affecting the price of wheat, for example, has been the level of stocks in the US and Canada and the fluctuation of supplies in the rest of the world, especially in countries with strong central planning policies such as the former Soviet Union and China (Mackie 1974: 18; World Bank 1985). Droughts in India, the former Soviet Union and China resulted in increased imports by these countries during widespread shortfalls in production of a number of agricultural commodities. Moreover, instability in world demand was reflected in the sharp rise and subsequent fall in per capita income growth in developed and developing countries (World Bank 1985).

Mackie believed that while all the factors mentioned above played a part in the 1973 surge in agricultural prices, the most important factor was supply shortages. He indicated that rapid growth in world import demand for US commodities was more directly related to shortfalls in production and low stock levels in the rest of the world than to rapid shifts in demand resulting from income growth or dollar devaluations. However, he did not discount the influence of factors other than the short supply of agricultural commodities. Furthermore, it seems that 'there was little evidence for attributing price increases in agricultural commodities during 1972 to speculative activity associated with the currency realignments in December 1971.

The food crisis since 2007

From this period the issue of rising global food prices moved to the forefront of international media attention and national and international political agendas. Since 2007 tens of millions more of the chronically food insecure were pushed into hunger and further poverty as a result of yet another sharp increase in food prices. Civil unrest was reported in locations all over the world. Developing countries, especially food importing countries, used various measures at national level to halt the crisis such as imposing export restrictions on food and using subsidies and price controls.

Households, faced with this crisis, were forced to find ways to cope. Coping mechanisms involved undesirable but often unavoidable compromises, such as replacing more-nutritious food with less-nutritious food, selling productive assets, withdrawing children from school, forgoing health care or education, or simply eating less (FAO 2009a: 4). The questions then are: what was the trigger for this latest crisis? How different was it from the crisis of 1972–1973? And what is the long-term outlook for food commodity markets?

The recent rise in food prices began around the year 2002, when global grain stocks began to decline steeply from 110 days' worth of food before the turn of the century to just over 60 days' worth just half a decade later in 2004 (Trostle, in Evans 2009: 12). From the outset this crisis was triggered by the same factors that caused the crisis in 1972 and 1973, with one exception – the use of food crops as biofuel, a factor that was constant for seven of the eight years since 2000 (ibid). The following are some of the key factors behind the recent boom, or the latest 'perfect storm'.

One major factor is that of sustained economic growth, especially in emerging economies (notably India and China), leading to a shift towards a more grain-intensive Western diet rich in meat and dairy products. Although this is an important factor, with a combined population of over 2.4 billion in both India and China there is no doubt that positive per capita economic growth in those countries will have its impact on global demand for food. However, the effect of changing dietary patterns in emerging economies may have been overestimated (FAO 2008; IFPRI 2008; Baffes 2009; Evans 2009). Goldman Sachs also show that while historical growth in global demand for food crops has been around 1.5 per cent a year, the figure is now 2 per cent and likely to rise to 2.6 per cent within a decade taking into account population growth rates (Currie 2007).

Recent analysis suggests that the policies which encouraged production of biofuels, such as support and subsidies, have been the single most significant driver of higher prices (Baffes 2009; Evans 2009).

In 2002 the US dollar began to depreciate, and as it devalued the price of oil increased – a trend that accelerated from 2004 onwards. High oil prices add directly to the costs of growing, harvesting and distributing farm produce, by increasing the costs of agricultural inputs such as fertilisers and transportation. The rising price of oil, and the role of speculators in maximising fear that the world is

Chapter 9 discusses gender and food security, focusing on approaches to policy analysis which can facilitate the processes of mainstreaming gender concerns in agricultural policies.

Chapter 10 provides a global perspective on food security, including aspects of agricultural trade and aid to agricultural development in low-income food deficit developing countries.

running out of extractive resources (especially crude oil), also helped to increase the attractiveness of biofuels as a substitute for oil in the US, the EU, Brazil and elsewhere (Evans 2009: 12).

Several studies have claimed that grain prices have been drastically inflated by manipulative financial speculation. The fear is that such trading has undermined the price-smoothing capacity of agricultural future markets, and increased the price risks encountered by consumers, producers and governments (Eugenio et al. 2009). Ronald Trostle, an economist at the US Department of Agriculture's Economic Research Service, notes that

> these new investors were not so much interested in agricultural commodities as they were using commodities to diversify their financial portfolios and observes that, while it is difficult to lay the blame for higher prices squarely at the door of speculators, investment funds' use of automated trend-following trading practices may well have served to increase price volatility. (Trostle 2008)

Commodity investors and hedge fund activity also seems to have played a minor role (World Bank 2008).

Another important factor has been weather-related supply disruptions. For example, in 2005 extreme weather in a number of major food-producing countries caused world cereal production to fall by 2.1 per cent in 2006 (FAO 2008). Australia was particularly affected, suffering its worse multi-year drought in a century. Russia and Ukraine, meanwhile, entered a two-year drought in 2006, and 2007 saw further impacts including a dry spring followed by harvest-time floods in Northern Europe, a hot and dry growing season in Canada with lower yields for wheat, barley and rapeseed, and droughts in southeast Europe, Turkey, northeast Africa and Argentina (ibid).

Finally, there is the effect of export restrictions imposed as a means of curbing domestic food price inflation in exporting countries. This has been matched by a move from importing countries to reduce their trade barriers so as to try to increase imports, build stocks and control inflation.

The increases in food prices since 2007 are not unusual, if viewed in the context of the history of grain prices over the last several decades. The behaviour of food prices for crops such as maize, rice and wheat during [2007–2012] is not qualitatively different from that of the early 1970s and of 1996–1997. The upward price increases occurred systematically in periods of unusually low levels of aggregate stocks (Eugenio et al. 2009; FAO 2011). Trends in demand due to income growth in China and India, droughts in some major producers of food and the growth of biofuel exacerbated by price increases in oil prices all have their part in explaining low stocks since 2007, although there was some food stock recovery during 2008. However, most writers agree that biofuel will be the most important driver of food prices for the future. According to Baffes (2009: 6):

> Among the many factors that will shape the long-term outlook for agricultural and food commodity markets are: the increased linkage between energy and non-energy commodity prices; biofuel mandates and subsidies, which are likely to play a key role in food markets; investment fund activity which is likely to continue or even intensify, implying that increased price volatility for most commodities will be the norm; economic growth prospects in developing countries where consumption of extractive and industrial commodities is growing faster; and changing weather patterns due to global warming. All these will affect production and the trading patterns of agricultural commodities.

Furthermore, the economic and financial crisis of 2009, which overlapped with the food crisis period, pushed the prices of basic staples beyond the reach of millions of poor people. Developing countries today are more financially and commercially integrated into the world economy than they were 20 years ago, and therefore they are more exposed to shocks in international markets (FAO 2009a). This argument was made by Mackie (1974: 20), in his concluding remarks on the causes of the first food crisis in 1973:

> The world appears to have entered a new era of uncertainty with respect to the availability of basic supplies of foods and raw materials. Uncertainty itself is familiar, but what is new is the high degree of interdependency of nations attained in recent years in production, consumption, and trade of agricultural products combined with low levels of stocks. This interdependency creates instantaneous disequilibrium in international commodity markets when either demand or supply of basic commodities is radically altered.

On the same note the FAO (2009a) describes how the current economic crisis is different from the previous crises, for two main reasons. First, the crisis is affecting large parts of the world simultaneously, and as such traditional coping mechanisms at national and sub-national levels are likely to be less effective than they were in the past. Second, since 2009 many countries have seen a substantial decline in the inflow of remittances, which has weakened the coping mechanisms of poor households.

Having discussed the causes of world food price volatility from the 1970s until present, the following section focuses on how world food prices influence domestic food prices and household purchasing power.

DOMESTIC FOOD PRICES

The three main factors affecting transitory food insecurity in low-income food deficit countries are: food production, the capability to import food and household purchasing power (World Bank 1985).

The stability of domestic food supplies is affected by factors such as: the resources available to the country in terms of land, labour and capital; trends and variations in rainfall (especially in countries where rain-fed agriculture is dominant); and the institutional capacity, both financial and technical, to enhance the productivity of these resources and sustain economic growth. However, the level of investment needed to promote food production is hampered by overall macroeconomic policy and the structural constraints affecting the agricultural sector. The first- and second-generation structural adjustment programmes of the 1980s influenced low-income countries and their governments' investment priorities, resulting in changes such as investing in export crop production at the expense of food production.

Four hypotheses proposed by the World Bank (2007)[4] could explain the constraints facing low-income developing countries, or as the World Bank labels them 'agriculture-based countries,' in promoting their agricultural and food sector:

- Agricultural productivity growth is intrinsically slow, making it hard to realise the growth and poverty-reducing potential of agriculture;
- Macroeconomic, price, and trade policies unduly discriminate against agriculture;

- There has been an urban bias in the allocation of public investment. As well as misinvestment within agriculture. The share of public spending on agriculture in agriculture-based countries (mostly in Africa) is significantly less (4 per cent in 2004) than in the transforming countries during their agricultural growth spurt (10 per cent in 1980). Comparatively, these levels of agricultural spending are insufficient for sustained growth; and
- Official development assistance to agriculture has declined since the mid-1980s.

The World Bank's *World Development Report 2007–2008* argues that, especially for Africa, rapid agricultural growth will be difficult and agricultural policies will remain distorted because of the legacy of colonial and post-colonial strategies. In addition, there is an inherently unfavourable agro-ecological base. Important aspects of this are: rapid soil degradation, low population density, poorly functioning markets, competition from the rest of the world, undeveloped infrastructure and low levels of fertiliser use.

Research evidence over the past two decades regarding rates of growth in agricultural output or value-added confirms that agriculture has grown more slowly compared to industry and services, although the gap is larger in the transforming countries and negligible in the agriculture-based economies. However, labour productivity in agriculture grew faster than in non-agricultural sectors in each of the three country categories due to better education (ibid).

To offset food shortages developing countries usually depend on world markets to import food, and they are often constrained by shortage of foreign exchange. As a result, their capability to import food has been highly volatile. Constraints such as debt repayment, fuel imports and tight foreign exchange reserves limit their ability to offset fluctuations in earnings generated from export crops which are subject to extreme price swings and volatility (World Bank 1985: 5).

The World Bank (1985: 34) outlined the impact of border prices on domestic markets during the 1973 crisis thus:

border prices have been less stable than domestic producer prices for some foods in many countries, if governments had transmitted the instability of border prices to domestic markets or had allowed domestic prices to vary in response to fluctuations in production, producers and consumers alike, particularly many poor people would have felt large shocks to their incomes and food budgets.[5]

Considering the most recent food crisis, which began in 2007, by the end of 2008 domestic prices for staple foods remained, on average, 17 per cent higher in real terms than two years earlier. This represented a considerable reduction in the effective purchasing power of poor consumers, who spend a substantial share of their income (often more than 40 per cent) on staple foods.

Another reason is the variability in the exchange rates of major trading countries. One of the reasons for the 1973 crisis was that major producers, among them the US, decided to reduce production to consumption level to reduce the farm bill and to improve farmers' incomes. Furthermore, the failure of trade negotiations, from the GATT to the Doha round, has contributed to the distortion of the global agricultural trading system and affected the food security of millions of people around the world in 2007 and beyond. However, a household's purchasing power is the most important factor determining an individual's ability to withstand shocks such as high food prices, and to be food secure or not.

HOUSEHOLD PURCHASING POWER

The concept of a household's access to nutritious food includes both the supply of food and the individual's ability to gain that food, in addition to the factors affecting the utilisation of food. Availability of food in the market does not guarantee a household's ability to command and acquire enough calories to live healthily, and to contribute to the well-being of their household and communities.

However, a household's purchasing power is influenced by the country's purchasing power parity if the country depends on imports for its food needs. The country's purchasing power is determined by border price criteria, such as the international exchange rate adjusted to the domestic exchange rate (Ellis 1992: 72–73).[6]

Aggregate data usually hide more than they reveal about how transitory food insecurity affects households. Incomes and food production vary much more across households and regions than across countries. The World Bank provided evidence from India in 1968–1970, for example, showing that at national level aggregate income, food production and food consumption were fairly stable. Yet a survey of the per capita income and spending of 4,000 rural households showed considerable instability from year to year.

Nearly half the households had at least one year in which their per capita income fell below 70 per cent of their three-year average. In about two-fifths of the households, total spending and spending on food showed similar deviations from the average.

In conclusion, Oshaug (1985: 5–13) argues that a society that enjoys food security is a society that reaches the 'food norm' – that is, a satisfactory level of consumption. This society should have developed internal structures which will enable it to sustain the goal of a satisfactory level of consumption in the face of crises threatening to lower the achieved goal of the 'food norm.' He identifies three type of households: enduring households, which maintain household food security on a continuous basis. Endurance can be defined as

> the capacity of a given social system and households to undergo a perturbation without a decline in the degree of progress made towards the 'food norm' (ibid.).
>
> Resilient households, which suffer shocks but recover quickly; and fragile households, which become increasingly insecure because of their vulnerability to external shocks (ibid.).

Most people living on US$1–2 a day per person (or less) would be considered as fragile households, depending on how the poverty line is measured in a given country, and these households are exposed to the volatility of both domestic and international food prices. Poor households suffering from chronic food insecurity on a regular basis are more likely to be vulnerable to the factors associated with transitory food insecurity, of which famine is the worst form. Table 1.2 shows a classification of those who are chronically food insecure and at risk of transitory food insecurity.

Table 1.2   A classification of chronically food insecure people by geographic location

Food insecure categories	Causes of hunger/ malnutrition	Percentage of undernourished	Geographic location
Low-income farm households	Small farm size, rain-fed cultivation; traditional inputs and methods of farming; low productivity (labour and land); degraded soil; remoteness from markets; weak diversifications; poor market institutions and infrastructures	50% of total (400 million)	Dry lands: Sahel, Southern Africa, South Asia, Near East, Brazil; Mountains: Mesoamerica, Andes, East Africa, Himalayas, South East Asia

continued

Food insecure categories	Causes of hunger/ malnutrition	Percentage of undernourished	Geographic location
Rural landless and low-income non-farm households	Inadequate income; weak social networks; lack of access to productive employment (poor skills); low wages	22% of total (176 million)	Asia, Central America
Low-income urban households	Inadequate income; lack of access to productive employment (poor skills); low wages	20% of total (160 million)	China, India, Zambia
Poor herders, fishers and forest people dependent on community or public resources	Climate change; pressure on pastures, forest and water resources; pollution; competition with expanding urbanisation and infrastructural development; unidentified legal rights of access	8% of total (64 million)	Dry lands: Africa, lowland Asia; forest regions or Amazonia, Himalayas, South East Asia
Cross-cutting above categories			
Pregnant and lactating women	Inadequate food and micro-nutrient intake; low level of education and knowledge	Several hundred million	South Central Asia, South East Asia and all chronically hungry and pregnant women in sub-Saharan Africa
Newborn infants	Inadequate foetal nutrition due to maternal malnutrition; cultural belief (Kwashiorkor)	30 million	South Central Asia, South East Asia
Children under five years	Inadequate childcare; poor feeding practices; infectious disease, dirty water; low social and economic status of women; poor health services	150 million	South Central Asia, South East Asia, Sub-Saharan Africa (East Africa, West Africa)
Micro-nutrient-deficient individuals	Teenage girls and women (iron deficient); nutrient-deficient diets; lack of protein, fruit, vegetables and low level of education (drop out of school)	2 billion	Widely distributed
Victims of extreme events (natural disasters, war and civil conflict) and high food prices	Low farm investment, disruption of food systems, loss of assets; loss of jobs, low wages, aid not delivered	60 million	Recent victims in Sahel, Horn of Africa Southern Africa
HIV/AIDS and other adult disabilities	Inability to produce or access food; increased dependency ratio; depleted social networks	36 million infected	Sub-Saharan Africa, but moving to Asia

Source: Adapted from Kracht (2005) and Shaw (2007).

2
Famine

Famine is the worst form of transitory food insecurity. More than one million people have died in famines since the world declared 'never again' following the Ethiopian famine of 1984. (Devereux 2007: 1)

Nevertheless, Devereux (2000: 3) made the point that 'during the twentieth century, vulnerability to famine appears to have been virtually eradicated from all regions outside Africa'.

Famine has been explained in terms of FAD, involving 'supply failure' (due to climate change, population pressure, subsistence farming systems and national agricultural policies) and temporary lack of access to food. In addition, there can be 'demand failure', due to instability in world and/or domestic food prices such as sudden increases in food prices that undermine the ability of low-income households or low-income countries to buy food.

There are other associated factors, such as political and civil unrest and wars. Contemporary famines, as Devereux puts it, can be caused deliberately (through acts of commission) or else are not prevented when they could and should have been (acts of omission). Even when a livelihood shock such as drought triggers a food shortage or sudden increases in food prices, it is the failure of local, national and international responses that allows the food shortage to evolve into famine (Maxwell and Frankenberger 1992; Devereux 1993; 2007; Devereux and Maxwell 2001).

Several recent contributions to the theories and explanations of famine emphasise the role of political factors. Devereux's list includes: the absence of mature democracy[1] and 'anti-famine political contracts';[2] complex political emergencies; and government's political and economic priorities. To these should be added the political and economic interests of international actors, including the major producers of food – these interests work against rather than in support of the interests of vulnerable populations. Scholars of famine emphasise that, throughout history, famines have affected those countries and populations that are politically marginalised as well as economically impoverished. These ideas all share a growing preoccupation with accountability, making politics central to explanations of famine causation, and to the failure to prevent famine (Devereux 2007; ÓGráda 2009).

This chapter discusses old and new explanations of famine, using Devereux's analyses of the paradigm shifts underlying the dominant pre-modern, modern and postmodern explanations.

FAMINE MORTALITY 1903–2011

Between 1901 and 2011, 35 famines occurred in 18 countries, at different times and in various locations, within East Asia, South East Asia, South Asia, Europe and Africa. Table 2.1 shows that more than 70 million people died in famines during the twentieth and early twenty-first centuries: estimates range from 71.1 million to 80.5 million (Devereux 2000: 6–9).[3] Causal triggers of these famines were: drought alone (on eight occasions); drought and conflict (nine times); and drought and government policy (twice, in the former Soviet Union in 1946–47 and in Somalia in 1974–75 and 2011). Government policy in China was the main cause of the 1958–62 famine, which killed an estimated 30 to 33 million people. Flood and market failure killed 1.5 million in Bangladesh in 1974, and flood and government policy killed about 3.5 million people in North Korea. Drought and locusts killed between 100,000 to 397,000 in Ethiopia during 1957–58.

The evidence suggests that contemporary famines are less widespread and less severe than the famines of the last century (Devereux 2007: 22). Evidence of progress is clear, since the total minimum estimate of deaths since 2000 is 162,897 people. These figures are based on the most recent famines: in Ethiopia in 2000, which killed an estimated 71,600–122,700 people (Salama et al. in Devereux 2009: 25); Malawi in 2001–2 (with 47,000–85,000 deaths) (Devereux and Tiba 2007); Niger in 2004–5 (between 3,297 and 47,755) (Devereux and Tiba 2007: 25; Rubin 2009). Reports from Somalia, since the UN declared famine in the summer of 2011, put the death toll among children at 29,000.

Table 2.1 clearly shows that famines have been successfully eradicated in Europe since the 1940s, following the end of peasant agriculture and the advent of the Industrial and Transport Revolutions. The Green Revolution and government policies of support for farmers in China, the former Soviet Union, East Asia, India and Bangladesh were important factors in conquering famine since the 1960s. Moreover, there has been no famine in Tanzania since 1919, in Rwanda since the 1940s, and in Mozambique since 1985.

Table 2.1   Estimated mortality figures in major twentieth- and early twenty-first-century famines

Regions	Years	Mortality	Causal triggers
Africa			
Nigeria (Hausaland)	1901–1906	5,000	Drought
Nigeria (Biafra)	1961–1970	1,000,000	Conflict
Tanzania (south)	1901–1907	37,500	Conflict
Tanzania (central)	1911–1919	30,000	Conflict and drought
West Africa (Sahel)	1911–1914	125,000	Drought
	1961–1974	101,000	Drought
Rwanda	1941–1944	300,000	Conflict and drought
Ethiopia (Tigray)	1951–1958	100,001–397,000	Drought and locusts
Ethiopia (Wollo)	1966	45,001–60,000	Drought
Ethiopia (Wollo and Tigray)	1971–1975	200,001–500,000	Drought
Ethiopia	1981–1985	590,001–1,000,000	Conflict and drought
Somalia	1971–1975	20,000	Drought
Somalia	1991–1993	300,001–500,000	Conflict and drought
Somalia	2011	29,000	Conflict and drought
Uganda (Karamoja)	1981–1981	30,000	Conflict and drought
Mozambique	1981–1985	100,000	Conflict and drought
Sudan (Darfur, Korodofan)	1981–1985	250,000	Drought
Sudan (South)	1988	250,000	Conflict
Sudan (Bahr el Ghazal)	1998	70,000	Conflict and drought
Malawi	2001–2002	47,001–85,000	Government policy
Niger	2004–2005	3,296–47,000	Market failure
Total		3,613,007–4,936,500	
Asia (East, South East and South)			
Bangladesh	1974	1,500,000	Flood and market failure
China (Gansu, Shaanxi)	1921–1921	500,000	Drought
China (northwest)	1927	3,000,001–6,000,000	Natural disasters
China (Hunan)	1929	2,000,000	Drought and conflict
China (Henan)	1943	5,000,000	Conflict
China	1951–1962	30,000,001–33,000,000	Government policy
Cambodia	1979	1,500,001–2,000,000	Conflict
India (Bengal)	1943	2,100,001–3,000,000	Conflict
India (Maharashtra)	1971–1973	130,000	Drought
North Korea	1991–1999	2,800,001–3,500,000	Flood and government policy

continued

Regions	Years	Mortality	Causal triggers
Total		48,530,005–56,630,000	
Europe			
Soviet Union	1921–1922	9,000,000	Drought and conflict
Soviet Union (Ukraine)	1931–1934	7,000,001–8,000,000	Government policy
Soviet Union	1941–1947	2,000,000	Drought and government policy
Netherlands	1944	10,000	Conflict
Total		18,010,001–19,010,000	
Grand total		70,153,013–80,575,500	

Calculation of the total and grand total is based on a range of lower and higher estimates.

Source: Devereux (2000: 1–10, Tables 1, 2 and 3; 2009). Also various web sources related to the recent death toll in Somalia.

DEFINING FAMINE

Famine as a concept is defined variously by writers from different disciplines, with each reflecting their own experience and/or academic interests. Famine as 'natural disaster' was defined by Mayer (1975: 572) as 'a severe shortage of food accompanied by a significant increase in local or regional death rate'.

This definition offers no quantifiable indicators for the causes or consequences of famine, in terms of destitution levels or number of deaths. Although Mayer's definition indicates the importance of location, he fails to pinpoint the severity or the significance of the underlying causes, such as the natural, political, and socio-economic factors. His analysis does not indicate to what extent famine is triggered by external factors, such as high food prices combined with poor purchasing power at national and household levels, political instability or conflict, both internal and external.

Sen (1981: 40) defines famine as: 'a particular virulent manifestation of starvation causing widespread death'. He points out that people start starving immediately after the collapse of all their exchange entitlements to food. Kumar (1990: 173) adapts Sen's definition and described famine as 'virulent manifestations of intense starvation causing substantial loss of life'. Both these definitions see famine as an event, and as a breakdown of 'biological' abilities and functions which leads to death (Howe and Devereux 2007).

However, households' responses to food shortages differ depending on their livelihood coping strategy, as most rural famines follow two or three harvest failures. Some households can survive for months or years, for example by eating less (adjusting their famine food reserves), and by using grain loaned by kin. They may stop sending their children to school, sell their small animals, and some family members might migrate in search of a job. In some cases people borrow money or take a grain loan from merchants or money lenders (pledging their farm land) and then, when they are unable to repay the loan, start moving from their homes and land in search of anything that is edible (Watts 1983; Frankenberger 1985).

Furthermore, Alamgir's (1980: 5–6) descriptions of ex-post famine includes the following observations: changes in the nutritional status of individuals, loss of body weight, and increases in the incidence of fatal diseases including mental disorientation; excess deaths in a region or in a country as a whole; increases in interregional migration by famine victims, leading to the uprooting and separation of families, and breakdown of social bonds (out-migration, destitution); transfer of assets; and increase in crime.

Most dictionaries agree on defining famines as: 'crises of mass starvation' characterised by food shortages, severe hunger and excess mortality. However, the implicit theory underlying this widely accepted combination of elements is not always adequate. Devereux (1993; 2001: 119) shows that:

1. Famines have occurred in situations where there was no food shortage at all. Sen notes that, 'during the Wollo famine of 1973, there was a modest increase in national agricultural output recorded by the National Bank of Ethiopia' (Sen 1981: 92). In the Antananarivo famine between 1985 and 1987 in Madagascar, overall food availability did not seem to be a major issue, since production per capita was rather better than both the preceding and following years (Garenne 2007: 178–80).
2. In some instances, excess mortality was caused by disease, not starvation. Preventable infectious diseases such as measles, diarrhoea, typhoid and diphtheria have been reported from famine-related disasters, for example in the Great Irish famine of 1845–50, and in Ethiopia and Somalia.
3. Some famines have produced no excess mortality at all. Victims of famines in Tanzania and Sudan talk about 'the famine that kills' (Iliffe 1979; de Waal 1989), as distinct from the famines that cause hunger and destitution but do not result in death.

These views were interrogated by writers who saw famine as a 'social process' (Rangasami 1985) and as a 'community crisis' (Currey and Hugo 1984). Currey's (1981: 123) definition was originally devised in 1976, and was the first definition of its kind (Devereux 1993: 14):

> Famine might be defined as the community syndrome which results when social, economic and administrative structures are already under stress and are further triggered by one, or several, discrete disruptions which accelerate the incidence of many symptoms, or crisis adjustments, of which one is epidemic malnutrition.

Cutler (in Devereux 1993: 15) introduces a social class dimension to the definition, in order to identify the likely victims and 'beneficiaries' of famine:

> Excess mortality is concentrated among certain classes, social groups and household members who are particularly vulnerable socio-economically or culturally. A corollary of this is the profit which can be made from famine by other dominant classes, social groups or households.

However, in relation to the impact of famine on displaced people, de Waal (1989) found no correlation, in Sudanese refugee camps in 1985, between individual wealth and the probability of death. Richer people, who had enough cash to buy the food they needed but were displaced into refugee camps by drought, were as likely as the destitute to catch a communicable disease through increased exposure, and to die. Evidence from the Great Irish famines also suggests that social workers and priests died from disease, not from starvation. De Waal calls this the 'health crisis' explanation of famine mortality, as distinct from the conventional 'food crisis' explanation (Devereux 2000: 12).

Howe and Devereux (2007: 30) examined the debate over whether famine should be conceptualised as a 'process' or an 'event', contrasting Mayer's (1975: 572) definition 'severe shortage of food with significant increases in local or regional death rates'. Walker (1989: 6) defines famine as:

> A socioeconomic process which causes the accelerated destitution of the most vulnerable, marginal and least powerful groups in a community, to a point where they can no longer as a group,

maintain a sustainable livelihood. Ultimately, the process leads to the inability of the individual to acquire sufficient food to sustain life.

This definition, like Curry's (1981) and Alamgir's (1981), emphasises the way famines typically develop: that is, as a socio-economic process which occurs over a period of time. However, it fails to focus on the political systems including institutional and administrative capacities – as well as on the development processes and government priorities pre- and post-famine. There is no doubt that government policies and investment priorities determine their level of commitment to public action and to prevent or deal with famine when it occurs.

Moreover, while Sen (1981: 47) writes of people being 'plunged into starvation', Walker (1989: 6) describes a more extended 'socio-economic process' leading to 'accelerated destitution' and – 'ultimately – death'. Rangasami (1993) identifies a three-phase 'famine process': 'dearth', or incipient famine; 'famishment' or maturing famine; and 'full-blown famine'. She suggests that appropriate and measurable indices of distress should be identified from the perspective of the victims, to describe this three-phase process (Howe and Devereux 2007: 30).

No doubt an operational definition of famine using clear indicators can be used to guide national governments and international emergency operations to provide timely and appropriate responses. The results of lack of understanding or of clarity about what is happening on the ground when famine strikes a community can lead to a serious outcome in levels of destitution and mortality.

OPERATIONAL DEFINITIONS OF FAMINE

Most definitions offer important insights, for example on the perspectives of famine-affected populations, and provide the academic grounding for the development of an instrumental definition, but their imprecision and conflicting theoretical stances limit their usefulness for practical purposes (Devereux 2007). As Sen (1981: 40) acknowledges, 'most definitions of famine merely provide 'a pithy description' of what happens during famines, rather than 'helping us to do the diagnosis – the traditional function of a definition'.

Howe and Devereux (2007: 30) state that most definitions of famine are ambiguous or descriptive, and lack clarity, and so provide no practical basis for planning interventions or for enforcing accountability. Furthermore, at the political level, the absence of an agreed definition has made it difficult to hold stakeholders to account, where appropriate. Thus an operational definition is required to assist national governments and donors to make an accurate diagnosis (ibid 2007: 31–45).

To establish the links over a period of time between a pre-famine deterioration in food security indicators among the most vulnerable individuals and households, and a famine situation, it is necessary to redefine famine. Therefore, I propose a more complete definition, which is adapted from Walker (1989: 6), Howe and Devereux (2007) and Devereux (1993) 2001; 2007: 29–45):

> Famine is a political and socio-economic process triggered by a multiplicity of complex factors which cause a rapid deterioration in the nutritional status of individuals, leading to hunger, social breakdown and destitution of the most vulnerable, marginal and least powerful groups in a community, to a point where they can no longer, as a group, maintain a sustainable livelihood. Ultimately, the political decision for public action is the most important factor in preventing vulnerability to famine in the first place, and in alleviating the suffering of famine victims when it happens.

The question then, is how do we prevent famine from happening? Is it enough to achieve international consensus on how to redefine famine to improve operational clarity (improving responses to famine) and political accountability (for famine prevention) Howe and Devereux (2007: 15)?

In relation to improving responses to famine (in terms of time and costs) and to providing indicators or evidence that can be utilised for political accountability, Howe and Devereux (2007: 31–45) made a significant contribution to the literature of famine and to the prevention of future famines. They proposed an 'instrumental definition' based on two complementary scales. The 'intensity scale' monitors the severity of famine conditions by combining outcome indicators (anthropometry and mortality rates) and food security descriptors (food prices and the adoption of coping strategies). Agreed thresholds for key indicators will identify when conditions have deteriorated from 'food security' to 'food insecurity', to 'food crisis' and ultimately to 'famine'.

Intensity and magnitude scales

'Intensity' refers to 'the severity of a crisis at a point in time, which varies from place to place over its duration', while 'magnitude' refers to 'the aggregate impact of the crisis on affected populations' (Howe and Devereux 2007: 36–43). The proposed scales draw on insights and indicators from the various strands of literature reviewed above, and should be understood as analytical tools aimed at diagnosing the situation in a specific area with chronic food insecurity conditions and great vulnerability to famine.

They differ from previous approaches, such as the Indian Famine Codes (see endnote 3) and the Turkana District Early Warning system in the following ways:

1. The scales are intended to provide general operational criteria for identifying famines for the purpose of comparing situations across the globe, while at the same time recognising that each food crisis is grounded in a specific context. This is done by selecting locally appropriate food security indicators which capture the complex experiences of famine-affected populations, to complement standardised anthropometric cut-off points.
2. In disaggregating intensity and magnitude, the scales capture a greater complexity of famine impacts than other approaches.
3. The scales offer a better diagnosis of a range of food insecurity situations, which should eliminate terminological debates about 'famine' or 'no famine', such as have caused fatal delays in several recent food crises.

Table 2.2 shows the intensity scale, and Table 2.3 shows the intensity and magnitude scales combined.

The intensity scale recognises that famines do not have a uniform effect over the entire geographic area inhabited by the affected population. Over time, the area and populations affected by food insecurity and famine will change – expanding and contracting in size, increasing and decreasing in intensity (Howe and Devereux 2007 36–9). The magnitude scale refers to 'the scale of human suffering caused by the entire famine crises which is practically difficult to capture in terms of measuring the impacts of a humanitarian crisis including its macroeconomic, social-cultural, psychological and other consequences' (ibid).

Howe and Devereux propose graduated scales, which can make crude estimates of the magnitude of a famine while it is ongoing, as well as classifying famines after the event. Mortality in the magnitude scale begins at 0 rather than 1, because the criteria used for famine conditions in the intensity scale include malnutrition rates that need not imply deaths, and because a rise in the crude

Table 2.2 Intensity scale

Levels[1]	Designation	Lives: malnutrition and mortality indicators[2]	Livelihood: food security descriptors[3]
0	Food security conditions	CMR < 0.2 and wasting < 2.3%	Social system is cohesive; prices are stable; negligible adoption of coping strategies
1	Food insecurity conditions	CMR ≥ 0.2 but < 5/10,000 per day and/ or wasting ≥ 2.3 but < 10%	Social system remains largely cohesive; price instability and seasonal shortage of key items; reversible 'adaptive strategies' are employed
2	Food crisis conditions	CMR ≥ 0.5 but < 1/10,000 per day and/ or wasting ≥ 10 but < 20% and/or prevalence of oedema	Social system significantly stressed but remains largely cohesive; dramatic rise in price of food and other basic items; adaptive mechanisms start to fail; increase in irreversible coping strategies
3	Famine conditions	CMR > 1 but < 5/10,000 per day and/ or wasting ≥ 20% but < 40% and/or prevalence of oedema	Clear signs of social breakdown appear; markets begin to close or collapse; coping strategies are exhausted and survival strategies are adopted; affected population identify food as the dominant problem in the onset of the crisis
4	Severe famine conditions	CMR > 5 but < 15/10,000 per day and/or wasting ≥ 40% and/or prevalence of oedema	Widespread social breakdown; markets are closed or inaccessible to affected population; survival strategies are widespread; affected population identify food as the dominant problem in the onset of the crisis
5	Extreme famine conditions	CMR ≥ 15/10,000 per day	Complete social breakdown; widespread mortality; affected population identify food as the dominant problem in the onset of the crisis

Source: Howe and Devereux (2007).

1 The idea of using a system of levels was originally suggested to Howe and Devereux by Hamish Young of UNICEF.

2 Wasting: The proportion of the child population (six months to five years old) who are below 80% of the median weight-for-height or have a Z-score weight-for-height below 2 (cf. NCH 1977).

3 These food security descriptors are examples of the types of experiences that may be associated with each intensity level, but not all of them have to be present in every situation that is given that intensity designation.

mortality rate (CMR) is not a prerequisite for a declaration of 'Level 3' famine.

This graduated approach is useful both for deciding the level of intervention and for differentiating between famines characterised by hunger and destitution but not necessarily by death, and others. It also challenges the reductionist position that famine equates to 'mass death by starvation' (Howe and Devereux 2007).

The intensity and magnitude scales are designed to be complementary. Any intensity level of 3 or above will register as a famine on the magnitude scale, even if it occurs in a very localised area, and even if no deaths are recorded, for example in a 'Category A' famine. In addition, these two scales highlight the fact that not every situation involving excess mortality is a famine. Howe and Devereux point out that 'Level 2' food crisis conditions may reach 'Level 3' or above in at least one assessment area, and they suggest that, as long as one population area experiences famine conditions, the deaths from other areas associated with the crisis should be included in the total mortality figures to determine the magnitude of the situation, even if the intensity only reaches 'Level 1' or 'Level 2' in some places.

Table 2.3 Intensity and magnitude scales with examples of classifications

Famine (year)	*Estimated mortality*[1]	*Location*	*CMR*	*Intensity classification*	*Magnitude classification and mortality range*[2]	*Phrase designation*
Sudan (1998)	70,000	Ajiep village	2.6/10,000 per day	Level 5	Category C (10,001–99,999)	Extreme famine conditions
		Rumbek town	3.7/10,000 per day	Level 3	Category C (10,001–99,999)	Famine conditions
Ethiopia (2000)	6,070	Gode town	3.2/10,000 per day	Level 3	Category B (1,001–9,999)	Famine conditions
Malawi (2002)	301–500	Salima district	1.23/10,000 per day	Level 3	Category A (1–999)	Famine conditions
		Mchinji district	0.21/10,000 per day	Level 1	Category A (1–999)	Food insecurity conditions

Source: Adapted from Howe and Devereux (2007).

1 These figures are 'snapshots' and do not reflect the trends in each of these locations. For example, the mortality rate in Malawi in 2002 is estimated to be between 47,000 and 85,000 (Howe and Devereux 2007: 41).

2 Famine description and mortality range A = minor famine (1–999), B = moderate famine (1,001–9,999), C = major famine (10,001–99,999), D = great famine (100,001–999,999), E = catastrophic famine (1,000,000 and over).

THEORIES OF FAMINE

In tracing the evolution of the concept of food security, three overlapping paradigm shifts seem to have taken place since the World Food Conference of 1974. Devereux and Maxwell (2001: 13–27) indicate that these shifts are reflected in the successive development of the term, from the global and national to the household and individual; from a food-first perspective to a livelihood perspective; and from objective indicators to subjective perception (see Chapter 1).

However, the intellectual progression in explaining the causes of famines has the same roots, and sees famine as a sequence of 'entitlement failures'. Devereux (2007) identified two major paradigm shifts: from the pre-modern view of famine in terms of FAD to the modern emphasis on failure of access to FED, and finally to a postmodern focus on failures of accountability and of national and international responses. Table 2.4 illustrates these shifts. However, all famines may have causal elements found in the pre-modern, modern and postmodern explanatory approaches.

Table 2.4   Evolution of famine thinking

Pre-modern: 'old famines' Failure of food supply	Modern: failure of access to food 1st paradigm shift	Postmodern: failure of response 2nd paradigm shift
Entitlement failures		
Production-base exchange entitlement:	Market-based exchange entitlement:	Transfer-based exchange entitlement:
Political and economic interests of major producers; countries and corporations	Political and economic interests of major producers; countries and corporations	Political and economic interests of major producers; countries and corporations
Food availability decline (FAD) theories: Demographic (Malthusian population pressure) Climate (drought, flood, El Niño, global warming Environment (desertification, soil fertility decline) Subsistence farming (peasant's agriculture)	Poverty (weak purchasing power) and food entitlement decline (FED): Fragmented or missing markets, weak infrastructure Market failure (supply/ demand, speculation/ hoarding)	Accountability failures: Government priorities Failure of institutions for public action Failure of informal safety nets – 'moral economy' Socio-cultural failures Callous disregard for the victims of famine Food aid failure

Source: Adapted from Devereux (2007: 12).

The following sections explore the theories and explanations of famine drawing on the work of Devereux, Sen, Maxwell, ÓGráda and others.

PRE-MODERN THEORIES: SUPPLY-SIDE FACTORS

Pre-modern theories of famine explain famine largely in terms of food shortages caused by population growth 'too many people, too little food' – and/or by climatic variations such as floods and droughts. These are labelled by Sen (1981) as food availability decline or (FAD) theories (Devereux 1993; 2000; 2001; 2007).

Food availability decline (FAD) – too many people, too little food

Demographic explanations of famines have generally been based on the work of the Reverend Thomas Malthus, whose essay of 1798, 'The principle of population: the future improvement of society', forecast that population growth would outstrip the world's food supply. As a result, demand for food will eventually outstrip potential food production. In Malthus' view, starvation acts as a 'natural check' on population growth and famine restores the balance between food demand and food supply.

Devereux (2001: 122) summarises the basic Malthusian arguments:

- Population and the demand for food increase at a parallel rate over time.
- Natural resources, especially arable land, are limited in supply. Land is not only scarce; it is also of variable quality: as population pressure causes more land to be cultivated, increasingly marginal soils will be brought into cultivation, leading to falling productivity.
- Rising demand for food can be met by either more extensive (land clearing by deforestation) or more intensive cultivation of land. Once the 'extensive margin' of cultivation has been reached it will become necessary to intensify production in order to increase yields per unit of land. But this too will eventually lead to falling productivity, as returns to labour and other inputs diminish, so that food production will eventually grow more slowly than population.
- Given fixed natural resources, the population must stabilise at the maximum possible level of food production. Therefore,

starvation acts as a natural check on population growth, with famine maintaining equilibrium between the need for food and food supplies.

The timing of Malthus' arguments, however, was unfortunate, for something started to happen around then, as industrialisation swept through what is now the developed world, and the fertility rate fell sharply – first in France, then in Britain, and then throughout Europe and America (*Economist* 31 October 2009: 29).

Recent statistical evidence shows that the fertility rate is falling and families are getting smaller in many developing countries. Half of humanity will have only enough children to replace the population, which means that the fertility rate of half the world will be 2.1 or below. This replacement level of fertility causes a country's population to slow down and eventually stabilise (ibid.).

Although Malthus' original propositions have been convincingly refuted by history, several 'neo-Malthusian' variants of the argument insist that famine can still be explained in terms of 'too many people, too little food'. These analyses tend to discount the significance of falling fertility, believing that there are too many people in the world so it is the absolute number that matters. They argue that, where the environment is fragile or degraded, famine follows from the fact that the regional carrying capacity has been fatally exceeded. Related to this is the economic argument that high population growth-rates perpetuate poverty at the household level, and famine vulnerability at the regional level, due to the excessive partition of land among heirs and the creation of high dependency ratios (Devereux 1993: 183).

ÓGráda (2009: 90), quoting Karl Marx's arguments in Das Kapital that 'the Great Irish Famine killed "poor devils only"', claims that this 'holds for all famines as mortality has always varied inversely with socio-economic status, but especially so during famines'.

Some argue that 'death control' is being practised in societies where 'birth control' is needed even more urgently, in that modern medicine keeps more people alive while the rate of decline in birth rates lags behind. Hence neo-Malthusians recommended birth control, by coercion if necessary. However, they have failed to realise the importance of children to poor families as an insurance against risk, and the fact that high fertility can be a response to poverty and vulnerability to famine, rather than a cause of it (Devereux 1993: 183).

The evidence shows that famine is not a 'Malthusian leveller'. Only a tiny percentage of a population affected by food shortages die as a consequence. Those most likely to survive are young and middle-aged adults, and almost all famines are followed by a post-famine 'baby boom', which rapidly compensates for the excess deaths. Moreover, Malthus failed to foresee the green revolution (which raised production), the transport revolution (which improved food distribution) or the information and communication technology, including mobile phones which has improved access to markets and has facilitated the early warning systems (Devereux 1993: 183).

Classical Malthusian theory is challenged by Böserup (1983). She argues that population levels determine agricultural methods, rather than agricultural methods determining population via the food supply. Population concentration encourages investment in rural infrastructure (roads, irrigation), which reduces vulnerability. Through economies of scale it facilitates more people, more investments, with the right policies in place that in turn stimulate technological innovation. More people means intensification of agricultural production: a shift to using the plough instead of the hoe; increased use of fertilisers (organic and non-organic); integration of crops and livestock; investment in irrigation; and increased use of rural labour, all of which leads to higher agricultural production per unit and higher incomes, which in turn lead to higher demands for goods and services from both rural and urban areas.

Simon (1996) also challenges the Malthusian catastrophic vision, citing first the existence of new knowledge, and educated people to take advantage of it, and second 'economic freedom', that is, the ability of the world to increase production when there is a profitable opportunity to do so.

George (2006) argues that Malthus did not provide any evidence of a natural tendency for a population to overwhelm its ability to provide for itself. He showed that even the main body of Malthus' work refuted this theory, indicating social causes for misery, such as 'ignorance and greed, bad government, unjust laws, or war, rather than insufficient food production'.

However, ÓGráda (2009: 122) asserts that:

Historically malnutrition and disease in so-called normal times were more potent positive checks on population growth in the long run than the 'Third Horseman'. One reason for this is that famines were probably not frequent enough to fulfil their

Malthusian mission. He [Malthus] also argued that famine offered no more than an ephemeral 'remedy' for overpopulation, unless survivors 'learned' from the tragedy that they had escaped, since the resultant demographic vacuum would quickly be filled. In the case of China, Malthus himself conceded that famines 'produced but a trifling effect on the average population'.

Vagaries of the earth's climate and famine

Historically, famine has been associated with 'natural events' such as droughts, flood, El Niño and freezing winters. While geography must have influenced the intensity and frequency of famines in the past, no part of the globe has been always free from famine, some regions have escaped more lightly than others. (ÓGráda 2009: 14)

Geographers, climatologists and other physical scientists have taken the lead in ascribing famines to the vagaries of the earth's climate. A common theme during the 1970s was that climate produces 'natural famine regions' (Devereux 1993: 35).

Cox (in Devereux 1993: 35) describes two global 'famine belts'. One, extending from the British Isles across Europe and Russia to northern China, corresponds to a region in which food production failures may occur because of dampness, cold, and shortened growing seasons. The second, extending from Africa and the Mediterranean littoral eastward through the dry and monsoon lands to China, is a belt of drought-induced famine.

Devereux (1993: 36) criticises Cox and other 'climate prophets of dooms' who believed that vulnerability to famine was likely to increase worldwide because of 'ecological imbalances' brought about by massive climatic changes, notably the cooling of the northern hemisphere, which has been 'implicated as a possible causal mechanism of drought in the Sahelian Zone of Africa'. He emphasises that:

Even if global cooling is true, though, the apocalyptic conclusion does not necessarily follow. Commentators who pursue purely climatic explanations fail to distinguish between the climatic crisis of drought and the socioeconomic crisis of famine. No famine can be explained by its trigger factor alone, particularly something as 'scientific' [that is, removed from its social, economic and political context] as a drought. Drought or flood causes crop failure; but vulnerability to drought or flood or any other trigger causes famine.

Meteorological drought is a 'specific percentage reduction in precipitation over a given period of time' (Glantz, in Devereux 1993: 38). An agricultural drought can be defined as a 'lack of adequate soil moisture to sustain crop growth and production' and 'this requires a certain distribution (not just a total amount) of moisture throughout the growing season' (Hansen and Glantz, in Devereux 1993: 38). Furthermore, a definition of agricultural drought must be sensitive to the energy moisture balance, as Visvader and Burton (1974) indicate: 'while a lack of precipitation is basic to a drought situation, modification of the environment or man's activities to increase water supply or decrease demand may either ameliorate or exacerbate the impact of the physical element of drought'.

Similarly, 'a period of water shortage becomes a drought only when cultural or biological activity becomes constricted' (Visvader and Burton 1974: 6). Thus, human action or inaction determines the possible consequences of drought or flood or other severe climatic conditions.

Drought or flood can cause food shortages in rain-fed agricultural areas of Africa and South Asia, but reduced production of food may affect a household's ability to get food in a number of ways: (1) reducing their own production and any sales thereof; (2) reducing their ability to get cash or wages in kind through work (reducing rural employment); and (3) reducing the purchasing power of any wages they get and the assets they have accumulated, by raising the price they have to pay for food (Devereux 1993: 39).

While these are serious consequences of climatically induced food shortages, this theory does not stand up under closer scrutiny (Devereux 1993: 182). The idea that a calamitous drought leads directly to famine is too simplistic, for the following reasons:

- Drought, flood or crop blight disrupts food production, not distribution. So the concept of FAD as a central cause assumes a totally closed economy;
- FAD implies that everyone is equally affected, but the rich rarely die during famines;
- People in drought-prone areas have developed a range of insurance mechanisms and coping strategies which help them to survive;

- Drought develops into famine in sub-Saharan Africa, if it is especially severe and protracted, if it operates in tandem with other threats to food security (notably war) and if coping strategies have been undermined or exhausted; and
- If interventions designed to prevent famine fail to materialise, are inappropriate, or arrive too late for example in the case of the Great Irish famines; the Great Bengali famine and so on.

A robust theory must explain why, in potentially life-threatening circumstances, food does not come in from elsewhere, in the form of either trade or aid. Finally, since drought does not always lead to famine (as it does not in the US, for example), the theory fails to distinguish between situations where people are vulnerable to drought and those where they are not (Devereux 1993: 182).

MODERN THEORIES: DEMAND-SIDE FACTORS

Exchange entitlement collapse (EEC)

Several writers had recognised the relationships between poverty, vulnerability and famine before the publications of Sen's book *Poverty and Famine* in 1981, in which he decisively shifted the focus of famine analysis from the supply-side FAD to the demand side (Devereux 1993: 183). Despite the amount of criticism it has received, Sen's theoretical approach has significant implications for policy-making and for poverty reduction strategies in developing countries.

This theoretical approach to food entitlement concentrates on people's lack of ability to command food by means legally available in the society, and views this ability as dependent on households' endowments in four areas, as outlined by Sen (1981: 46–51):

1. Trade-based possibilities through commodity exchange, or 'exchange entitlement'.
2. Production-based opportunities, or the right to own what one produces with one's own (or hired) resources.
3. Own-labour entitlement. This includes all trade-based and production entitlements derived from the 'sale' of one's own labour power.
4. Inheritance and transfer entitlement. Refers to the right to own what is willingly given by others, including gifts and bequests,

as well as transfers by the state. This last endowment is seen as entitlement vis-à-vis the state.

Sen (1981: 47) demonstrates that:

> Famine can and does occur with plenty of food in the region or country, because people have differential access to this food, and its distribution can shift unfavourably even if aggregate food availability is adequate and constant or rising. Households' vulnerability to starvation depends on their unique entitlement to food.

Viewed from this perspective, a person starves either because he does not have the ability to command enough food, or does not use his/her ability to avoid starvation – they choose not to work or not to eat. Sen (1981: 48) emphasises that ownership of food is one of the most primitive property rights, and that in every society there are rules governing this right.

Devereux (1993: 69; 2001) highlights some elements of the strength of Sen's theoretical approach. He argues that Sen has shifted the analysis, from conventional supply-side analyses of food crises, towards an analysis of lack of capability and ability to access food. This is 'demand failure' in the strictest sense.

His approach identifies which groups of people will be affected by various threats to availability of, or access to, food (that is, the poor and vulnerable). Sen's analysis of famines which occur in 'boom' periods as well as during 'slumps' indicates that a boom famine is characterised by failures of exchange or trade entitlements for some people because of food price-rises or the marginalisation of certain occupational groups. A good example is the 2007 rise in food prices, and the number of people both in rural and urban areas, including middle-class people in Africa, who became dependent on food aid or 'food for work' programmes.

In the words of Devereux, a boom for some means greater vulnerability for others, if it takes the form of uneven economic expansion. 'Slump famine', by contrast, is typified by direct entitlement failures, the most obvious example of which is crop losses following drought. Those dependent on others for their income (say, landless labourers on cash-crop farms) will also suffer during slump famines.

Sen's approach explains famine as a normal market process, given that markets respond to purchasing power rather than to needs.

Sen cites cases where food was actually exported from an area while people starved. This clearly cannot be explained by the pure FAD approach, but it can be explained by the failure of moral obligation on the part of the government and also by the influence of governments' priorities and producers' and traders' interests.

Sen refutes what he calls 'Malthusian pessimism' and 'Malthusian optimism', both of which he believes fail to address the real, underlying causes of famine: poverty and vulnerability.

Devereux (1993: 72) points out the extent to which entitlement analysis differs from FAD approaches, by highlighting how Sen has challenged the conventional famine-relief model by emphasising the long-term policy implications of public action on poverty and vulnerability:

> Moving food into famine areas will not in itself do much to cure starvation, since what needs to be created is food entitlement and not just food availability. Indeed, people have perished in famines in sight of much food in shops. This was widely noted in the Bengal famine of 1943. (Sen 1982: 48)

According to Devereux (1993: 76) Sen's theoretical approach to famine analysis has been challenged by many writers, despite its immediate and widespread acceptance in the early 1980s as the new dominant theoretical approach. Moreover, writers such as Brett-Crowther (1983: 94–5) questioned the book's practical value and its academic validity.

However, Sen (1981: 48) himself presents four limitations to his entitlement approach, none of which, in his view, undermines the basic theory. He points out that while it is an approach of some generality, it makes no attempt to include all possible influences that can in principle cause starvation. He outlines these four limitations as follows:

1. There can be ambiguities in the specification of entitlements. Even in capitalist market economies, entitlements may not be well defined in the absence of a market clearing equilibrium,[4] and in pre-capitalist formations there can be a good deal of vagueness on property rights. In addition, related matters such as communal land ownership or interlocking factors markets significantly affect entitlements (da Corta, in Devereux 1993: 76; Devereux 2001).

2. While entitlement relations concentrate on rights within the given legal structure in a particular society, some transfers, such as looting or brigandage, involve violation of these rights. In circumstances where such extra-entitlement transfers are substantial, the entitlement approach to famines will be defective. However, he acknowledges that most recent famines seem to have taken place in societies with adequate 'law and order', and without anything illegal about the process leading to starvation. He cites the example of how the state in Bangladesh protected well-stocked food shops, while many people died and were denied food because of lack of legal entitlement.

3. People's actual food consumption may fall below their entitlements for a variety of other reasons, such as ignorance, fixed food habits, or apathy – people sometimes choose to starve in the short term rather than sell their productive assets, in order to enhance their future entitlements (Sen 1981; Devereux 2001).

4. The entitlement approach focuses on starvation, which has to be distinguished from famine mortality, since in some cases famine deaths are caused by epidemics, which have patterns of their own. The epidemics are, of course, induced partly by starvation, but also by other famine characteristics, for example population movements, or a breakdown of sanitary facilities.

Devereux's 2001 article, 'Sen's entitlement approach: critiques and counter critiques' examines Sen's own four limitations: starvation by choice; disease-driven rather than starvation-driven mortality; ambiguities in entitlement specification; and extra-legal entitlement transfers. He concludes that Sen's theoretical approach is significantly weakened, both conceptually and empirically, by its methodological individualism and by its privileging economic aspects of famine above socio-political determinants.

Devereux did not refute Sen's theory as did Bowbrick (1986), or dismiss it as a theoretical failure as did Rangasami (1985) and Fine (1997). He states that:

a complementary analysis is required, one that recognises the importance of non-market institutions in determining entitlements, famine as social process and epidemiological crisis, and violations of entitlement rules in the complex emergencies that typify most contemporary famines. (2001: 245)

Devereux points out some of the weaknesses in Sen's theoretical approach. For example, intra-household distribution of food is not determined by any recognisable 'entitlement' basis. Children have no legal claim over food, so perhaps the notion of 'dependency entitlement' should be introduced even though it would be difficult to quantify. Other non-income sources of food include 'relief entitlement' or 'latent entitlement' sources of food or income which become operative only when normal sources of entitlement fail. These might include social entitlements such as claims or donations from other households, and food aid and other crisis-triggered transfers.

Devereux (1993: 191) suggests adding a political dimension to Sen's economic analysis, that of 'enfranchisement', which is the degree to which an individual or group can legitimately participate in the decisions of a given society regarding entitlement: 'Famines should raise questions about the relationship between entitlement and enfranchisement in any society, at any moment in history'.

In fact, Sen's (1999) second major, and broadly accepted, contribution to the analysis of famine occured when he asserted that democratic institutions together with a free press provide effective protection from famine. The rationale is that electoral political dynamics (the competitive struggle to win over public opinion and crucial votes) will induce the incumbent government to take timely and adequate action in the face of a famine disaster (Rubin 2009: 700).

Rubin's qualitative and quantitative study 'The merit of democracy in famine protection: fact or fallacy?' calls into question the strength of the link between democracy and famine protection. He states that 'famines have occurred in electoral democracies where the political dynamics at times ran counter to providing protection from famine, citing evidence from Bihar, India, in 1966, Malawi in 2002 and Niger in 2005'. The article concludes that 'to fully grasp the complexities of famine, one should replace mono-causal political explanations (such as democracy protects against famine) with general tools for context-specific political analyses'.

Market failures

Devereux (1993: 86) examined the relationship between famine victims and their local markets when food is scarce: that is, the role of traders in either exacerbating or alleviating a localised subsistence crisis. He describes how well-functioning markets for goods operate: demand by consumers and supply from the markets must operate effectively and simultaneously.

Moreover, the markets can contribute to or create the conditions for famine in two ways. The first scenario is when effective demand fails to materialise, which is related to the inability of certain groups of people to secure adequate food because they lack adequate purchasing power, despite the existence of functioning markets for food and other commodities. This is labelled as 'effective demand failure' or 'pull failure'. The second might occur when the market is unable to meet the effective demand for food in a region, even though the necessary demand exists. This is labelled 'response failure' (Sen 1985: 1).

Pull failure must be clearly distinguished from response failure when the contribution of markets to famine is considered. Starvation resulting from pull failure can be seen as the outcome of normal market processes, while pull failure as a problem arises because markets do not, and cannot, respond to needs, but only to purchasing power – a factor which may contribute to famines if poor people lose their ability to buy adequate food (Sen 1985: 2):

> 'Pull failure' is not, strictly speaking, a 'market failure' at all, since the market has no pre assigned role of giving everyone 'pull' to get what they need. Those who think of this as a market failure are much too respectful of the market; it is not that kind of institution with any commitment to equality or justice. In contrast, 'response failure' is a failure of the market in its institutional role.

ÓGráda (2009: 158) points to another factor:

> Failure of food markets per se was not responsible for famines, at least in early modern Europe. At the same time, it should be emphasised that markets were no panacea: again and again, market forces lacked the power and speed to override severe harvest failures in backward economies.

Moreover, a dependence on the markets for food is dangerous if markets are unreliable, so that 'response failure' during a food crisis is possible. Markets can fail to function well either inter-temporally[5] or spatially. According to ÓGráda (2009: 143):

> most populist critiques of how markets worked during famines focused on the intertemporal aspect. They held that traders often, if not always, tended to underestimate the size of the harvest in poor years, and thus engage in 'excessive' storage. The claim implies an asymmetry in speculators' expectations about the state of the harvest shortfall.

Devereux (1993: 187) points out that:

> Hoarding food, whether for precautionary or speculative reasons, can magnify food shortages and price rises. Exaggerated fears of future shortages result in panic hoarding beyond what is justified in reality.

Desai (in Devereux 1993: 88) adds that 'vulnerability is a function of economic distance from food production'. His assumption is based on the fact that the risks for the poor [groups such as casual workers, the landless and the urban poor] of market dependence are greater than the risks farmers experience in agriculture, even in difficult climates. It is generally accepted that wage rates and employment opportunities in rural areas are closely associated with year-to-year agricultural performance. Famine is frequently a rural problem, because in bad years farm wage rates fall and workers are laid off or not hired, while farmers are at least assured of whatever food they manage to harvest (Devereux 1993: 88).

Shepherd (in Devereux 1993: 89), using evidence from Sudan, suggests that markets worsen the position of the poor by aggravating demand failure if the distribution of food is left to 'free market forces':

> Private mercantile control over the distribution of staple food grains has meant that food deficit areas, such as the semi-arid zones, and parts of Southern Sudan, often do not receive the amount of grain needed to maintain a reasonable stability of prices. Merchants will sell in areas where there is purchasing power. This means that food deficit areas also tend to be low income areas. The real tragedy is that low income areas are poorly supplied in drought years when livestock mortality is high and savings cannot easily be mobilised. Famine may result, not because of a scarcity of food, but because of poor distribution of available food.

Moreover, the crisis of famine presents opportunities for the rich and powerful to increase their power and wealth through market mechanisms. As Devereux (1993: 90–1) explains, citing Hartmann:

> while to most people scarcity means suffering, to others it means profit. The obverse of impoverishment is accumulation, and famines accelerate polarisation within communities, as the poor

are forced to transfer their assets to the rich at unusually low prices. Such 'distress sales' are a common feature of most, if not all, famines.

This is in response to Ravallion's (1987a: 59) argument that hoarding at the early stages of famine will improve grain availability later on and can ameliorate a food supply crisis by accurately anticipating it. Devereux (1993: 93) suggests that, throughout the history of famine and in many locations across the globe, hoarding and speculation by traders and producers was an act of self interest, with the sole motive of maximising their profits, especially during anticipated food shortages. Thus there is strong evidence to counter the belief that 'hoarding smoothes out food shortages'.

In the case of the Bengal famine in 1974, the expectation of food scarcity following the floods was made worse by a US embargo on food aid, and by the government's difficulties in importing grain from the world market. Producers and traders overreacted to an anticipated cutback in the government's public distribution as imports were squeezed during 1974.

Sen (1981: 76) elaborates further in the case of the Great Bengali famine of 1943:

Demand forces were reinforced by 'indifferent' winter crops and by vigorous speculation and panic hoardings. The hoarding was financially profitable on the basis of even 'static expectations': rice prices had more than doubled in the preceding year. There was an abnormally higher withholding of rice stocks by farmers and traders from the winter harvest of 1942–43; the normal release following the harvest did not take place. A moderate short-fall in production had by then been translated into an exceptional short-fall in market release.

ÓGráda (2009: 184–5) sheds new light on the Bengali famine:

At the height of the Bengal famine, an editorial in the Calcutta Statesman pointed to an uncanny similarity between official reactions to incipient famine in Bihar and Orissa in 1866 and Bengal in 1943. In both cases the authorities denied that there was a genuine dearth, 'large stores are being in the hands of dealers who are keeping back stocks out of greed'; they refused to recognise 'advancing calamity'; and in both cases disaster followed. In the case of Bengal, the lack of convincing evidence for significant speculative hoards and the socioeconomic backgrounds of the 'losers' support the case for a dearth. A major difference between the two famines, though, is that in 1943 the authorities were engaged in a global war that they were in some danger of losing.

ÓGráda (2009: 184–5) cites *The Economist*, in response to the *New Statesman* and *Nation* when they first raised the spectre of famine in India in January 1943, with a concise statement of British wartime priorities: 'the best way to end famine is speedy victory and, however hard the decision, food ships must come second to victory ships'. And so wartime priorities made Bengal starve in the second half of 1943.

Market fragmentation

ÓGráda (2009: 157) states: 'the historical record suggests that the integration of markets and the gradual eradication of famine are linked'. Moreover, Devereux (1993: 94–5) explains:

> If markets are fully integrated and functioning perfectly, supplies of food could simply be brought in from other markets in surplus areas, with little effect on prices or consumption in either area. Yet dramatic rises in local food prices, which reflect market fragmentation, are symptomatic of food shortages, and have been incorporated as crisis indicators in many famine 'Early Warning Systems' (EWS) for this reason.

He emphasises:

> The notions of a fully integrated and a totally isolated 'island' economy should be regarded as two extremes on the spectrum of actual possibilities. In reality, the extent to which regional food shortages are translated into local food price rises will depend not on whether markets are integrated or fragmented, but on their degree of integration.

A market fragmentation theory of famine has been advanced by Seaman and Holt (in Devereux 1993: 97). They argue that 'prices rise in a series of ".ripples" around a food shortage region, as those afflicted migrate to neighboring markets where food is more readily available, as evidenced in the Bengali famine of 1974 and the Ethiopian famine of 1983'.

'The price ripple hypothesis reflects the reality of the breakdown of the markets and market signals that typically accompanies a crop failure in isolated, self-provisioning communities' (ibid). This problem still exists in most low-income developing countries where poor infrastructure impedes the flow of trade from self-provisioning farmers to regional markets.

Devereux (1993: 98) asks the question: 'why do traders not bring grain into markets where people are desperate for food?' He suggests two compatible explanations, one reflecting demand or 'pull factors' the other supply or 'response factors'. The first point relates to inequalities in wealth distribution within famine villages:

> Following a local production failure, food prices will start to rise. But high prices do not have the identical effect on all consumers. It is the relatively wealthy who exert most of the real upward pressure on food prices, while the poorest will rapidly be forced out of the market. Hence the brunt of the reduction in supply inevitably falls on the poor, because of their acute sensitivity to food price rises. (ibid)

The second point relates to the 'transaction cost' a trader would face in supplying famine villages with grain:

> Traders would not necessarily respond, even to unusually high prices, because they would recognise this signal as illusory. It would require costly reorientation of marketing routes to start supplying remote villages which were normally self-sufficient with grains; there would be only a few wealthy consumers willing to pay very high prices; and the market would not last beyond the next harvest, when prices and demand would fall back to normal levels. All these factors add up to a much smaller profit potential than the high prices initially suggest. (ibid)

Devereux (1993: 98) concludes: 'the combined effect of these two sets of factors suggests a disaggregated explanation of the Wollo famine, one that recognises the role of both "FAD" and "FED" approaches. Both the "demand/pull" and "supply/response" failure have their merits; and explanatory power'.

However, despite major improvements in infrastructure, transport facilities and communication technologies in developing countries – there are more than 600 million mobile-phone users in Africa, for example (*Economist* 6 January 2011) – many rural areas in the developing world still suffer from low population density, and have isolated and inaccessible communities. This has severe consequences during food shortages, or in the context of any other factors that directly affect food prices.

POSTMODERN THEORY: THE FAILURE OF ACCOUNTABILITY

Politics is central to 'new famine' thinking and analysis in four distinct ways (Devereux 2007: 7–9):

1. Famines are related to political regimes. Most twentieth-century famines occurred under authoritarian, unaccountable regimes, colonial administrations, military dictatorships, and one-party states, or during wartime. Five of the worst famines of the century took place in Stalin's Soviet Union, Mao's China, Pol Pot's Cambodia, Mengistu's Ethiopia and Kim Jong-il's North Korea.

2. Recent famines are often connected with conflict, but in more complicated ways than historical conflict-famines. In the 1990s, the phrase 'complex political emergencies' was coined to characterise the relationship between the 'new wars' and famine. Wars disrupt all components of a food system – agricultural production and food stores, trade routes, and aid flows – but in complex emergencies starvation is not only a by-product, it is also often an intended consequence of conflict.

   Two key insights that challenge 'old famine' thinking are that complex emergencies produce beneficiaries as well as victims (Keen 1994; Devereux 2007: 8). Furthermore, Duffield and Deng (in Devereux 2007: 8) indicate that asset ownership does not necessarily provide buffers against livelihood shocks, but can increase vulnerability to famine as wealthier people are targeted during counter-insurgency attacks.

3. The factors that create famine have become 'globalised' to an unprecedented extent. Several 'new famines' have followed directly from the exercise of economic and political leverage by powerful countries and global institutions against weak and vulnerable countries, intended to correct bad government policies or to undermine a dictator. 'A most dramatic instance of political leverage creating famine conditions was the "sanction famine" in Iraq in the 1990s' (Gazdar 2007: 127).

4. The fourth political factor in contemporary famines is the role of the 'international social safety net' and the humanitarian

industry in famine prevention (Noland, in Devereux 2007: 197–221). The emergence since the Second World War of the global humanitarian industry has played a significant role in reducing famine deaths across the world. However, despite the rapidly increasing technical, logistical and institutional capacity to prevent famine their work has not been accompanied by a corresponding strengthening of accountability (ÓGráda 2009: 220).

The politicisation of famine: the example of Ethiopia

Lautze and Maxwell (2007: 240–1) examine the politics of famines in Ethiopia, shedding new light on the way famine is defined in terms of political containment or in terms of political empowerment:

> The sensitivity surrounding the term 'famine' in Ethiopia is not a benign debate about semantics, but rather serves a highly functional purpose. Famines defined as 'events' have largely been proven to be containable, albeit at a considerable (and increasing) effort and expense. Famines defined as the logical outcomes of longer-term processes have hardly ever been dented by the efforts of the past two decades – as evidenced by the interlocking vulnerabilities and rising number of the people who are chronically food insecure.

Donors' concerns about political stability tend to preclude honest and constructive critiques of the government of Ethiopia's long-term recovery programmes. Declaring a famine was also a complicated question for the Ethiopian government, and famine has contributed to the downfall of Ethiopian regimes:

> The government's Disaster Prevention and Preparedness Commission (DPPC) are charged with preventing famines of the 1984–1985 type: that is, those types of famine that make regimes fall. In both the 1999–2000 and the 2004 crises, the DPPC fulfilled its mandate well; neither crisis was allowed to develop into famine that threatened the political order. (Lautze and Raven-Roberts 2004)

Lautze and Maxwell (2007: 223–42) conclude their article, 'Why do famines persist in the Horn of Africa? Ethiopia, 1999–2003' thus:

Clearly exposures to the vagaries of global politics and the world market have far surpassed the vagaries of weather as the driving force of vulnerability in Ethiopia (and in most other low-income food deficit countries). The question now remains whether there is adequate impetus from any of the key actors in Ethiopia – the government, donors, international organisations and affected populations – to effect the radical transformation in the systems of vulnerability identification and strategies required for alleviating risks and vulnerabilities across multiple time frames.

Non-governmental organisations: accountability?

Strong civil society movements that promote diverse non-governmental organisations are the prerequisite for good governance. Part of the challenge is how the state and civil society organisations coordinate their efforts in their engagements with people. There are over one million NGOs in the United States, and by the mid-1990s about one million NGOs were operating in India, 210,000 in Brazil, 96,000 in the Philippines, 27,000 in Chile, 20,000 in Egypt and 11,000 in Thailand (World Resources Institute 2003). Many NGOs have established strong programmes and presence in food policy and hunger prevention in recent years, although they have yet to convert these into firm positions in terms of delivery and actively shaping overall policy integration (Lang and Heasman 2004).

However, NGOs face a number of challenges in their work delivering effective aid programmes, whether it is short-term relief or long-term development, and in being accountable to their beneficiaries (a requirement in order to fulfil their obligations to their public and private donors). The challenges were found to be both financial and administrative, including time and money constraints, problems in the area of operation in terms of logistics and workloads, and issues with management, including staff awareness and capacity to implement and accept the challenges for both upward and downward accountability.

They have 'undoubtedly succeeded in raising global awareness of poverty and underdevelopment'. Moreover, 'the transition from ad hoc philanthropy to enduring bureaucracy has not been without its downside' ÓGráda (2009: 220).

ÓGráda (2009: 220), points out some of the challenges such as lack of meaningful cooperation with other similar NGOs and UN agencies in terms of sharing information and the coordination of field activities. One can argue that this is because each agency is individually accountable to their core source of funding, and thus upward accountability becomes a priority to secure further funding. The above constraints (that is, finance, administration and technical capacity) put pressure on NGOs to follow disaster emergencies rather than engage fully with partner governments in working to prevent disasters.

Moreover, the disaster relief and long-term development programmes of NGOs face dilemmas related to low levels of funding, which force them to spread their activities thin and wide. Thus, many NGOs have become increasingly reliant on public funding, and have in effect been coopted by governments as intermediaries to distribute food and development aid.

ÓGráda, in his recent book *Famine, a Short History* (2009), sounds a note of optimism in his predictions for the regions most exposed to the threats of major famines:

> The recent history of famine is not easily squared with the World Food Programme's (WFP) claim that food emergencies are twice as numerous today as they were in the 1980s, a decade in which famine mortality was much higher. NGOs also tend to paint a bleak and depressing picture of emergencies without end. The evidence suggests otherwise, though: probably for the first time in history, only pockets of the globe, such as parts of Africa, Afghanistan, and North Korea, now remain truly vulnerable to the threat of major famine. Endemic malnutrition is a distinct and more intractable issue.

To conclude, according to ÓGráda (2009: 282) 'the prospect of a famine free world hinges on improved governance and peace. It is as simple – or difficult – as that'. There is a need to create food entitlement through cash for work as opposed to food for work and not just food availability, through sustainable progress towards alleviating poverty and vulnerability to future crises.

In relation to FAD, moving food into famine areas will not in itself do much to address starvation. Devereux (1993) suggests that when food shortage is localised rather than nationwide, which is a normal pattern in most famines, more effort should be made to procure food from surplus regions in the area instead of automatically shipping in tons of wheat and other produce from Western Europe or North America. This will stimulate local production and trade and avoid disincentive and dependency effects.

Chapter 3 focuses on the supply side of food, examining the world food system and its ability to feed the anticipated nine billion people who will inhabit the planet by 2050. It will highlight the limitations of existing trends and approaches to stabilise food production and to combating hunger.

3
The World Food System: Challenges and Options

This chapter links the debate about food insecurity to two schools of thought. The first is exemplified by Lang and Heasman's (2004) book, *Food Wars: The Global Battle for Mouths, Mind and Markets*. In it, they suggest that food policy can be understood as a product of the tension between three competing paradigms. The 'productionist paradigm' came to full dominance during the last 50 years of the twentieth century, with its core ethos of 'production almost at all costs' but is now giving way to two significant new approaches.

One, which Lang and Heasman term the 'life sciences integrated paradigm' (LSIP), is premised on integrating the life sciences into food policy. The other approach, which they term the 'ecologically integrated paradigm' (EIP), sees food supply as rooted in people's social and ecological needs. Market power and access to market define LSIP through corporate control and are powerfully supported by states and by corporate funding. The EIP approach, on the other hand, is dominated by smaller players, occupies a multi-billion dollar organic niche, and has been led and created by consumers, with little support from states or large corporations. The EIP framework, which is represented by strong movements in developing countries, promotes environmental sustainability based on ecological principles, a holistic perspective on population health issues, and the promotion of social justice in food systems.

The second school of thought is exemplified by Collier's (2008) article, 'The politics of hunger: how illusion and greed fan the food crisis', which labels the EIP and its strong emphasis on organic farming as an approach led by romantics who have portrayed the food crisis as demonstrating the failure of scientific commercial agriculture, and who advocate the return to organic small-scale farming thus counting on abandoned technologies to feed a prospective world population of nine billion. He sees the real challenge not as the technical difficulty of returning the world to cheap food, but the political difficulty of confronting the lobbying interests and the illusions, as he sees them, on which these current policies are based.

Collier proposes three politically challenging steps. First, contrary to the 'romantics', he is convinced that the world needs more large-scale commercial agriculture, not less. Second, the world needs more science: the European ban and consequential African ban on genetically modified organisms (GMO) have slowed the pace of agricultural productivity growth in the face of accelerating growth in demand. He argues that ending restriction could be part of a deal, a mutual de-escalation of folly that would make the third step possible: in return for Europe lifting its self-damaging ban on GM products, the United States should lift its self-damaging subsidies on domestic biofuel production.

Holmén (2006: 473) rejects both the productionist and the 'romantic' or anti-modernist point of view, pointing out that:

> African agriculture and food security are under attack on two fronts. On one side a joint onslaught by transnational agribusiness corporations, governments in rich countries where these corporations are based, and international organisations under their control, such as the World Bank and the World Trade Organisation (WTO). They all strive for acquiring control of food chains and to force Africa to open its borders for overwhelming foreign competition, which will only deepen poverty and extend dependencies. On the other front, Africa is under attack from supposedly well-meaning Western 'anti-modernists' and romantics, who sometimes make good diagnoses of existing evils but like quack-doctors, tend to offer lethal cures for perceived illnesses.

This chapter examines the world food system and a number of key drivers for change in terms of the approaches used in food production worldwide. It goes on to discuss these changes, elaborating on the productionist, the life sciences, and the ecologically integrated approaches, highlighting the advantages and limitations of each. Finally, some suggestions are made for using affordable and environmentally sustainable approaches to improve the productivity of small farmers in low-income food deficit regions in developing countries.

WHAT IS THE WORLD FOOD SYSTEM?

The twentieth century witnessed one of the most significant agricultural revolutions since settled agriculture began around 10,000 years ago. At that time, the Earth's population numbered five million people. Today, it has increased over a thousand-fold to around 6.7 billion (Trostle 2008), and on 1 November 2011 the UN declared the world's population to have reached seven billion. However, the roots of this revolution were planted in England from the sixteenth to the eighteenth centuries, during which the population of the country trebled, allowing the introduction of the new social innovation of more efficient agricultural management practices through to a relentless process of technological development, and leading to major agricultural changes in how food was grown, processed, distributed, and consumed (Evans 2009).

Since the mid-twentieth century, the world food system has been undergoing a revolution in the nature of the food supply-chain, which is characterised by significant increases in productivity and the commercialisation of farming, greater reliance on technical change as the main source of growth, and a greater degree of integration of production with the markets and control systems for processing and distribution (FAO 2002a; Lang and Heasman 2004: 140–1). These changes are driven by, and interact with, rapid urbanisation and the rapid industrialisation of the food industry.

In this context, de Haen et al. (2004: 133) argue that the traditional picture of agriculture in developing countries, of small-scale producers serving largely local markets, is no longer the case, and that there is an increasing need to focus on largely urban markets which are served by sophisticated supply-chains, sourcing goods in both developing and developed countries.

The following section provides a discussion of their description of the drivers for such change in the emerging world food economy:

1. *The slow-down in population growth and fertility rate*: the world population average growth-rate was 1.35 per cent per annum in the second half of the 1990s, and is expected to decline to 1.1 per cent between 2010 and 2015 and to 0.5 per cent by 2045–50 (UN Habitat 2001). Statistical evidence shows fertility rates are falling and families are getting smaller in many developing countries (see Chapter 2 on demography and famine).

2. *Income growth and reduction in poverty*: per capita income growth in developing countries as a whole will increase from 2.4 per annum between 2001 and 2005 to 3.5 per cent between 2006 and 2015. The incidence of poverty will be reduced from 23.2 per cent in 1999 to 13.3 per cent in 2015. However, to date these rates have varied across world regions – there

has been great progress in East Asia, but little progress in sub-Saharan Africa (FAO 2010).

3. *Increasing average food intakes alongside high hunger levels*: daily per capita caloric intake in developing countries is estimated to increase from an average of 2,681 kcal in 1997–99 to 2,850 kcal in 2015. Under 'business as usual', undernourishment will decline from 20 per cent in 1992 to 11 per cent in 2015, but any reductions in the absolute number of undernourished people will be modest, from 776 million in 1990–92 to 610 million in 2015. However, this estimate is far from meeting the World Food Summit target of halving the number of malnourished people by 2015 (MDG 1).[1] In fact, the number of undernourished people increased from 850 million to about one billion, following the world food-price crisis since 2007 (FAO 2010).

4. *Slower rates of growth in agricultural production*: the growth of demand for agricultural products, and therefore of production, will slow down as a result of slower population growth and reduced scope for consumption increases in places where food consumption is already high. For developing countries, production growth has declined from an average of 3.9 per cent per annum in 1989–99 to 2.0 per cent from 1999 to 2002 (FAO 2002a; de Haen et al. 2004). New evidence suggests that food consumption has increased, and dietary habits have changed, following per capita income growth in countries such as China and India. Moreover, diverting food crops to biofuel will contribute further to increasing the volatility of world food prices.

5. *Changes in product composition*: between 1997 and 2015, wheat and rice production in developing countries will grow modestly (by 28 and 21 per cent respectively). However, significant increases are expected in coarse grains (45 per cent), vegetable oils and oilseeds (61 per cent), beef and veal (47 per cent), mutton and lamb (51 per cent), pig meat (41 per cent), poultry meat (88 per cent), and milk and dairy production (58 per cent) (FAO 2002a; de Haen et al. 2004). It should be noted, however, that these figures are estimates based on previous three- or five-year averages, and mostly do not take into account climate variations, oil prices, or the prices of agricultural inputs.

6. *Production growth, based mostly on yield growth*: yield improvements will account for about 70 per cent of production

growth, land expansion for 20 per cent, and increase cropping intensity for the rest by 2030. Nevertheless, FAO projections show that the arable area in developing countries will increase by almost 13 per cent (120 million hectares) and water withdrawals for irrigation by 14 per cent by 2030.

7. *Increasing farm sizes*: as the opportunity cost of family labour rises, small family farm operations for subsistence production become increasingly unprofitable, and landless tenant farmers gradually find their way to the urban industrial and service sectors. Small landowners will likewise find it more profitable to sell or lease landholdings, and will cultivate them only if they have the ownership rights to do so. However, in situations where access to land is through a communal system, farmers are unlikely to be able to sell the land for which they have user rights only. Other factors such as job opportunities outside farming, the farmer's age, number of dependents, education level, and knowledge of the labour market, all determine farmers' decisions to sell their land and move from rural to urban areas.

8. *Growing agricultural trade deficits*: agricultural trade surpluses in developing countries are shrinking, and by 2030 there will be an overall deficit of about US$31 billion, with a rapid rise in imports of cereals and livestock products, and a decline in imports of vegetable oils and sugar. These trends are already becoming prominent in world markets, and a permanent food crisis has effectively been unfolding for decades. In 2010, food prices increased by 5 per cent between July and August. This was due to the short-term supply shocks to basic food commodities, which among other things were caused by the Russian wildfires and the subsequent ban on wheat exports.

9. *Urbanisation*: it is anticipated that world population growth between 2000 and 2030 will be concentrated in urban areas (UN Habitat 2001). On average, across the globe the urban population will be 50 per cent of the whole by 2030 and will exceed the rural population from that point on (de Haen et al. 2004).

10. *Dietary transitions*: as developing countries become richer, and populations become increasingly urbanised, a shift towards a higher-energy diet is already taking place. This includes increased consumption of livestock products such as meat, milk and eggs, as well as vegetable oils and, to a lesser extent, sugar. No doubt as highly populated countries such as China and India become wealthier and more urbanised, demand for

these products will increase, putting pressure on world markets for both food and animal feed. This dynamic has been identified by many writers as one of the factors contributing to increasing food price volatility since 2007.

11. *Market structures*: the first half of the twentieth century was marked by the industrialisation of both agriculture and processing, the second half will be remembered as the decades of retailing industrialisation. These power shifts in the food economy have contributed to the contemporary conflict within the food system between the 'productionist' and 'consumerist' sectors: agribusiness versus consumer business; primary producers versus traders; food processors versus health goals. Lang and Heasman (2004: 139) state that 'In many parts of the world, including Latin America, Asia and Africa, supermarkets are emerging, and along with them changing patterns of food procurement in urban areas'.

Professor Marshall Martin[2] sees 'three drivers of change that will shape the future of food supply globally: first, environmental quality; second; the industrialisation of agriculture, as farming continues to shift from a rural lifestyle to an agribusiness sector with a "chain mentality"; and third, according to Martin, will be firms that can link the food chain and added value in order to benefit economically' (Lang and Heasman 2004: 137–8).

Lang and Heasman (2004) argue that 'developing countries are confronted with the real world of "food politics" which has a number of key battle grounds; the outcome of these global conflicts is of immense significance to the health of individuals, societies and the environment'.

The following sections describe Lang and Heasman's three paradigms that characterise world food system, namely: the productionist paradigm; the life science integrated paradigm (LSIP) and the ecologically integrated paradigm (EIP), and elaborates on their limitations, drawing on the work of Lang and Heasman (2004); Holmén's (2006) paper, 'Myths about agriculture, obstacles to solving the African food-crisis'; and Madeley's (2002) book *Food for All: The Need for a New Agriculture*.

THE PRODUCTIONIST PARADIGM

The overarching goal of the productionist paradigm was to prioritise increasing the quantity of food to meet the needs of growing populations, which was to be achieved by increasing output through enhanced productivity of land, labour and capital. Its origins lie in the industrialisation of food over the last 200 years, and it was based on the agricultural revolution of the eighteenth, nineteenth and twentieth centuries and the concomitant advances in agricultural technologies. These have included the introduction of the Green Revolution (GR) package, which entailed an intensive application of complementary amounts of HYV seeds, fertilisers and water.

Moreover, developments in transport and in information and communication technologies (ICT) have promoted radical changes, enabling and enhancing the capacity of food processors to preserve, store and distribute food across the globe (Lang and Heasman 2004: 19; Evans 2009). As Lang and Heasman put it: 'Colleges of agriculture; extension services and other state and private sector supports were gradually incorporated into this paradigm, which came to dominate food policy after the food shortages and failures of supplies in the pre-World War II period'.

Food shortages, hunger and malnutrition worldwide during the mid-twentieth century led both the US and EU to adopt, from the 1960s on, a policy of increasing investment in GR technology, both by giving incentives to farmers through subsidies and export supports, and through continued progress in crop research. The result has been a significant increase in per capita food production in most developed countries, and some regions of developing countries, which brought about a situation characterised by fewer but larger farms, large-scale mechanisation, and a heavy reliance on fossil fuels (see, Conway 1999; Emerson 2001; Lang and Heasman 2004: 19; Evans 2009: 7).

In all developing countries, the adoption of modern crop varieties increased substantially during the first 20 years of the GR. Figures aggregated across all crops show that usage rose from 9 per cent in 1970 to 29 per cent in 1980. By the 1990s, the figure was 46 per cent, and by 1998, 63 per cent. Moreover, in many areas and for many crops, first-generation modern varieties have been replaced by second- and third-generations of modern varieties (Evenson 2010: 3–7).

However, yield increases cannot be attributed wholly to varietal improvement, as the productivity impacts of crop genetic improvement research were not 'completed' in any sense by the 1980s. For example, FAO data indicate that for all developing countries, wheat yields rose 38 per cent, and even cassava yields rose 13 per cent from 1980 to 2000. In absolute terms (measured in kg/ha), yields for many crops rose more in the 1980–2000 period than in the 1961–80 period (ibid: 6). Table 3.1 describes the main features of the productionist paradigm (Lang and Heasman 2004).

Table 3.1   Features of the productionist paradigm (PP)

Drivers	Major producers were driven by state's support to raise food output through intensification of food production on large-scale farming. State's support was motivated by political and economic interests. It was also envisaged that increasing food supplies would provide the conditions for world food security.
Key food sector	The anticipation of high demands for food was key to driving the commodity markets to respond with high-input agriculture for mass production and processing for mass markets.
Industry approach	The industry approach of using homogeneous products (monoculture/one crop), with high specialisation in terms of the applications of science (HYV seeds, chemical fertilisers, pesticides), meant that major producers pursued higher quantity and productivity (throughout) over quality.
Scientific focus	The application of chemical fertilisers, and ranges of pesticides, herbicides and insecticides, with significant involvement from pharmaceutical companies and agricultural research institutions.
Policy framework	Largely set at high political level including agricultural ministries as policymakers and implementers with a heavy reliance on subsidies and export support.
Consumer focus	The support and subsidies for mass production of food aimed at dominating world markets with cheap food stuffs. For marketing purposes, the food industry invests in producing homogeneous products to satisfy consumers' tests on the one hand and provide convenience for women in terms of cooking time with high response to specification. This approach assumes the safety of the foods produced.
Market focus	Aimed at international and national markets. Export-led trade domination which inevitably created trade tensions. The new products led to the emergence of new consumer choice and a shift to branding.
Environmental assumptions	Assumes limitless natural resources (land, water and so on). Cheap energy for inputs and transportation provided the ground for the expansion of the monoculture industry. Consequently, externalisation of waste/pollution became an issue.
Political support	Historically strong but declining, as reflected in policy battle over subsidies (and export support) both within major producers countries and at WTO negotiations. Farmers' lobby in developed countries still strong in demanding no change to the status quo.
Role of knowledge	Agro-economists as important as scientists.
Health approach	Marginal interest; assumes that health gains follow from sufficiency of supply.

Source: Adapted from Lang and Heasman (2004).

Evenson (2010: 21) argues that the political economy of 'food security' has two dimensions: global and local. From a global perspective, the GR achieved an extraordinary success. Food production per capita outstripped a period of unprecedented population growth. On average, global prices of most food and feed commodities were lower in real terms than at any time in history, apart from the surges in food prices during the 1970s, the mid-1990s and since 2007. However, he asserts that 'in order to ascertain if the GR had an impact on reducing poverty, and if its benefits were equally distributed among farmers and rural labourers, it is essential to evaluate its success from a local perspective'.

The GR undoubtedly did raise the productivity of land and labour and, depending on a country's macro- and microeconomic policies and regulations, may have had some impact on wages. However, Evenson also states that: 'for the poorest countries, the GR, late and uneven as it was, the only game in town'.

Limitations of the productionist paradigm

At the beginning of the twenty-first century, the overall outcome of the 'GR model' of agricultural production (or PP) is in crisis (see, GRAIN 1997; Madeley 2002: 14–19; Lang and Heasman 2004: 19–20; Macdonald 2004). It has been criticised and even rejected by many writers advocating an agro-ecological or 'ecologically integrated model' of agriculture which they are convinced that developing countries need to adopt in order to conserve soil, water, and energy, and promote agricultural and environmental sustainability. They further argue that this change of direction can promote equality in terms of income distribution, since it is scale-neutral, cost-effective and is based on local knowledge and inputs. Box 3.1 summarises some of the major limitations they have identified.

Further criticism and counter criticism focuses on the problems of specialisation and monoculture, which are often assumed to be an automatic outcome of the use of the GR package. Inter-cropping is often suggested as a more ecologically sound agricultural practice than those associated with scientific–industrial agriculture. Holmén (2006) argues that to some extent this is a false dichotomy since such agriculture does not of itself exclude inter-cropping. The two are often combined, though more often in horticulture than in staple food production. The problem with combining inter-cropping and intensive agriculture is that inter-cropping is more labour-intensive. Hence, it can be only maintained on a large scale if labour costs

Box 3.1   Major limitations of the productionist paradigm

- Despite their significant successes in raising production, an estimated 800 million smallholders, who support 1.9 to 2.2 billion people in the world, remain directly or indirectly untouched by modern agricultural technology (Madeley 2002; FAO 2010). This may be because of: lack of resources and/or weak resources and supports; weak institutional capacity; lack of scientific knowledge among farmers; poor extension services; weak, unintegrated and under-funded research; and weak market access.

- The overall objective, as pursued by major producing economies such as the US, was to increase production and eliminate global hunger and promote global food security (the policy during the mid-1960s to mid-1980s was driven by the desire to 'feed the world'). Nevertheless, during this period, and despite all the efforts of national governments, international agencies and NGOs since the first World Food Conference in 1974, the number of hungry people has increased. In fact, the mountains of surpluses have been used to weaken the self-sufficiency policies of many developing countries. They were urged to open their local markets to global trade (Lang and Heasman 2004) and their governments were pressurised to phase out all food production subsidies from the mid-1980s.

- The burden on tax payers of subsidies and export support was draining the budgets of all 29 countries of the OECD of US$327 billion annually (OECD 2001; Madeley 2002: 14). This huge sum – the equivalent of the annual output of sub-Saharan Africa, or nearly the entire public expenditure of Britain – comprised US$114.5 billion of EU production support. Moreover, in October 2010, the Common Agriculture Policy (CAP) budget remained stable at €55 to €60 billion a year, despite opposition from those EU countries which believed it should not consume up to 40 per cent of the total EU budget (*Irish Times* 8 October 2010).

- It is a known fact that one quarter of the EU's farmers with large farms get three-quarters of the CAP subsidies. Small-scale farmers – those with less than 1,000 acres in industrialised countries – have found that they cannot make a living from agriculture, and frequently their land has been sold to larger entities, often large corporations (Altieri, in Madeley 2002: 10–19). The number of farms in OECD countries has been in decline since the late 1930s, and farm incomes have fallen by 72 per cent since the

▶

1960s (Madeley 2002), with most small farmers depending on income transfers to survive.

- The success of the productionist paradigm has been at a huge cost to the environment, through soil erosion, pollution by pesticides, salinisation, the force-feeding of animals, and excessive use of fertilisers and pesticides. In addition it has created social problems, such as the elimination of the family farm, the concentration of land resources in production, the growth of agribusiness and its attempts at corporate control of the food chain and farm production, and the marked change in rural–urban migration patterns.
- The effects of spreading this type of agricultural production to developing countries are now clear. In China, the modernisation of agriculture has already led to the uprooting of more than half the rural population in the last two decades. Pastoralists in West Africa have been displaced by cheap meat imports from Europe, while Indian farmers – who grow traditional oil-seeds such as sesame, linseed and mustard – are being driven under by soya imported from the US. Mexican beef producers are losing ground to US producers, whose inroads into Mexico's markets have tripled since the North American Free Trade Agreement (NAFTA) was ratified (Madeley 2002:10–19).
- This type of agriculture, with its costly machinery and its intensive use of expensive oil, cannot be sustainable. If total world agricultural production and food processing were based on European and North American levels of energy use, says George McRobie, co-founder of the Intermediate Technology Development Group 'known oil reserves would disappear off the face of the earth in 30 years' (Madeley 2002: 18).

Sources: Lang and Heasman (2004); Madeley (2002).

are low, and if consumers are willing to pay a higher price for food staples. In these circumstances, inter-cropping would have a greater chance of surviving an agricultural intensification process (ibid).

Issues of biodiversity have become increasingly salient in recent times. Agricultural modernisation, because of its increased specialisation, threatens the biodiversity of plant species, and a monocultures mode of production is an added risk to all life-supporting systems (Abramovitz and Kane, in Holmén 2006). However, Holmén points out that this is not confined to 'modern' agriculture alone: compared to a natural, 'wild' landscape, even a 'traditional' inter-cropped field means reduced local biodiversity. Indeed, over millennia, the careful selection of preferred plants and plant characteristics, while gradually making it possible to feed an ever-growing human population, has inevitably resulted in a loss of biodiversity. Research by Holmén (2006) and Djurfeldt et al. (2003) in sub-Saharan Africa revealed that, in fact, poor smallholder subsistence farmers have less crop diversity than larger, more wealthy and market-oriented farm households using external inputs, who are more diverse in their agricultural practices.

Furthermore, the claim that modern agriculture offers only a handful of uniform varieties (de Grassi and Rosset 2003: 33) or even very few varieties (Shiva, in Pringle 2003: 37; Holmén 2006: 461–2), does not stand the test of closer scrutiny. While large agribusiness corporations may have an interest in limiting the number of varieties released, since this could enhance profits, such restrictions do not apply to publicly owned crop research.

In this context, nearly 300 new varieties were released between 1966 and 1990. Evenson and Gollin (2003: 3) found that 'by 2000 more than 800 modern varieties had been released in 11 crops studied' in public crop research programmes in Latin America, Asia and Africa. More varieties can be produced and released from public institutions depending on the levels of funding available to these institutions. 'The fact is, neither externally nor within agriculture is it inevitable that "modernisation" of agriculture will lead to genetic erosion' (Egzhabier, in Djurfeldt et al. 2003; Holmén 2006). In fact, seed varieties have been produced with new characteristics, such as higher potential yields and better resistance to drought, pest and insects (Larsson et al., in Holmén 2006: 467). Also, a wider choice of seeds now exists, offering greater adaptability to varied agro-ecological conditions. Contemporary GR technologies include new varieties of nitrogen-fixing seeds and farming conservation practices such as minimum tillage, biological pest control, and improved fallow. These developments all aim to reduce the need for both fertilisers and pesticides (Holmén 2006: 467–8).

However, Holmén (2006: 467–8; acknowledged that the GR has not been successful everywhere. In Asia, where it was small-holder-based and more equitable and inclusive, it included a large and increasing part of the population in the development process. Since the technology is scale-neutral it has strengthened the relative position of small farmers, who utilised the technology package of new seeds, fertiliser and irrigation more intensively than did the large landowners.

In other parts of the world, such as the low-income food deficit countries in Africa, the GR was considered unsuitable because Africa has a multitude of small and highly varied agro-ecological systems. In addition, vested interests in those countries have prevented the full implementation of the GR there. Holmén (2006) argues that contemporary technologies allow new crop varieties, especially GMOs, to be tailored to food crops and small agro-ecological systems, and to be combined with organic and other alternative types of agriculture so as to establish more sustainable food systems. Green and gene technologies do not have to be presented as an either/or choice, since there is great potential for achieving more by using them together.

Holmén (2006: 471–4) concludes that the crucial issue now is not the choice between 'organic' and chemical (or biological LSIP) farming, but rather how to achieve the best results by combining the two forms of technology. Successfully combining modern technology and ecologically sustainable agriculture will require the knowledge and application of sustainable agricultural practices.

Moreover, the capacity and the knowledge already exist to combine scientific and organic methods for more ecologically sound pest control, such as the use of 'integrated pest management' (IPM) and the efficient use of fertiliser by combining fertilisers with biological nitrogen fixation (green manure and mulch). Thus, modern technologies, in combination with enhanced farmer knowledge and involvement in developing such technologies, can do a lot for low-income food deficit countries in Africa and elsewhere.

However, Lang and Heasman (2004: 21) believe that the future of the world's food system will rely more upon the biological rather than the chemical sciences to deliver its vision for production, even though the chemical sciences will continue to play a prominent role in the medium term. The industrial nature of the PP is being softened and reshaped by the new biological thinking that is the LSIP.

THE LIFE SCIENCES INTEGRATED PARADIGM (LSIP)

Lang and Heasman (2004: 21) indicate that there are two possible competing paradigms for the future of food, namely the LSIP and the EIP. Both present visions for the future that are informed by science, and both are seeking to transform the PP. Both predict that the twenty-first century will be the century of biology (Rifkin, in Lang and Heasman 2004). This new paradigm is already giving rise to new controversies, for example over 'genetically modified foods and cloning' (Lang and Heasman 2004: 21). They describe the new languages that are injecting new 'bio-words' into the lexicon: there is now bioprocessing, bioprospecting, bioprivacy, bioextinction, biodiversity, bioscience, bioinformatics, biovigilance, biosafety, bioterrorism, and of course, biotechnologies'.

The LSIP is an emerging scientific approach that depends on the application of advanced new biological technologies to food production methods, food processing and consumer products (Lang and Heasman 2004; Lemaux 2009).[3] Although the terms 'biotechnology' and 'genetic modification' are commonly used interchangeably, GM is a specific set of technologies that alter the genetic make-up of organisms such as animals, plants, or bacteria. It involves combining genes with different organisms from both the plant and animal kingdoms, and is also known as recombinant DNA or DNA technology. The resulting organism is said to be 'genetically modified', 'genetically engineered', or 'transgenic' (Lemaux 2009). GM products (current or those in development) include medicines and vaccines, foods and food ingredients, feeds, and fibres (US Department of Energy 2010).

In 2009, the US grew over 97 per cent of the global transgenic crops, and some 14 million farmers were cultivating these crops, 700,000 more than in 2008. Of these, 90 per cent (13 million) were small farmers in developing countries such as China, India and Brazil, among others. During the first 12 years of commercialisation, 'biotech crops' yielded a net profit of US$44 billion around the world (Política Y Gobierno 2010).

The majority of these crops were herbicide- and insect-resistant soybeans, corn, cotton, canola, and alfalfa. Other crops grown commercially or field-tested are: a sweet potato resistant to a virus that could decimate most of the African harvest; rice with increased iron and vitamins that may alleviate chronic malnutrition in Asian countries; and a variety of plants able to survive weather extremes. On the horizon are bananas that produce human vaccines against infectious diseases such as hepatitis B; fish that mature more quickly; cows that are resistant to bovine spongiform encephalopathy (mad cow disease); fruit and nut trees that mature quickly; and plants that produce new plastics with unique properties (US Department of Energy 2010).

Although the growth of GMO crops is expected to plateau in industrialised nations, it is increasing in developing countries. The next decade will see exponential progress in GM product development as researchers gain increasing and unprecedented access to genomic resources that are applicable to organisms beyond the scope of individual projects (US Department of Energy 2010).

GMO plus

GMO plus nutrigenomics promises a targeted fix to the diet and health policy problem, based on an acceptance that both micronutrients and macronutrients alter the metabolic programming of cells, and on an understanding of how diet is a key factor in disease (Müller and Kersten, in Lang and Heasman 2004: 24). The commercial as well as the academic search is one for bio-active ingredients which could be exploited for health purposes (nutrigenomics.ucdavis.edu: 2012).

As Guy Miller, head of Galileo Laboratories Inc., a US biotech company working in this area, explains in Lang and Heasman (2004: 23):

> By being able to elucidate the genetic profiles of individuals, diets will be formulated from crop to fork to confer prevention or retard disease progression. As basic science advances converge with e-commerce, new opportunities will emerge to deliver to consumers, whose genetic susceptibility to specific diet and disease are known, products tailored to individual dietary needs.

Although the science and technology potentially shaping the LSIP are at the cutting edge, equally powerful scientific arguments are being put forward by its critics, who protest that it is little more than a modernisation of the PP, with the same weaknesses and potential for causing damage (Lang and Heasman 2004).

The question is: how relevant is this paradigm to the 1.2 billion poor individuals in developing countries who have never seen a fork in their lives, or the many poor people who are dependent on state benefits in the industrialised countries? Also, how realistic is it to promote GMO among the 2 billion small-scale subsistence farmers who would never be able to afford the cost incurred in using such technology without any state support? There is also the question of the cost to tax payers of such support, as the burden of the productionist paradigm on national budgets in industrialised countries is well attested.

There is no denying that advances in science are a welcome return on investment (in the US mainly of private money, although there is some investment of public money). However, it must be cost-effective, and the outcomes must cause no harm to human beings, as well as being equitable in terms of access. For example, many poor people in industrialised countries cannot afford to pay for hospital treatment, let alone pay a fee of US$400 to have a nutrigenomic test.

While the LSIP and its nutrigenomic promises reflect an individualised policy approach which focuses on looking after one's own health, it says little about the need to alter the environmental factors which lessen the chances of whole population groups taking adequate exercise or consuming a wholesome diet (Nuffield Trust, in Lang and Heasman 2004). Moreover, Lang and Heasman (2004: 24) state that:

It is an unusual Food War in relation to health, in that large companies not usually associated with humanitarian activism are now advocating that its technologies, particularly genetic modification, be rapidly implemented in order to 'feed the world'.

Technologies for GMO offer dramatic promises for meeting some of the twenty-first century's greatest challenges, but like all new

---

Box 3.2   LSIP and genetically modified organisms: features and benefits

- *Drivers*: it is a scientist-led approach to integrate the food supply chain (from production through to consumption) with tight control by agricultural corporations.
- *Key food sector*: reliance on large-scale farmers and intensive use of capital (by the agro food industry), with food retailers usually dominating the supply chain.
- *Crops*: it claims to enhance the taste and quality of food, in addition to increasing yield, reducing maturation time, and improving resistance to disease and pests.
- *Animals*: it aims at improving the productivity of animals and increasing yields of meat, eggs and milk. Research focuses on improving feed efficiency to enhance health and productivity, and adopting better diagnostic methods of diseases.
- *Environment*: the LSIP claims to be environmentally friendly, as GMO crops can enhance the conservation of soil, water and energy (by using less fertiliser, bioherbicides, bioinsecticides and bioprocessing for forestry products). This process can provide better natural waste management and more efficient food processing.
- *Society*: claims to increase food security (supply of food) for growing populations.

Sources: US Department of Energy (2010) and Lang and Heasman (2004).

technologies, they also pose some risks, both known and unknown. Controversies surrounding GM foods and crops commonly focus on human and environmental safety, labelling and consumer choice, intellectual property rights, ethics, food security, poverty reduction, and environmental conservation (see Boxes 3.2 and 3.3).

Box 3.3   Key limitations of the LSIP and GMO

- *Health and safety*: potential human health impacts, including allergens, transfer of antibiotic resistance markers, and the still unknown effects of nutrigenomics.[4]
- *Potential environmental impacts*: including, unintended transfer of transgenes through cross-pollination, still unknown effects on other organisms (for example, soil microbes), and loss of flora and fauna biodiversity.
- *Consumer focus*: this technology is geared towards the production of champion products, structured to appeal to an individual's health and choice.
- *Access and intellectual property*: the domination of a few companies in world food production can increase dependence on industrialised nations by developing countries. Concerns are also raised over biopiracy, or foreign exploitation of natural resources in developing countries. In addition to being top-down, expert-led and backed by trade and finance ministries in developed countries, it may present some challenges to the regulatory framework of the food industry and public policies.
- *Market focus and ethics*: aims for industrial-scale application of biotechnology, primarily for agriculture but increasingly in manufacturing (enzymes are not just applicable to GM). It uses a mixture of chemical and biological inputs. Opponents of this technology claim that it is a violation of natural organisms and that it is tampering with nature by mixing genes among species (objections raised against consuming animal genes in plants and vice versa).
- *Labelling*: not mandatory in some countries (for example, the United States). Mixing GM crops with non-GM products confounds labelling attempts.
- *Political support and society*: it is fast-developing in both developed and developing countries, but there are divisions among both rich and poor countries about how to interpret this technology. In most cases new advances may be skewed to benefit rich countries.

Sources: US Department of Energy (2010) and Lang and Heasman (2004).

Opponents of the LSIP and GMOs according to Lang and Heasman (2004) and the US Department of Energy (2010) Genome Programme highlight some of the controversies and limitations of this technology in Box 3.3.

However, it is unrealistic to suggest that the productionist/ industrial paradigm has run its course, despite its failure to promote and sustain socio-economic development, as evidenced in such phenomena as rural depopulation, the high cost to governments and tax payers of the required capital investment, and the loss of employment through mechanisation and the intensive use of technology.

It would be unwise for developing countries to dismiss these concerns as the luxuries of the affluent in their drive to improve their agriculture and food production, with or without international investment to maintain the existing global value-chain (Lang and Heasman 2004: 33). Lang and Heasman (2004: 25) state that 'concerns over the impacts of LSIP on human health and the environment are what brought to greater prominence a politically much weaker, and, until recently, highly fragmented body of scientific knowledge which we call the Ecologically Integrated Paradigm (EIP)'.

THE ECOLOGICALLY INTEGRATED PARADIGM

Robertson's (1979) book *The Sane Alternative* outlined five scenarios for the future that could be applied to food and public policy. These were: business as usual; disaster; totalitarian conservatism; hyper-expansion and sane human ecology. Gussow (in Lang and Heasman 2004) believes that the 'business as usual' scenario will ultimately lead to ecological disasters. Considering the track record of totalitarian conservatism, he postulates that it is likely to engender mass resistance. He suggests that within any democratic public food-policy framework there are only two meaningful scenarios to consider, namely, 'hyper-expansionism' – with the world of food becoming dominated by big business, biotechnology and factory farming, among others – or 'sane human ecology', which is characterised by small-scale production and low input (Lang and Heasman 2004: 28).

Madeley (2002: 18), under the title of 'Learning from Whom?' argues that agriculture is more than just another industry. In his view, modern 'western style' agriculture (the PP or the LSIP as Lang and Heasman label them) has neglected the principles of traditional husbandry, turned farms into factories, and driven small farmers from their land. Its intensive use of fertilisers, pesticides, water and energy is causing serious damage to the environment and human health, and has imposed major costs on tax payers and governments. Hence, 'it is unsustainable'.

We live in the era of hyper-expansionism, and it will stay with us unless consumers decide otherwise. Consumers, however, especially in developed countries, do have the power to radically alter their dietary habits and to turn en masse towards agro-ecological products – in other words, to the intensive knowledge-based organic farming which is growing in both developed and developing countries.

Both the historical record and research evidence suggest that dependence on world markets for food is dangerous because of the many factors associated with determining food prices, such as the political and economic interests of major producing countries and multinational corporations (see Chapter 1 in this book for details), as witnessed in the trends from the first world food-price crisis in 1973 through to the mid-1990s and to the most recent crisis from 2007 onwards. Developing countries should claim their rights to food sovereignty, and decide on the most relevant approach to address the issue of ensuring a food supply that is both cost-effective and sustainable.

Lang and Heasman (2004: 26–7) state that the EIP is:

> Grounded in the science of biology, but it takes a more integrative and less engineering approach to nature. Its core assumption recognises mutual dependencies, symbiotic relationships and more subtle forms of manipulation, and it aims to preserve ecological diversity. It takes a more holistic view of health and society than the more 'medicalised' one of the LSIP.

In contrast to the PP and the LSIP, Lang and Heasman (2004: 32) summarise the main features of the EIP as set out in Table 3.2.

Agro-ecology

According to Pretty (2002: 1-4), 'the EIP corresponds closely to the body of thinking described as agro-ecology'. Agro-ecology, or the 'new agriculture', offers a new vision of food production for farmers in both developing and developed countries. This approach aims to develop techniques that are grounded in a rediscovery of local skills and traditional knowledge, but which can be applied in tandem with modern understandings, in order to meet food

Table 3.2   Features of the ecologically integrated paradigm

Drivers	Environmental sustainability concerns; aim at energy/waste reduction; conserving and building biodiversity to minimise risks; reduction of certain chemical inputs.
Key food sector	Integration of all, but emphasis on whole farm systems approach (land and watersheds); biodiversity enhancement to stabilise and maximise yields over the long term.
Industry approach	Aims to move organic foods from marginal to mainstream; nervous about increasing the scale of production and capacity for quality controls.
Scientific focus	Multidisciplinary approach used by integrating biology, ecology and agro-ecological technology instead of chemicals.
Policy framework	Partnership of ministries collaborative institutional structures needed. It promotes advantages of decentralisation and teamwork.
Consumer focus	Citizens not consumers; improved links between the land and consumption and greater use of transparency.
Market focus	Regional and local focus – 'bio-regionalism'; nervous about export-led agriculture; favours smaller companies but increasingly adopted by larger ones.
Environmental assumptions	Resources are finite; need to move away from extensive monoculture and reliance on fossil fuels; need to integrate environmental, nature and conservation policy with industrial and social policy.
Political support	Weak, but low base strengthening in many countries; some merging of fragmented 'movements' claiming high ground.
Role of knowledge	Knowledge-intensive rather than input-intensive; skills needed across whole supply chain. Knowledge is power and it can empower small farmers and women in particular.
Health approach	Promotes diet diversity and presents itself as 'healthy' alternative but as yet on a weak evidence base.

Source: Adapted from Lang and Heasman (2004).

production requirements (Lang and Heasman 2004). The challenge, according to Altieri (in Madeley 2002: 41) is 'to find ways to increase investment and research in agro-ecology and to scale up agro-ecological processes that have already proven successful'.

Around the world there are many examples of initiatives to promote sustainable agriculture. Some of these are classified as organic or semi-organic, others as 'low external input agriculture', while some go further into the category of permaculture. Madeley (2002: 42–51) emphasises that low external input agriculture does not mean low-output agriculture, but that it can, on the contrary, be highly productive.

Permaculture

Permaculture spread rapidly in the last two decades of the twentieth century and has often proved highly productive in terms of overall farm output. The practice is knowledge-intensive, and there are now permaculture institutes in most developing countries. It is defined by Mollison; in Madeley (2002: 43) as 'the conscious design and maintenance of agriculturally productive ecosystems, which have the diversity, stability and resilience of natural ecosystems'. In brief:

- It makes no use of inputs from outside a farm's immediate locality;
- It can be practised in rural and urban areas, and can be either subsistence farming or market-oriented;
- It varies from one location to another depending on the agro-ecological systems. They usually involve the careful integration of trees, crops and livestock, and use mulches and green manures (ground-cover plants) to protect the soil and to build up soil fertility. Tree crops are used for food and fodder, as well as for controlling soil erosion;
- Permaculture is more 'energy conscious' than normal organic farming. In fact it is doubly organic because its emphasis on 'recycling' makes sure that nutrients continue to evolve to the benefit of the farm. Box 3.4 gives an example of increasing rice yields in Madagascar using a sustainable agricultural system.

However, and in response to critiques of the EIP, Lang and Heasman (2004: 33) state that 'it would be wrong to dub the EIP as reactionary, anti-science or anti-business'. Or, moreover, as a romantic approach attempt with abandoned technologies to feed the future nine billion people who will inhabit the earth in 2050 (Collier 2008: 68).

Collier (2008: 69) takes a defensive stand against the EIP, arguing that 'most poor people are farmers who are largely self-sufficient. They may buy and sell food, but the rural markets in which they trade are often not well integrated into global markets, and so are largely detached from the surge in prices. Where poor farmers are integrated into global markets, they are likely to benefit'. It is important to ask who is likely to benefit? On this account, Ellis (1996: 6) states that

Markets provide both opportunities and pressures for peasants. Engagement in them may lead to higher living standards or more diverse consumption, but at the same time it exposes them to the possibility of ruin either from adverse price trends or from the exercise of unequal market power. Thus the relationship of peasants to the market contains a continuous tension between the risky advantages of market participation and the more conservation of a non market basis for survival.

Most low-income food deficit countries, with large numbers of small farmers in the population, are unable to compete with large-scale, efficient and heavily subsidised and supported agricultural industries. Likewise, they cannot engage fully with global markets because of the historical, geo-ecological, and socio-economic constraints which

---

Box 3.4   A new method of rice production in Madagascar

For thousands of years, lowland rice has been grown under flooded conditions, to ensure water supply and reduce weed problems. But while rice can survive in water, it is not an aquatic plant. Farmers in Madagascar noted that root growth was far greater if the plant was not kept continually submerged in water. The plant receives more oxygen and nutrients from the atmosphere and derives greater benefit from the warmth of the sun.

Using the 'system of rice intensification' (SRI), the soil is kept continuously wet only during the reproductive stage when the plant is producing grains. During the rest of the growth cycle, the rice fields are irrigated in the evening and left dry during the day.

Using their own seeds, some 20,000 farmers in Madagascar have now adopted this method, and yields have proven to be sustainable. The previous yield of around 2 tonnes per hectare shot up to around 8 to 10 tonnes per hectare, without the use of chemical fertilisers, pesticides or expensive seed varieties, and by breaking some of the conventional 'rules' of rice management.

After being evaluated by Cornell University in the United States, the system has spread to other countries, including major rice producers in Bangladesh, China and Indonesia. In China, yields of 9 to 10.5 tonnes per hectare were achieved in the first year of the system, compared with the national average of 6 tonnes per hectare.

Source: Madeley (2002: 44).

have impeded their progress towards the higher growth-rates which would enable them to compete at a global level.

Lang and Heasman (2004: 28-34) sum up the debate of the 'food wars' by showing how the aim of increasing production at all costs will be the inevitable opponent in the protracted struggles over food security, because its methods have been demonstrated to be unsustainable and harmful to both human and environmental health. Only two new contenders will battle it out for future dominance: the LSIP and the EIP. Both are science-based, and both make claims to environmental and human health benefits. They agree with Thomas Kuhn; in Lang and Heasman (2004: 33), who coined the notion of paradigm shifts in science and acknowledged that two paradigms can coexist. This may be the case with food supply, in which case an ever-present danger is that there will be a polarised food supply shaped by competing paradigms. The tragedy would be if this supply became polarised around choices available only to the food-rich, which were then effectively at the expense of the food-poor.

It has been estimated that, if present trends in demand for food products continue, 'international agricultural trade will increase substantially, with developing countries' cereal imports doubling by 2025 and tripling by 2050' (Rosegrant and Cline 2003: 1917). Depending on the countries of the North to feed the South is not a viable option, since low-income food deficit countries do not have the capacity to take advantage of global markets or the purchasing power to import food at any cost to offset their food shortages.

However, the influence of the PP has in fact increased dependency, both directly and indirectly. In a state of dependency, low-income countries have few or no incentives for development – both the literature and the history of development show that agricultural development and food self-sufficiency are intimately connected with, and may even be a condition for, development in a broad sense. This is particularly true when agricultural development is based on smallholders and family farms (Djurfeldt et al. 2003; Lipton 2005; Timmer 2005; Holmén 2006). Thus it is essential to increase food production in food deficient regions.

World Bank policy over most of the last four decades has emphasised that ensuring food availability should be achieved by means of food imports, to be paid for by export earnings from the sale of other goods. It has gradually become clear that this may not be an appropriate solution to the problem of food insecurity in developing countries (Holmén 2006). However, in its *World Development Report 2007–2008: Agriculture for Development*, the World Bank (2007) rediscovered agriculture as 'a road to development':

> If we want to meet the Millennium Goals of halving extreme poverty and hunger by 2015, the agricultural sector must be placed again at the centre of the development agenda.

As Vanhaute (2008: 39) explains that:

> this implies new investment in the [agricultural sector] after decades of negligence, and [the provision of] support to small farmers. At the same time, countries [receiving this support] must deliver on vital reforms such as cutting distorting subsidies and opening markets. In this way, the report tries to reconcile new forms of national development with the old mantra of open borders and free trade.

The International Assessment of Agricultural Knowledge, Science and Technology for Development (IAASTD), a World Bank and FAO report (in Vanhaute 2008: 39) put the issue more clearly, stressing that 'business as usual is no longer an option'.

Agricultural progress, 'has to place greater emphasis on safeguarding natural resources and on 'agro-ecological' practices. These include using natural fertilisers and traditional seeds, intensifying natural processes and reducing the distance between agricultural production and consumer' (IAASTD in Vanhaute 2008: 39).

Direct dependence on large-scale imports is also politically unacceptable, because when food is controlled from abroad it leaves little room for policy choices. It has therefore been suggested that the FAO's concept of food security in terms of food availability should be replaced by 'food sovereignty', which emphasises self-reliance (Windfuhr and Jonsén 2005; Djurfeldt et al. 2003). Moreover, what enabled Asia to significantly reduce poverty was a deliberate strategy that aimed to achieve national self-sufficiency in food crops. There is therefore much to support Herman and Kuper's (2003: 3) claim that both the US and the EU must 'abandon their sacrosanct vocation to feed the world'.

In conclusion, poverty and vulnerability are the root cause of food insecurity and famine, and it is a product of the peasants' world[5] in low-income countries. The following chapter clarifies the meaning of peasants, their main characteristics and the future of peasant farming within the overall constraints imposed by their agro-ecological environment and by both national and international political and economic policies.

4
Peasant Farming:
Current and Future Challenges

The potential of agriculture to contribute to growth and poverty reduction depends on the productivity of small farms. This chapter focuses on the question of food supply in low-income food deficit countries where the numbers of malnourished people are high. It describes the meaning of 'peasants', and identifies their main characteristics and the constraints imposed by both national and international political and economic systems on their livelihoods. The chapter will also elaborate on the future of peasant farming in these contexts.

THE PEASANTS' WORLD

Most literature on peasants' economics estimate that over two billion people belong to peasant farm households, and most of them live in developing countries where they comprise up to 70 per cent of the population, especially in the low-income food deficit countries of sub-Saharan Africa and Asia. It is estimated that 85 per cent of these small farmers are farming less than two hectares of land in countries as diverse as Bangladesh, China, Egypt, and Malawi (Von Braun 2003; Anríquez and Bonomi 2007; World Bank 2007: 90).

Globally, after five centuries of an emerging capitalist world economy and two centuries of the true globalisation of that system, about 50 per cent of the world's population can still be considered peasants. This figure in fact marks a fundamental shift for the first time in world history, as less than half of the population lives 'from the land' (Vanhaute 2008: 42) (see Table 4.1).

Moreover, Ellis (1996: 3) indicates that:

in some regions, peasant farm households are disappearing under pressures of landlessness and concentration of farm holdings; in others they are a relatively stable feature of the rural social structure; and in still others they are created anew by the economic and social forces which bear on agricultural production.

Hobsbawm (in Bernstein 2003: 3) points out that:

> The most dramatic change of the second half of this century,
> and the one which cuts us forever from the world of the past,
> is the death of peasantry, which had formed the majority of the
> human race throughout recorded history. The disappearance of
> peasantries in the global transformation that took place from
> the 1950s onward, extended industrial capitalism beyond its
> historic heartlands of western and central Europe and North
> America. Only three regions of the globe remained essentially
> dominated by their villages and fields and by peasant farming:
> sub-Saharan Africa, South and continental South East Asia, and
> China. These regions of peasant dominance comprised half the
> world's population in the 1990s.

Bernstein (2003: 3) explains that the death of the peasantry is thus
somewhat exaggerated, and discusses the different versions of 'the
death of the peasantry' as described by Hobsbawm among others.
First, those peasant societies do persist in the world of mature
capitalism, and such persistence should be celebrated in various
forms of agrarian populism as the effect of qualities of peasant
resilience and resistance. Second, some writers arguably consider
'the peasantry' as a pre-capitalist mode of production and existence.

Table 4.1 Rural populations 1951–2030: absolute numbers and percentages of
population, globally and by region

	World population (billion)	Rural population (billion)	World (%)	Africa (%)	Asia (%)	Central and South America (%)	North America (%)	Europe (%)
1950	2,540,000	1,790,000	71	85	83	58	36	49
1970	3,700,000	2,370,000	64	77	77	43	26	37
1990	5,290,000	3,020,000	57	68	68	29	25	29
2000	6,120,000	3,270,000	53	64	63	25	21	27
2010	6.910,000	3,410,000	49	60	57	21	18	26
2030	8,320,000	3,350,000	40	50	46	15	13	21

Sources: UN (2007) and Vanhaute (2008: 43).

Ellis (1996: 3) argues that

> peasant populations occupy the margins of the capitalist world
> economy. With one foot in the markets and the other in subsistence

they are neither fully integrated into the market economy nor wholly insulated from its pressures. They are rarely prosperous, often precarious, and contain among them some of the poorest people in the world.

DEFINING 'PEASANT' AND PEASANT SOCIETIES

Peasant farming societies have been defined from social, anthropological, economic and cultural perspectives. Wolf (1966: vii–8) defines peasant societies as 'those which represent the transition from relatively dispersed, isolated, and self-sufficient communities to fully integrated market economies ... they stand midway between the primitive tribe and industrial society. Peasant households as a social group are always part of a larger economic system', and are considered by Smith and Wallerstein (1992) 'as an institution of the world economy'.

These institutions have different forms and play different roles in different social settings – they are components of the broader world, regional and national economic systems, but are also shaped by those systems. Smith and Wallerstein (1992) argue that 'peasant's households are non-capitalist islands within the big capitalist sea'. Moreover, they are functional and even indispensable for the working of that social system, as they provide cheap labour, subsistence and protection to their societies, and they thus lower the overall social costs in national income (Vanhaute 2008: 41).

Ellis (1996: 51) elaborates further:

> Peasants in varying degrees have the capability, via their access to land, for simple reproduction outside the dominant mode. Nevertheless, participation in market transactions means that they are never wholly independent of capitalist relations, and the more enmeshed they become in market exchanges the more they must conform to the dictates of productive efficiency set in the capitalist market place.

From an economic point of view, peasants may be defined in part by their varying rather than total commitment to the market (which also implies a varying capacity to withdraw from the market and still survive), and in part by the incomplete character of the markets[1] in which they participate. It is this that ties together such distinct components as transition, subordination, subsistence, and the peculiarities of the access of peasants to factors of production (such as land, labour and credit) (see, Wolf 1966: 13; Ellis 1996: 10). Moreover, Ellis (1996: 10) defines peasants as 'households which derive their livelihoods mainly from agriculture, utilise mainly family labour in farm production, and are characterised by partial engagement in input and output markets which are often imperfect or incomplete'.

He clarifies further:

1. Peasants are engaged in the purposive pursuit of personal or household goals like any other economic agents, and their actions take place and are modified by their social context.
2. Ellis indicates the inadequacy of terms such as 'traditional' 'subsistence', and 'small farm' to describe the peasant farm household.[2]
3. He also implies that peasants cease to be peasants when they become wholly committed to production in fully formed markets – they become instead family farm enterprises. Given the heterogeneity of social and economic change, the mode of transition cannot be sharply defined.

Moreover, the World Bank (2007: 91) describes

> smallholder farming as a small-scale farm operated by a household with limited hired labour and remains the most common form of organisation in agriculture, even in industrial countries. The record of superiority of smallholder farming as a form of organisation is striking, although many countries have tried to promote large scale farming, believing that smallholder (peasant) farming is inefficient, backward, and resistant to change.

Ellis (1996: 51) highlights two opposing lines of reasoning about the persistence of peasants, describing first the Marxist position as set out by Lenin, who believed that the pressures on peasant farming created by capitalist production relations must, inevitably, result in its disappearance as a distinct form of production. The process by which this occurs is called *social differentiation*, in which peasant communities are predicted to disintegrate into the two social classes: capitalist farmers and rural wage labourers. The reason this may happen are manifold, but they include such factors as:

- The institution of private ownership of land;
- The differential adoption of improved cultivation practices by different individual farmers;

- The enforced abandonment of their holdings by peasants unable to compete in the market with their more advanced neighbours;
- The foreclosure by creditors on farmers who have run into debt; and
- The increasing employment of wage labour by those farmers who are successful.

Ellis (1996: 50) agreed with Friedmann (1980) in emphasising that the transition from peasants' farming to a commercial family farm situation can happen when most of the conditions for well-functioning markets are fulfilled: diversity and abundance of information; many buyers and sellers; good transport and infrastructure; mobility; inputs such as certified seeds, chemical fertilisers and herbicides or pesticides; outlets; and consumer goods. In addition, there is a single, most important condition: active demand from both processors and consumers. Moreover, he stresses that the transition can occur quite quickly under conditions of sustained economic growth, while it may halt, or even go into reverse, when countries experience stagnation or economic collapse.

The other line of reasoning, according to Ellis (1996: 52), is that family farm production, of which peasant farming is a major type, possesses an internal logic which permits it to resist the pressures of capitalist production relations and thus enables it to reproduce itself indefinitely. Components of this position include:

- Peasant farmers' capability to maintain their needs of simple reproduction due to their control over means of production, especially land;
- The prevailing social norm of reciprocity, rather than individual profit maximisation, among peasant farmers;
- Their ability to utilise their own family members to overcome market pressures;
- The natural or technical factors constraining farm production, which make agriculture unattractive to capital investment. These can include: the length of the production cycle; weather conditions and the variability of rain; the risk of output failure; as well as lack of access to modern technology or to best practice in soil and water conservation;
- Functional advantages for capitalism (cheaper food, less risk) from leaving agriculture in the hands of peasants (related to points 3 and 4 above); and

- Household production has inbuilt flexibilities with respect to cropping patterns, labour use, and sources of income between farm and off-farm activities.

Vanhaute's (2008: 42) paper 'The end of peasantries? Rethinking the role of peasantries', attempts to understand policy concerns regarding the relationships between peasants' declining role in food production and the prospect of long-term food insecurity at both local and global levels. He defines peasants as:

Members of rural, agricultural households, who control the land they work, either as tenants or as smallholders, who are organised generally in households and in village communities that meet most of their subsistence needs (production, exchange, credit), who pool different forms of income, and who are ruled by other social groups, which extract a surplus either directly via rents, via (non-balanced) markets, or through control of state power (taxation).

Vanhaute (2008: 48) stresses that the modernisation of agricultural production in Europe, which in the nineteenth century provided the conditions to escape poverty and famine, 'went chronologically hand in hand with the end of European peasantry'. In this view, famines are related to peasant societies and to so-called backward economies, while modernisation leads (inevitably) to the end of famines (Braudel, in Vanhaute 2008: 48).

WORLD CAPITALISM AND AGRARIAN CHANGE

Europe's position in the transformation of the capitalist world-system during the nineteenth century is explained by Vanhaute (2008: 48). First, despite the unprecedented increase of land and labour productivity in agriculture, Europe became a net importer of basic foodstuffs in order to feed its own population. For example, around that time Great Britain had to import 70 per cent of its bread grains and 40 per cent of its meat from outside Europe. The cost of these huge imports could only be paid for by the profits of the Industrial Revolution.

Second, Europe disposed of an important part of its own surplus labour through migration to the periphery of the world system[3] – the non-European world. During the nineteenth century, some 40 to 50 million Europeans left the old continent. Thus, Europe's escape from hunger is a result both of the spectacular transformation of its old society, which created huge financial surpluses, and (as the centre of the nineteenth-century world-economy) of using its own periphery for migration (Vanhaute 2008: 48–9). However, a very high price was paid both by India and Ireland for Great Britain's hegemony at this period, and for the resulting commitment to laissez-faire economic policies.

In the twenty-first century, the big difference is that present-day weak economies lack the power and opportunities: (1) to import basic foodstuffs on the basis of self-regulated trade terms; and (2) to export their surplus population to new peripheries, or to contemporary (core/developed) countries (Vanhaute 2008: 48–9).

McMichael (2006: 415) argues that the contradictions of neoliberal capitalism express themselves through agrarian relations in various forms of 'accumulation through dispossession', concentrating and centralising agribusiness capital, privatising states, redistributing social resources away from the labouring classes and from peasantries, and degrading the environment. But they are also expressed in the politicisation of the 'margins', where capitalist circuits of social reproduction are tenuous and unstable, and infuse class with gender, racial and ethnic oppressions. However, Ellis (1996: 53) highlights the fact that:

> Lack of accumulation in the peasant economy may occur, not due to the limited material motivation of peasants but because capitalist production relations continuously push peasants back towards 'simple reproduction squeeze' it may include rents of various kinds, price squeezes, devaluation of peasant labour, and taxes.

Ellis (1996: 56) points out that:

> if peasants are exploited, it is more likely to be a function of non-capitalist social relations or the unequal exercise of market power, than a function of capitalism per se. Much of the supposed exploitation of peasants, price squeezes in particular, corresponds to the normal working of the capitalist economy in which only the most efficient producers survive in the longer run. One major exception to this is when the state uses prices to squeeze surplus from peasants.

However, McMichael (2006: 415) emphasises that 'the contemporary global agrarian question is pivotal to all other social arrangements'. It manifests itself in global struggles for land, sovereignty and security (Vanhaute 2008: 53). Moreover, Amin (2003: 271) states that, 'the agrarian question, far from being solved, is now more than ever at the heart of the major challenges which humanity will face during the twenty-first century'.

Josling (2009: 160) elaborates on the policies of the EC in the mid 1950s that were premised on the need to support European agriculture, which could not compete with domestic industry for labour and capital, or with production from overseas farms that were larger and perhaps less constrained by social and environmental factors. The instruments used were designed to insulate domestic producers from developments in world markets, since world prices were seen as too volatile to be a basis for stable domestic markets.

Vanhaute (2008: 56) believes that 'in one way or another, the future [for agrarian change in developing countries] lies in new peasantations which means an old age trend must be adapted'. He points out the following reasons:

First, a new conceptualisation is needed, one not based on a dualistic, linear, evolutionist modernisation view, but as part of a global perspective on the origins, growth, and functioning of the capitalist world-system.

Second, peasant societies are the best guarantee against large-scale human disasters. During and after famines, for example, peasant societies have absorbed the tensions and acted as a buffer to protect against mass starvation. That is why famines within peasant societies were short-term events, confined to restricted geographical areas [although caused by long-term processes of poverty, vulnerability and food insecurity, and confined to restricted geographical areas].

Thirdly, structural and global food security will not result from the expansion of a global free-market ideology, because food security in one part of the world was, is, and will be at the cost of more insecurity in other parts (Vanhaute 2008: 56). Vanhaute stresses that food security must be based on a diversity of more secure food systems, which must be embedded in local and regional rural communities that are interconnected, but also protected [by national legislations and appropriate food policies and trade rules], and in control of their own land and resources. Thus, international food policy must be based on the promotion and support of diverse, productive, and sustainable food systems [at all levels].

Fourthly, in the expansion of the global capitalist system, the existence of peasantries was, and still is, crucial (for the survival of vulnerable communities). However, to understand the new agrarian questions one needs a new historical knowledge of the role of peasantries within capitalist transformations. Vanhaute (2008: 54) argues that:

> Global capitalist transformation seems not to have followed the 'British way', in which a dissolving peasant society is replaced by a capitalist agriculture, as suggested by (Eurocentric) modernisation stories. The 'continental' variant, which 'skims' the peasants until their basis of survival becomes too weak, is the dominant path that most of the peasantries of the world have followed and still follow.

Moreover, the World Bank (2007: 92) asserts that:

> One of the major trends in the expansion of the capitalist world system is the undermining of the eventual disappearance of small scale, diversified, community based agricultural systems. As agriculture becomes more technology driven and access to consumers is mediated by agro-processors and supermarkets, economies of scale will pose major challenges for the future competitiveness of smallholders.

Ellis (1996: 52) explains further the forces influencing peasants' household production:

> There are various forces influencing the long run viability of peasant households' production and the interplay between these forces determines the fate and survival of peasant societies. In certain conditions the forces of disintegration are observed to dominate; in others the forces of stability or persistence seem to prevail. In contemporary agrarian societies the relative strength of these opposing forces is influenced by two more factors: one is the intensity of the pressure imposed on peasants to yield a surplus which is captured by other social groups. The second is the role of the state in contributing to the stability or instability of peasant production.

However, 'the peasants are back' on the agenda, since the World Bank (2007) has recently rediscovered, after 25 years, agriculture as a 'road to development': 'if we want to meet the Millennium Goals of halving extreme poverty and hunger by 2015, the agriculture sector must be placed again at the centre of the development agenda' (Vanhaute 2008: 39). The question remains as to whether this statement implies new investment in the agricultural sector (especially the food sector), after decades of negligence and lack of support to small farmers.

PEASANTS AND THE THREE WORLDS OF AGRICULTURE

The FAO estimates that agriculture provides employment to 1.3 billion people worldwide, 97 per cent of whom live in developing countries (FAO 2006). It is also a major source of income for rural households. In agriculture-based countries, farm crops, livestock income and agricultural wages generated between 42 and 75 per cent of total rural income. On-farm income comes both from production for self-consumption and from sales of agricultural products to the market (World Bank 2007: 26). Most rural dwellers depend on agriculture for their livelihoods, directly or indirectly. Thus a more dynamic and inclusive agriculture could dramatically reduce rural poverty and hunger.

The question is: how does agriculture get moving in low-income food deficit countries? First, this section provides an overview of the three worlds of agriculture, as described by the World Bank report of 2007 and the process of transformation from agriculture-based to urban-based economies. It will also elaborate on the constraints and key challenges of prioritising peasant farming for investment within countries' national development policies.

However, the constraints experienced by a typical peasant family in low-income countries indicate clearly the level of investment needed to eliminate those constraints and release peasant farmers' agricultural potential. Ellis (1996: 11–12) compares the economic situation of a typical farm family in an industrial market economy with that of the peasant farm family, in relation to the conditions essential to the production process (Box 4.1).

AGRICULTURAL CONTRIBUTION TO ECONOMIC DEVELOPMENT

The World Bank (2007: 26) suggests that at the macro level the process of economic development is one of the continuous redefining of roles and inter-relationships of agriculture, manufacturing, and

Box 4.1   Comparison of farming conditions in industrialised and developing countries

Conditions for farm families in industrialised countries:

- Credit is generally available from developed financial markets (banks, credit agencies and so on) at competitive market rates of interest for all economically viable enterprises.
- Variable production inputs (fertiliser, seed, fuel, chemicals) from many different sources are available in whatever quantity an individual farmer might wish to purchase them.
- Knowledge of the latest available technologies is widespread and discussed at length in farming magazines and other contexts such as radio, television, and electronic media.
- There is a freehold market in land, so that the potential exists for new entrants to begin farming and for unsuccessful farmers to exit from agriculture.
- Information on prices of both inputs and outputs is available, typically on a nationwide basis, reflecting the high degree of integration of markets and communications including mobile phones and sophisticated satellite technology.

For the peasant farm family only a few, and possibly none, of these conditions are likely to prevail:

- Capital markets are fragmented or non-existent and credit is obtained from local landlords, merchants, or moneylenders at rates of interest which reflect the individual circumstances of each transaction, not a market clearing condition. Microfinance institutions may exist but in most cases they vary in terms of operation, coverage (number of borrowers which they can serve and location), rates of interest and sustainability.
- Credit and rates of interest may be tied to other factor prices such as land and labour within dependent economic relationships, thus factor markets may be locked together contractually rather than being independent (for example, credit is linked to input supplies and marketing of harvest).
- Variable production inputs may be erratically available or unavailable, their quality may vary, and access to them may involve formal or informal systems of rationing.

▶

- Market information is poor, erratic, fragmented and incomplete, and the cost for the farm household of acquiring information beyond the immediate confines of village or community is high.
- A freehold market for land does not always exist, and where it does, non-market rights of access or non-price forms of tenancy are likely to predominate over open market transactions in land.
- Markets and communications in general are not well integrated, and, depending on place and infrastructure, there are varying degrees of isolation between local communities, regions, and the more developed segments of the national economy. However, as mobile phones spread throughout developing countries, farmers are making great use of the information that is available about commodity prices, and are thus able to expand their market potential.

Source: Adapted from Ellis (1996: 12)

services. However, two empirical pieces of evidence characterise this structural transformation.

First, at low levels of development, the shares of agriculture in gross domestic product (GDP) and in employment are large (up to 50 per cent in GDP and up to 85 per cent in employment), but they decline as countries develop.

Second, there is a large and persistent gap between the share of agriculture in GDP and the share of agriculture in the labour force. In other words, despite the fact that the employment share in agriculture is very high, its contribution to GDP is still comparably low.

Historically, these patterns of structural transformation have been observed in most developed countries, as agricultural growth was the precursor to the acceleration of industrial growth, very much in the way that agricultural revolutions predated the industrial revolutions that spread across the temperate world, from England in the mid-eighteenth century to Japan in the late nineteenth century (Bairoch 1973). Similar transformations are currently taking place in some regions of developing countries which are experiencing growth, such as dairy farming in China and Kenya; aquaculture in Bangladesh, vegetable production in Mexico for supermarkets in Latin America and for international markets; coffee production in Rwanda; horticulture in Chile, Guatemala, and Senegal; and so on (World Bank 2007: 26).

The World Bank (2007: 29–30) used the evolving role of agriculture in fostering growth and reducing poverty to classify developing countries into three development-related categories: agriculture-based; transforming; and urbanised. The categorisation is based on the share of aggregate growth originating in agriculture and the share of aggregate poverty (US$2.15 a day) in rural areas where agricultural production is dominated by smallholder peasants. Three clusters of structurally different economies emerge, each with distinct challenges for agricultural policy-making.

Agriculture-based countries

In this group of countries, mostly in sub-Saharan Africa, agriculture contributes significantly to growth, as more than 600 million people live in these countries, 49 per cent of them on less than US$1 a day, and in rural areas 68 per cent are smallholders involved in both staple food crops and the agricultural export sector. The staple crop sector is the largest sub-sector and produces mostly for the domestic market. The non-staple crop sector produces for export, and is often dominated by traditional commodities, but increasingly it also includes new dynamic sub-sectors of high-value products such as vegetables, flowers and fish.

The key policy challenge is to help agriculture play its role as an engine of growth and poverty reduction (World Bank 2007: 30–5).

Transforming countries

More than two billion people, about three-quarters of the rural population in developing countries, live in the rural areas of transforming countries including most of South and East Asia, North Africa and the Middle East, and some regions of Europe and Central Asia. During 1993–2005, agriculture contributed 7 per cent to economic growth, constituting 13 per cent of the economy, and employing 57 per cent of the labour force. Despite rapid growth and declining poverty rates in many of these countries, poverty remains widespread and largely rural, with more than 80 per cent of the poor living in rural areas.

In the transforming countries, natural resources are coming under growing pressure, both from agriculture and from the competition for land and water from rapidly growing urban populations and non-agricultural sectors. The rising urban–rural income gap, accompanied by unfulfilled expectations, creates political tensions (de Gorter and Swinnen 2002; Hayami 2005; World Bank 2007: 30).

The key policy challenge is to invest and promote agriculture and the rural non-farm economy in order to reduce poverty and narrow the urban–rural divide (World Bank 2007: 30–5).

Urbanised countries

Agriculture makes up only 6 per cent of the urbanised economies, while the agribusiness and food industry, and agriculture-related services, can account for 30 per cent of GDP. Although almost three-quarters of the population of urbanised countries live in urban areas, 45 per cent of the labour force still works in agriculture. Most countries in Latin America and many in Europe and Central Asia also fall into this category (World Bank 2007: 28 and 37).

The key policy challenge is to include the remaining rural poor as direct producers and to create employment for them (World Bank 2007: 30 and 37).

As the World Bank report (2007: 30) indicates, there is no unique route for a country to move along, from being an agriculture-based country to one which is urbanised, and eventually to move to the high-income category. However, both China and India moved from the agriculture-based category to the transforming category in the 1970s, further reducing the share of rural poverty, as did Brazil, a country in the urbanised category. Table 4.2 provides data on demographic and economic characteristics of three types of developing countries as described by the World Bank.

INVESTMENT AND ECONOMIC INCENTIVES FOR AGRICULTURAL GROWTH

Agriculture can be the engine for growth and poverty reduction for agriculture-based countries, but for this to happen, it is essential to have sustained investment to maintain progress. Unfortunately, in countries where the socio-economic role of agriculture is largest, public investment in agriculture, measured as a percentage of agricultural GDP, is lowest (about 4 per cent), while it is largest in urbanised developing economies (about 15 per cent) (Fan and Rao 2003). Table 4.3 provides comparative data for all three developing country categories.

Table 4.2   Demographic and economic characteristics of three developing country types, 2005

	Agriculture-based countries	Transforming countries	Urbanised countries
Population			
Total (million)	615	3,510	965
Rural (million)	417	2,220	255
Rural poverty rate (US$2.15 a day) (%)	83	73	36
Rural poverty rate (US$1.08)	51	28	13
Share of rural population (%)	68	63	26
Annual population growth, 1991–2005 (%)	2.5	1.4	1.0
Geographical distribution of rural population (%)			
Sub-Saharan Africa	82.2	13.6	4.2
South Asia	2.2	97.8	0.0
East Asia and Pacific Islands	0.9	96.1	2.9
Middle East and North Africa	8.0	92.0	0.0
Europe and Central Asia	0.0	12.0	88.0
Latin America and Caribbean	2.2	9.7	88.1
Labour force (in 2004)			
Total (million)	266	1,780	447
Agriculture (million)	172	1,020	82
Share of agriculture (%)	65	57	18
Economy			
GDP per capita, 2000 (US$)	379	1,068	3,489
Annual GDP growth, 1991–2005 (%)	3.7	6.3	2.6
Agriculture			
Agriculture value added per capita, 2000 (US$)	111	142	215
Share of agriculture in GDP (%)	29.0	13.0	6.0
Agriculture's contribution to growth, 1991–2005	32.0	2.9	2.2
Annual agricultural GDP growth, 1991–2005 (%)	4.0	7.0	5.0
Annual non-agricultural GDP 1991–2005 (%)	3.5	7.0	2.7

Sources: Adapted from World Bank (2007: 31–2, Tables 1.1 and 1.2). FAO (2006) for labour force data. Chen and Ravallion (2007).

Note: Averages are weighted and based on 74 countries with at least 5 million people, except for agriculture value added which is based on 71 countries because of missing information. Data are for 2005 unless otherwise noted.

Table 4.3 Public spending on agriculture in three country categories

	Agriculture-based countries[1]		Transforming countries		Urbanised countries	
	1980	2004	1980	2004	1980	2004
Public spending on agriculture as a share of total public spending (%)	6.9	4.0	14.3	7.0	8.1	2.7
Public spending on agriculture as a share of agricultural GDP (%)	3.7	4.0	10.2	10.6	16.9	12.1
Share of agriculture in GDP (%)	28.8	28.9	24.4	15.6	14.4	10.2

Source: World Bank (2007).

1 Figures for agriculture-based countries are based on 14 countries (12 from sub-Saharan Africa), those for transforming countries on 12 countries, and those for urbanised countries on 11 countries.

Hayami and Honma (2009: 68) indicate that:

> Significant growth in agricultural protection began when Japan, Korea, China and Taiwan, entered the middle-income stage of economic development. Statistical observations are found to be consistent with the hypothesis that the success of rapid industrialisation that advanced these economies beyond the middle-income stage resulted in a decline in agriculture's comparative advantage associated with the growing income disparity between farmers and employees in non-agricultural sectors. In several cases, demand from farmers for a reduction of farm and non-farm income disparity materialised in the form of increased assistance to agriculture. This was manifest predominantly through rapid and sustained growth in broader protection of agricultural products.

They support Schultz's statement that 'as economies advance from low to high-income status, agricultural policies tend to shift from taxation to subsidisation of agriculture. In this regard, Japan, Korea, China and Taiwan, are clear examples' (in Hayami and Honma 2009: 68).

According to Hayami and Honma (2009: 70), resource endowment to some degree determined the course of modern economic growth and development in Japan, Korea China and Taiwan, as well as the evolution of agricultural policies including relative and nominal rates of assistance.

Moreover, they argue that 'the reasons behind the success of Taiwan, China, Korea and Japan in maintaining economic growth was due to pertinent borrowing of technology from advanced economies' (ibid). This is what Gershenkron (Hayami and Honma 2009: 70) reveals, in 1962, that 'the later the industrialisation of an economy begins, the larger the scope for economic growth through technology borrowing'. But why were Japan, Korea, China and Taiwan particularly successful in technology borrowing, among the many countries that were late starters? One commonly cited reason is 'the fact that these resource-poor countries were heavily endowed with cheap but relatively well educated labour, a situation that made technologies fairly efficient and smoothed the way for borrowing of capital and knowledge-intensive technology'.

They conclude that the nominal rate of assistance (NRA)[4] for selected individual commodities, and the relative rate of assistance (RRA) between agriculture and industry, show that the growth of agricultural production in Northeast Asia, together with the decline of industrial protection rates, caused the RRA to rise in the three economies over the five post-war decades under investigation. The agricultural protection level continued to grow even after 1980 in all three economies, despite an apparently decreased need for agricultural support to prevent widening rural–urban income disparity – a common problem in the high-income stage of economic development, particularly for the widening income gap between agricultural and non-agricultural sectors when a country reaches middle-income status (ibid: 110).

Hayami and Honma suggest that if the income gap had been dealt with more appropriately at the middle-income stage, problems caused by agricultural protection in the high-income stage could have been significantly reduced. Thus greater attention needs to be paid to the widening rural–urban income gap problem in the middle-income stage – the so-called 'disparity problem'. The challenge at that stage of development is to find a compromise between two conflicting needs: on the one hand, the need to reduce the farm-income gap, and on the other, the need to supply low-cost food to a larger number of workers in urban areas, when the government capacity to raise sufficient revenue from non-agricultural sectors is weak and when import restrictions effectively tax net buyers of food.

AGRICULTURAL POLICIES IN AGRICULTURE-BASED DEVELOPING COUNTRIES

This book is primarily concerned about key challenges regarding how to get agriculture in general, and food production in particular, moving in agriculture-based regions in developing countries. This is to ensure food availability on the one hand, and to provide job opportunities for the growing numbers of economically active people in agriculture-based regions of developing countries on the other.

With regard to sub-Saharan Africa, despite long periods of sustained agricultural growth in recent years, due to prices and market liberalisation (Badiane 2010) many price distortions remain. However, with 60 per cent of sub-Saharan Africa's workforce still employed in agriculture, and more than 80 per cent of the region's poorest households depending directly or indirectly on farming for their livelihoods, agricultural and trade policies have significant influence on the pace and direction of change in Africa (see, Chen and Ravallion 2007 1-15; World Bank 2007: 27; Anderson and Masters 2009: 323).

In this regard, the World Bank highlights the unsatisfactory performance of agriculture – and specifically food crops – in sub-Saharan Africa, especially when contrasted with the Green Revolution in South Asia.

In the mid 1980s, the African cereal yields were comparatively low and poverty was comparatively high. Fifteen years later, in South Asia, yields had increased by more than 50 per cent and poverty had declined by 30 per cent. In sub-Saharan Africa, yields and poverty were unchanged. Food security today remains challenging for most countries in Africa, given their low agricultural growth, rapid population growth, weak foreign exchange earnings, and high transaction costs incurred in integrating domestic and international markets. (World Bank 2007: 26)

Moreover, Anderson and Masters (2009) agreed with the account provided by Krueger et al. (1991) of African governmental policies in the 1960s and 1970s. These were macroeconomic, sectoral, and trade policies that increasingly favoured urban households and export crops (coffee, cocoa, tea, cotton, and so on) at the expense of food crops. African government policies of increasing investments in urban areas have also affected food imports indirectly by creating incentives for rural people to migrate from rural to urban areas.

At the same time, lower world food prices were the result of farm policies in developed countries, which should be considered as a factor contributing to the high level of food imports observed in Africa.

Furthermore, in most sub-Saharan countries over the last 40 years the share of labour in agriculture has declined dramatically, despite modest growth in per capita GDP. This has been the case in Nigeria and in Latin America since 1980. This trend is consistent with the observed urbanisation of poverty in these two regions. By contrast, the reallocation of labour out of agriculture has been very slow in China, partly because of restrictions on labour mobility, which, given rapid growth outside of agriculture, is consistent with an increase in the rural–urban divide (World Bank 2007: 27).

Anderson and Masters (2009: 324) considered the situation in sub-Saharan Africa, providing macro-level analysis of agricultural policies in 21 countries, including large countries such as Ethiopia and Egypt, and focusing especially on the level of NRAs and RRAs. Their study indicates that the level and dispersion of agricultural NRAs confirm that there has been substantial reform toward less distortion of incentives. They suggest that there are still many opportunities for policy changes that would be both pro-poor and pro-growth, for raising income for low-income farmers and for improving resource allocation within and between countries.

The main findings of their study can be summarised as follows:

• African governments have removed much of the earlier anti-farm and anti-trade policy biases, which had worsened in the late 1960s and 1970s, primarily through increased taxation of exportable products. Reforms in the 1980s and 1990s reversed that trend, and average rates of agricultural taxation are now below the levels of the early 1960s.
• The substantial distortions that remain continue to impose a large tax burden on Africa's poor. In 2000–4, the burden of taxation averaged US$6 billion per year, or US$41 per person working in agriculture. Even this lower amount is appreciably larger than public investment or foreign aid into the sector.
• African farmers have become less taxed, in part because of the changing trade orientation of African agriculture. Reduced taxation of farmers has occurred partly because of a decline in the share of output that is exportable and a corresponding rise in the share that is import-competing. Protection from imports for these products has fluctuated but remains positive, which

helped net sellers of protected products, especially those less efficient than many other possible interventions.

- Trade restrictions continue to be Africa's most important instruments of agricultural intervention. Domestic taxes and subsidies on farm inputs and outputs, along with 'none product specific' (NPS) agricultural subsidies or tax credits, are a small share of total distortions to farmer incentives. As a result, price policy trends for consumers tend to mirror the agricultural policy imposed on producers.
- Differences in NRAs and RRAs across commodities and countries are still substantial. Moving towards more uniform rates within the farm sector and between countries within the region could still yield substantial increases in the efficiency of resource use. However, this requires higher levels of, and more vibrant, inter-regional trade.

Anderson and Masters also pointed to the fact that neither increasing food prices nor subsidising production can address the rural–urban gap. They suggest some measures, such as increasing the rural–urban mobility of some members of farm households, enabling full-time or part-time off-farm employment and the repatriation of part of these higher earnings back to those remaining on the farm. However, normal flow from rural to urban areas is happening at various rates depending on the government regulation (see, Otsuka and Quisumbing 2001; World Bank 2007).

In addition, there is a need for targeted social policy measures, including assisting poor households (non-farm as well as farm households) and providing public investment in sectors such as education and health, rural infrastructure, and agricultural research and extension.

Collier and Venables (2007) highlight the sources of comparative advantage in these countries:

1. *Comparative advantage from factor endowments.* Most African and other agriculture-based economies are relatively rich in natural resources, but poor in skilled labour, suggesting a comparative advantage for unprocessed primary products. In some countries, a combination of natural resources and human capital endowments point to comparative advantage in processed primary commodities, even though other factors may have prevented the development of the agricultural processing sector to date.

2. *Comparative advantage from the difference in productivity costs.* These are determined by the business environment, infrastructure (roads, electricity, communications), and institutions (legal, financial, regulatory) that influence the efficiency of operations for firms and industries. The business environment is more important for manufacturing and high-value services because they use these factors more intensively. World Bank Investment Climate surveys support the contention that indirect costs inherent in a poor business environment are higher on average in Africa than in their competitors in the developing world.

3. *Comparative advantage from dynamic economies of scale.* The very existence of economies of scale puts latecomers at a disadvantage in competing with countries that have already developed their industrial base. Agriculture-based economies have largely missed the expansion of labour-intensive manufacturing that spurred development in Asia in the 1980s. There is still debate about the likelihood that Africa will emerge as a significant exporter of manufactured goods. However, based on current and emerging comparative advantage, a diverse portfolio of processed and unprocessed primary-based exports (including services such as tourism) will remain the main option for generating foreign exchange in the medium term.

Many countries in the agriculture-based category have declining per capita domestic production of food staples. Burundi, Ethiopia, Kenya, Madagascar, Nigeria, Sudan, Tanzania, and Zambia all had negative per capita annual growth rates in staple food of 1 to 1.7 per cent from 1994–2004. Staple crops in most agriculture-based countries are largely rain-fed and hence experience large fluctuations caused by climatic variability (World Bank 2007: 95).

At national level, stagnation or decline in domestic production, and large fluctuations in food production, clearly create serious problems of food availability. Importing food is one option, but when countries are constrained by a lack of foreign currency and weak purchasing power, their capacity to import is limited (World Bank 2007: 95). Their exposure and vulnerability to wide fluctuations in world food prices make it even harder for these countries to depend for food either on world markets or on food aid, since food aid itself is erratic in volume and subject to availability and cost.

Poor infrastructure means high costs for the transport of food to isolated areas, even when capital and coastal cities are well served by international markets. Thus problems in food availability from low domestic production or lack of imports translate into large spikes in domestic prices and reductions in the real incomes of poor consumers, many of whom are farmers. Even in countries that engage in trade, transportation and marketing, the costs result in a large gap between import and export parity, within which domestic prices can fluctuate without triggering trade. Price variability, which is already high even in capital cities with mostly liberalised markets, is exacerbated in inland and more remote regions (World Bank 2007: 95).

PEASANT FARMING: CONSTRAINTS AND CHALLENGES

Peasant households engage in diverse 'portfolios' of on-farm and off-farm activities, such as farming, labour and migration, but one of these activities usually dominates as a source of income. The relative importance of each differs across the three country types described above (World Bank 2007: 75). This report distinguished five livelihood strategies:

1. *Market oriented* smallholders who derive most of their income from actively engaging in agricultural markets. Commercialisation is most help to those small farmers with easy access to urban and export markets, who benefit from good infrastructure, human capital, technology and risk assistance. However, even if small farmers use their resources more efficiently than larger farmers, there can still be disadvantages in being small. While smallholders have an advantage in overcoming labour supervision problems, other factors can erase their competitive advantage. Yields on small farms often lag behind gains on larger farms, which tend to apply more fertiliser or other inputs, and these gaps may increase over time (IFAD 2001: 175).
2. *Subsistence-oriented farmers* who depend on farming for their livelihoods but use the majority of their produce for home consumption. Even if subsistence farmers use their resources more efficiently than larger farmers, they will still be disadvantaged as mentioned above.
3. *Labour-oriented farm households* that derive most of their income from waged work in agriculture or in the rural non-farm economy, or from non-agricultural self-employment.

4. *Migration-oriented households* that choose to leave the rural sector entirely, or depend on transfers from members who have migrated.
5. *Diversified households* that combine income from farming, off-farm labour, and migration. Diversification is often prescribed as a way of reducing the vulnerability of farmers (particularly poor ones) to fluctuations in prices and production, while many small farmers see commercialisation as the way out of poverty. The importance of growing cash crops and food crops simultaneously is illustrated in studies carried out in countries including India, the Philippines, Guatemala and seven sub-Saharan African states (see, Von Braun and Kennedy 1994; Killick et al. 2000; IFAD 2001: 174).

Subsistence farming is the dominant strategy pursued by rural households in agriculture-based countries, while the labour and migration-oriented strategies are more common in urbanised and transforming countries (World Bank 2007: 76).

Although the agricultural sector is dominated by private enterprises – peasant farming, medium size farms and large farming businesses – the state and its market institutions can promote pro-peasant farming growth, especially in the food sector. Public and private investments can facilitate the creation of dynamic food markets for both the production of food crops and food processing.

However, market and state failures to support peasant farmers can undermine their ability to contribute to agricultural growth and poverty reduction. With such market and state failures, initial asset endowments affect the efficiency of resource use (in terms of land allocation, tenure arrangement, provision of credit and enabling the market to supply most needed inputs, in addition to strengthening marketing channels and so on), and thus the well-being of households (World Bank 2007: 82). Many markets in rural areas of agriculture-based countries fail to support efficient production outcomes due to lack of access to resources and services. They also suffer from inequality because of the extreme asymmetry of relations between, on the one hand the large numbers of small producers and consumers and, on the other, the small number of buyers and sellers.

The International Fund for Agricultural Development (IFAD 2001: 161) points to the multidimensional factors hindering peasant farmers' attempts to realise their full potential:

- *Physical factors*: particularly the distance of the peasants from markets, but also including the quality of infrastructure generally. Badly maintained (or only seasonally available) roads give rise to high transport costs, while there may be weak communication systems for disseminating information on markets, products and prices. Other physical factors include the low value-to-weight ratios of much peasant farmer produce (which makes transporting it to market difficult and costly), the perishable nature of much agricultural produce, and a lack of storage facilities, all of which increase the transaction costs for both buyers and sellers.
- *Political factors*: peasant farmers' inability, due to their weak bargaining power, to influence the terms and conditions of their market participation. This weak position relates to their lack of skills and knowledge of how the market works or why prices fluctuate, their lack of adequate information on market conditions, prices and quality of goods, and the difficulties of organising collectively.
- *Structural factors*: mainly a lack of market intermediaries. Many rural communities (particularly those in more remote areas where population densities are low) have such limited demand for production inputs, or have so little to sell or barter, that especially small traders do not find it worth their while engaging with them as they face high transaction costs arising from physical remoteness, which affect demand for small farmers' produce and the prices they receive.
- *Geographical externalities*: arising from living in a poor area with a weak natural resource base, where the soil may be overused and there is heavy dependence on rain-fed agriculture.
- *Failures of the state*: to provide public goods such as infrastructure, communication systems and supports. This could enable small farmers to take advantage of price and trade liberalisation. Many states have withdrawn from activities such as input supplies, production support, financial services and marketing, to create space for the private sector to enter, believing that it would operate more efficiently. Although progress in achieving market liberalisation in agriculture-based countries is now substantial, especially for domestic food crops, there are some major exceptions. In much of sub-Saharan Africa, private sector development has been slow and faltering, and the withdrawal of the state has resulted in a vacuum which has not been adequately filled by the private

sector. Reforms in many cases have been beneficial to large and small farmers who are geographically close to markets, and to farm labourers (through increased employment and or wages), but farmers in remote areas have, at least in the short term, been left worse off.

However, marketing cooperatives (MCs) can still be considered an important vehicle to enable farmers to take advantage of economies of scale in transportation and storage so as to reduce the cost of marketing produce. Politically, MCs can give farmers greater control over trading activities than reliance on private traders alone, particularly in remote areas, and it enables farmers to raise their profit margins through reducing the costs of marketing their produce and increasing their selling prices. This can happen if these MCs are efficiently managed (requiring a knowledge of business skills, training and finance, and that they are free of corruption and state interference).

Moreover, imperfect competition in those markets might favour land concentration in larger farms. For example, imperfections in credit and insurance markets prevent small farmers from adopting more productive capital-intensive techniques or higher-value products. These imperfections, in combination with transaction costs, can also prevent markets for land sales and rentals from allocating land to the most efficient users (see, Feder 1985; Kevane 1996; World Bank 2003; Zimmerman and Carter 2003; World Bank 2007: 91).

These complexities indicate the need to consider the interrelationships of policies regarding land, capital and risk for small farmers, since land is a key asset for poor people, and inequality in the ownership of land has far reaching consequences for the well-being of society and its organisation for generations to come. As agriculture becomes more technology-driven, and access to consumers is mediated by agro-processors and supermarkets, economies of scale will pose major challenges for the future competitiveness of smallholders.

These different mechanisms can all reverse the small-farm labour advantage, or make it irrelevant, leading to a potential decline of the family farm. The 'perceived crisis' in smallholder agriculture is manifested by such evidence as: suicides of heavily indebted farmers in India; the long-term stagnation of food crop productivity in Africa; the role of poor indigenous farmers in the political instability of many Latin American countries; and increased rural–urban income disparities in South and East Asia. But there are many policy instruments to help smallholders increase their competitiveness, as long as governments do not tilt the playing field against them (World Bank 2007: 92).

In conclusion, heterogeneity in the smallholder sector implies that a group of entrepreneurial smallholders is likely to respond when markets offer new opportunities. Improved access to assets (physical, natural, financial, human and social), access to new and ecologically integrated technology and better incentives can allow more smallholders to become market participants in staples and high-value crops. In addition, smallholders can act collectively to overcome high transaction costs by forming producer cooperatives.

Part II of this book examines the constraints facing smallholders in relation to access to resources for improving their production and productivity. These constraints are land, labour, credit, and water for livelihoods. It also includes a discussion of questions relating to gender and food security.

Part II

Challenges and Options
for Food Security

5
Access to Land

For the rural poor, the key to sustainable livelihoods and poverty reduction is access to assets that are legally secure. If they are denied the rights of secure access to land, to water and to other crucial resources such as credit, inputs and technology, their ability to invest in better resource management is likely to be undermined. 'Unfortunately, in most developing countries, there are still serious unresolved issues of access to land, of appropriate land reform, and of agrarian reform' (de Janvry et al. 2001: 1).

Land policies and land reforms are important elements in macroeconomic and political decision-making. From the 1960s to the early 1980s, agricultural policy in most developing countries was based on protecting markets, controlling prices, and subsidising agricultural services and inputs, while state controls, intervention and regulation were used to protect land immobility. It was envisaged that land reforms would lead to a more equitable distribution of land, and broader, more efficient participation of peasant farmers, and that this would increase agricultural productivity (Ellis 1992: 195–7).

This chapter examines the diversity and types of land tenure systems available to farmers in developing countries. It explores the pressure for land reforms from socio-economic and demographic perspectives and elaborates on the old and new constraints experienced by smallholders in access to land. It discusses the problems associated with state-led land reforms and examines 'market-led agrarian reform' (MLAR), which has gained worldwide prominence since the early 1990s, elaborating on the main problems associated with this policy regarding people's access to land in low-income countries. A further section deals with the constraints facing women's access to land within the context of the various land tenure systems, and concludes with some discussion on the old and new challenges faced by smallholders in access to land, including so-called 'land grabbing'.

PRESSURE FOR LAND REFORM

Ellis (1992: 199) suggests that pressure for land reform can arise due to the growing disparity between the fixed, but often highly unequal, structure of land ownership, and the rapid socio-economic changes otherwise taking place in society. These changes include:

- High population growth, increasing poverty, and growing disparities between rural and urban areas. In fact, where population growth is rapid, the benefit from once-and-for-all land distribution will eventually disappear, since the average landholding per head of the agricultural population will decline across all agriculture-based groups, especially in the smallholder category, unless there is a significant redistribution of population from agriculture to non-agricultural activity. Continuous subdivision and fragmentation of landholdings under inheritance laws may also aggravate the problem (IFAD 1992).
- The pre-reform ownership structure may be inefficient, due to the existence of idle lands and extensive land-use methods producing low output per unit area, which may be associated with absentee ownership and the microeconomic inefficiency of share tenancy systems.
- Increasing mobility – both people's physical mobility between urban and rural areas and their social mobility within the power structure of the rural community.
- Development of markets resulting from external demands for certain commodities such as tea, coffee or biofuel for export, and an overall increase in demand for food production.
- Income growth and increasing disparities between those who have and those who have not, accelerating social change in rural areas which in some cases may reach an explosive level.
- Modernisation of the agricultural sector through new technology (for example, large-scale mechanisation), which can result in a high level of landlessness.

Before examining land reforms there is a need to provide a brief overview of the land tenure systems in developing countries.

According to the FAO (2007a: 1), land tenure is an important part of countries' social, political and economic structures. It is multi-dimensional, bringing into play social, technical, economic, institutional, legal and political aspects that are often ignored but must be taken into account. Land tenure relationships may be well defined and enforceable in a formal court of law or through customary structures in a community. Alternatively, they may be relatively poorly defined, with ambiguities and open to exploitation. The FAO (ibid) defines land tenure as:

> The relationship, whether legally or customarily defined, among people, as individuals or groups, with respect to land. (For convenience, 'land' is used here to include other natural resources such as water and trees). Land tenure is an institution, that is, rules invented by societies to regulate behaviour. Rules of tenure define how property rights to land are to be allocated within societies. They define how access is granted to rights to use, control, and transfer land, as well as associated responsibilities and restraints.

The FAO (2002: 1) points out that land tenure constitutes a web of intersecting interests. These include:

- Overriding interests: when a sovereign power (for example, a nation or community has the powers to allocate or reallocate land through expropriation and so on);
- Overlapping interests: when several parties are allocated different rights to the same parcel of land (for example, one party may have lease rights, another may have a right of way, and so on);
- Complementary interests: when different parties share the same interest in the same parcel of land (for example, when members of a community share common rights to grazing land, and so on); and
- Competing interests: when different parties contest the same interests in the same parcel (for example, when two parties independently claim rights to exclusive use of a parcel of agricultural land. Land disputes arise from competing claims).

According to the FAO (2002: 1), land tenure is often categorised as:

- Private: the assignment of rights to a private party who may be an individual, a (household), a group of people, or a corporate body such as a commercial entity or non-profit organisation. For example, within a community, individual families may have exclusive rights to residential parcels, agricultural parcels and certain trees. Other members of the community can be excluded from using these resources without the consent of those who hold the rights.

- Communal: a right of commons may exist within a community where each member has a right to use independently the holdings of the community. For example, members of a community may have the right to graze cattle on a common pasture.
- Open access: specific rights are not assigned to anyone and no-one can be excluded. This typically includes marine tenure where access to the high seas is generally open to anyone; it may include rangelands, forests, and so on, where there may be free access to the resources for all. (An important difference between open access and communal systems is that under communal systems non-members of the community are excluded from using the common areas).
- State: property rights are assigned to some authority in the public sector. For example, in some countries, forest lands may fall under the mandate of the state, whether at a central or decentralised level of government.

INSTRUMENTS OF STATE-LED LAND REFORM

The highly political nature of land access and land reform must be emphasised at the outset. Land reform seldom involves making minor adjustments to the socio-economic environment, and historically many land reforms have attempted to change the social relationships arising from property ownership, and alter the existing patterns of wealth, social status, and political power in a society. Thus, land reforms tend to give rise to conflicts between the powerful political groups (such as new revolutionary governments) seeking to put land reform into effect, and those equally powerful members of society (Ellis 1992: 195).

Land reform has political, social, and economic objectives. Political objectives include: (1) consolidation of the new state after revolutionary political change (such as the post-Castro revolution in Cuba, or Iraq post-1958 and post-1967); (2) undermining the power of the land-based elite by liberal socialist political groups in power; or (3) defensive land tenure change by conservative political forces wishing to maintain the status quo. Social objectives are to do with social equality, the emancipation of social groups living in conditions of servitude, and the sweeping away of non-market barriers to social change. Economic objectives include income distribution, employment, and productivity (Ellis 1992: 215).

This chapter uses Ellis's definition of land reform: 'the redistribution of property ownership in land or other right of access to the use of land' (1992: 196). Land reform may involve the following criteria:

- Reforming the contractual aspect of the land tenure system, and determining the rules/criteria and regulations of people's access to land;
- Determining the ownership structure of land (for example communal ownership, private ownership, long lease or rent); and
- Determining the size, structure and location of land holdings (for example, types of cultivation, and perishable v. non-perishable crops), cost of transport, climatic conditions (rain-fed v. irrigated land) (see, Warriner 1969; Lipton 1974; World Bank 1974; Ellis 1992: 194; IFAD 2001).

Agrarian reforms, according to Ellis (1992: 197), are 'the whole host of legal, institutional, and social changes that accompany, result, or "ought to occur" from land reform'. While Herring (in Ellis 1992: 195) believes that

> agrarian reforms transform rural society through alteration in property structure and production relations, (for example between state and peasants, land lord and peasants, transnational companies and peasants). They include a re-distribution of power and privilege, and it involves legal, institutional and social changes in the agrarian economy. (Ellis 1992: 195)

Instruments of state-led land reform

Ellis (1992: 204–5) identifies three main groups of land reform instruments. These are: (1) instruments of tenancy reform; (2) instruments of land redistribution; and (3) instruments of land settlement. Tenancy reform does not involve the redistribution of existing private titles to land, it merely means changing the rules concerning legal and illegal types of contract between landowner and tenant.

Tenancy reform typically means the prohibition of certain feudalistic types of tenancy – by imposing a ceiling on a landowner's share in tenancy contracts. In practice, the effectiveness of these instruments is compromised by the diversity and unwritten nature of the relations between landowners and tenants in many rural situations. Further instruments of tenancy reform are to convert feudal or semi-feudal tenancy arrangements to a cash rent basis, and to impose rules on landowners regarding the security of tenure of their tenants.

On the other hand, land settlement does not involve the redistribution of property rights in land under existing cultivation. However, land settlement does alter a country's overall ownership distribution of land. It involves creating new farms – either owner-operated or leased – on new lands (frontier settlement), on previously unutilised state lands, or in sparsely populated regions (for example, the transmigration programme of the Indonesian state, designed to relieve land pressure on Java by establishing farm settlements in islands of low population density) (Ellis 1992: 197). Land settlement criteria in most cases include: decisions on the size of holdings, the amount of capital (usually in the form of credit) required to get started, and the payment rules for these loans, as well as decisions on whether to lease or sell the land. Ultimately, land prices will depend on the overall objectives of land settlement policy in a given country (Ellis 1992: 197–205).

Land redistribution does mean reallocating the ownership of land between people, and the rules for this are a great deal more difficult to formulate and implement than in either of the other more modest types of land reform. Warriner (1969: 17–22), identifies four main components: expropriation, compensation, exemption, and distribution.[1]

However, land distribution involves land reform legislation which must also include the criteria and instruments for post-reform land allocation. It involves criteria concerning maximum and minimum sizes of holdings, unless land is reassigned to former tenants with no planned changes in holding size. A failure to set minimum farm sizes could mean the advent of a large number of holdings that are below family subsistence in output, and with fragmentation in later years these might become uneconomic to operate (Ellis 1992: 207). A failure to set a maximum farm size has the reverse effect of reducing the total number of holdings available, and of permitting fewer, larger, farmers a relatively high standard of living while other rural dwellers may remain landless and extremely poor. Ellis adds that both minimum and maximum criteria are, in practice, rather insensitive instruments given the variability in soils, climate, topography, crop choices, and other features of agricultural zones (ibid: 207).

Moreover, the process of redistribution must take into account the costs of the transition from land ownership patterns involving large holdings by small numbers of people, to a new structure with multiple smallholdings intended to improve the livelihoods of the new owners/tenants. In this context, the evidence on the higher productivity of smaller farms shows that redistribution can often improve aggregate production, while also redressing the problems of inequitable access (IFAD 2001: 73).

State-led land reform: old and new constraints

Cassman et al. (in World Bank 2007: 63) indicate that:

Throughout most of history, agriculture grew by bringing more land under cultivation, driven by population growth and expanding markets. But in the more densely populated parts of the world, the land frontier has closed. In Asia, land scarcity has become acute in most countries, and rapid urbanization is reducing the area available for agriculture. The urbanized countries of Latin America and Eastern Europe and Central Asia are relatively land-abundant because of lower population densities and a declining agricultural population. In Latin America there is further scope for agricultural land expansion, driven by export markets, but this is often at the expense of cutting subtropical and tropical forests and woodlands.

In sub-Saharan Africa, high rural population growth is driving expansion into forest or grazing land – creating conflicts with traditional users – or into areas subject to human and animal diseases. Even so, there is considerable room for land expansion in some sub-Saharan countries, but it will require large investments in infrastructure and human and animal disease control to convert these lands to productive agriculture.

In most cases, productivity growth of available land is often undermined by pollution, salinisation, and soil degradation from poorly managed intensification, all reducing potential yields.

In the agriculture-based countries of sub-Saharan Africa, where peasant farming is still the prevalent form of production, access to land is characterised by the communal tenure systems which now coexist with emerging private African ownership, in addition to continued private ownership by white settlers. State law is generally based on colonial law, and covers collective ownership, tenancy, rangelands and other common property. However, in many countries with such legal systems, large portions of land held under customary tenure do not enjoy legal protection (Ellis 1992; Pinckney and Kimuyu 1999).

Problems associated with communal land tenure systems

The World Bank (2007: 139) points out that:

> many African jurisdictions considered most land to be 'state land' and those who had cultivated such land for generations received only precarious tenure rights and could lose their land to make room for strategic investment with little or no compensation.

Moreover, the World Bank (2007: 138–42) elaborates further on some of problems associated with the communal systems in agriculture-based countries:

• Communal access is often associated with a lack of legal title to the land, which then cannot be used as collateral to access credit;
• Land in this system is regarded as a tied asset, so users have no right to sell;
• Peasant users are not allowed to build fences, including green belts of trees and shrubs, for conserving water and soil;
• Communal ownership makes it difficult to establish practical rules for urbanisation or for industrial and commercial enterprises, and can also create problems for extending infrastructure; and
• Communal access creates relatively few problems when the population is stable or low, but high population growth will eventually undermine equality objectives because of land partition, and may also lead to conflicts between clans and tribes.

Many writers agree that ownership of land with proper title can provide farmers with the collateral and incentives to access credit and invest in order to improve land management. Secure land rights also help rural credit markets to develop, because land is considered to be good collateral (World Bank 1989; 2007).

Pinckney and Kimuyu (1999) conducted field research in Kenya and Tanzania in an attempt to find out whether formalising land titles for smallholders had enabled them to access commercial credit and make improved investments in land management. Their research focused on two villages in the coffee zones of Kenya and Tanzania, where policies were markedly different. Kenya, working on World Bank advice, encouraged farmers to own their land with proper titles, while Tanzania still believed that communal access was best for farmers and prioritised equality of access to land over ownership. They investigated the effect of giving land titles in Kenya on farmers' access to credit, highlighting the issue of using the land as collateral. Their study findings showed that:

- There was no difference in the outcomes of the two radically different land policies;
- Neither community was able to use land as collateral for formal-sector loans;
- Since security of tenure was not enhanced by ownership, there was no additional incentive to invest;
- Neither community showed evidence of small inefficient farmers selling out to larger, more efficient farmers; and
- In neither community did land purchases or sales cause increasing inequality in relation to the ownership of local land among the households in the sample.

Moreover, to explain whether land title alone can help give small farmers access to credit, Musembi (2007: 1457–78) points out that de Soto's (2003: 6–39) arguments linking the formalisation of land ownership to access to credit have been discredited by empirical evidence such as the study by Pinckney and Kimuyu (1999) and in other places, including de Soto's native Peru (Hendrix 1996). Moreover, recent studies from Argentina and Peru concede that factors other than lack of title make the poor risk-averse, and that biases in the commercial lending sector still persist, so that poor people with title are no more likely to obtain loans from commercial banks than those without (*The Economist*, in Musembi 2007: 1457–78).

The reasons why smallholders' access to credit has not improved significantly with formal titling are summed up by Musembi (2007: 1466) as follows:

- Based on a cost–benefit analysis, commercial banks tend to shun small-scale (particularly rural or agriculture-dependent) land-holders. Evidence from Tanzania shows that the amendment to its 1999 Land Act – which for the first time permitted the outright sale of land, in order to make it easier for smallholders to use their land as collateral – did not provide the necessary guarantee (of 20 acres) for the commercial banks to give loans. Thus title in itself does little to change these institutional biases.[2]

• The situation is influenced by the existence of a vibrant informal micro-scale lending network. Since the credit obtained from informal institutions is not secured on land, it is attractive in a context where people fear losing their family land.

• Musembi (2007: 1457–78) finds out that many registered landowners had not collected their official documents of title from the land registries several years after they had been formalised (with the parcel number and sketch map issued to them following demarcation).

• It is difficult to identify and measure the impact of tenure reform on productivity, as shown by inconclusive research conducted in the Njoro area in Kenya, because the richer and 'more productive' farmers, who were most likely to benefit from titling programmes were also the ones more likely to seek title and leverage loans (Pinckney and Kimuyu 1999).

The World Bank (2007: 139) considers that individual titling is still appropriate in many cases, but that it needs to be complemented by new approaches to securing tenure, and it points out that:

earlier interventions to improve tenure security focused almost exclusively on individual titling, but this can weaken or leave out communal, secondary, or women's rights. Moreover, the process of titling can be used for land-grabbing by local elites and bureaucrats.

The report suggests that moving to more formal types of tenure can be made possible through a well-defined and transparent process, as has happened in Mexico for example, where certified individual land plots in ejido[3] communities can become fully transferable freehold land through a qualified vote by the assembly. The fact that fewer than 15 per cent of ejidos choose full titling shows that many users view the benefits of maintaining communal relations as greater than the benefits deriving from the individualisation of rights (see World Bank 2007: 140, Box 6.1), for a case study of benefits from community-driven certification in Ethiopia).

However, three decades of land reforms have produced only mixed results, ranging from partial success to total failure. Among the many reasons cited for the failure of agrarian reforms are: insufficient political support; the high economic costs of land redistribution; the weakness of the institutions responsible for issuing land titles and administering registration processes; the centralisation of the process and a lack of participation on the part of beneficiaries; and the severe flaws inherent in a policy of land distribution with ceiling area retention by landowners which concentrated land-holding once again in the hands of the powerful (Ellis 1992; IFAD 2001). The following section will elaborate further on some of the problems associated with state-led land reform.

Problems associated with state-led land reform

Lahiff et al. (2007: 1421–3) discuss the grounds on which the World Bank's neoliberal critique of conventional state-led agrarian reform has been put forward under three main headings: distortions in the land market, poor programme design, and excessive cost of implementation.

First, most state-led reform programmes have introduced a range of distortions to land and agricultural markets through restrictive measures such as ceilings on land size and restrictions on land rentals and land sales. It is generally agreed that these have failed to achieve the desired result of a more equitable distribution of land (Binswanger and Deininger in Lahiff et al. 2007).

Second, state-led agrarian reform programmes are generally inefficient and ineffective, with all responsibility for funding and implementation being assumed by the state through its centralised and bureaucratic requirements to implement land reform. A state supply-driven approach, motivated by a political agenda, results in two undesirable outcomes: the acquisition of lands that are not suitable for resettlement, and the inclusion of households that are not 'qualified' to become land reform beneficiaries. This is because political affiliations and other non-economic factors may lead to the inclusion of beneficiaries who already own land, or who have little interest in farming, while those in greatest need, or with the greatest ability to farm, may be overlooked.

The expropriation of large productive farms that are then subdivided into smaller, less productive farms, leads to efficiency losses in agriculture (this is particularly pronounced in the case of Zimbabwe). This strategy may provoke resistance or evasive action (such as the registration of an owner's land in many different names, bribery, or side agreements made between landowners and tenants). The beneficiaries in most cases are unaware of their rights and obligations, because of the complexity of the documentation and problems regarding legal title. In some cases, courts find loopholes and rule in favour of landowners (Ellis 1992; Lahiff et al. 2007).

IFAD (2001: 73) indicates that it is not easy to correct asset inequalities through redistribution programmes as redistribution can disrupt the economy, deterring saving (including capital flight) and impeding growth, especially in increasingly open markets. But while this might sometimes be a risk, the risk of neglecting the rural poor can be even greater, creating rural conflict, environmental degradation and expanding mega-cities. Furthermore, failure to carry out farm-level planning before land transfer commences contributes to poor productivity on resettled land, and to failure on the part of state institutions and agricultural services to adapt and to deliver support services in a coordinated and timely manner (IFAD 2001).

Third, state-led programmes are accused of being excessively expensive and breeding large and unaccountable bureaucracies as operational costs are compounded by the need to provide support and subsidies. The high levels of default on loan repayment by farmers has added to operational costs and further undermined the sustainability of such programmes (see, Ellis 1992; Binswanger and Deininger 1997; Johnson and Rogaly 1997: 61; Lahiff et al. 2007).

However, past experience shows that tenancy reforms which do not involve land redistribution or changes of land title have a negligible impact on tenancy status, income, efficiency and technical innovation. It also shows that there are serious flaws in those land distribution programmes that are based on ceiling area retentions by landowners. The direct transfer of freehold ownership to peasant farm families – as in South Korea, Taiwan and Japan – has worked much better in terms of stability, income levels and efficiency (Ellis 1992; World Bank 2007: 142).

Moreover, one of the state-led objectives of land reform is to increase agricultural production and achieve food security. However, output increases cannot be attributed to land reform alone unless the social, economic and agronomic factors can be accounted for. The absence of appropriate state policies in areas such as irrigation, inputs and credit, efficient markets and marketing systems, and research and advisory services, have contributed to the lack of success of land reform in many cases (Ellis 1992).

With the adoption of structural adjustment programmes (SAPs) in the mid-1980s, and in the context of political and economic liberalisation, the role of the state in many countries has been drastically reduced. This has meant the reduction of state intervention in the provision of agricultural services and the protection of rural markets and price controls, as well as the elimination of subsidies. The expectation was that removing state control and intervention would free the market for private sector actors to take over agricultural services, thus reducing their costs, improving their quality, and eliminating their regressive bias (Bardhan et al. 2000; Kanbur and Lusting 1999; de Janvry et al. 2001).

However, as the World Bank (2007) notes, too often this did not happen:

> In some places the state withdrawal was tentative at best, limiting private entry. Elsewhere, the private sector emerged only slowly and partially, mainly serving commercial farmers but leaving many smallholders exposed to extensive market failures, high transaction costs and risks, and service gaps.

Moreover, imperfect markets and service gaps can impose huge costs in foregone growth and welfare losses for smallholders, threatening their competitiveness and, in many cases, their survival (World Bank 2007: 139–57):

> In practice, macroeconomic reforms implemented as part of SAPs have often produced only a weak supply response from agriculture, undermining one of the main objectives of these reforms. Many poor rural households have been unable to gain sufficient access to land, when this could be their best option out of poverty. The result is the reproduction of poverty and inequality, which further led to inefficiencies through disincentive effects and negative externalities.

There is therefore a need for a new type of agrarian reform that will enhance the capacity of a state's institutions to fill the vacuum left by the reduction in direct state participation, and to develop efficient and productive agricultural alternatives for rural producers. For instance, agricultural cooperatives can play an important social and economic role in filing the vacuum left by the state's direct intervention in the past. In this respect, land reform must involve the development of a comprehensive institutional framework, inclusive of public, private and civil society participation, that ensures rights, equality and security. Therefore, it should be a priority for land reform to: (1) remove obstacles that discourage or inhibit farmers' investment in their land; (2) provide a comprehensive set of rules and a legal framework for land access; (3) clarify individual rights; and (4) put in place adequate systems for regularisation and land titling, which are seen as important mechanisms for ensuring security, and which favour investments in the agricultural sector by producers (World Bank 1974; 2007; IFAD 2001).

MLAR has gained worldwide prominence since the early 1990s as an alternative to the state-led approaches widely implemented over the course of the twentieth century (Lahiff et al. 2007). The following section describes MLAR and highlights some of the problems associated with this type of reform.

MARKET-LED AGRARIAN REFORM (MLAR)

According to Lahiff et al. (2007: 1423):

> like other versions of agrarian reform, MLAR should ... be seen not just as a means of re-distributing land or alleviating rural poverty, but as part of the wider (market-oriented) structural adjustment of national economies being implemented as part of neoliberal globalisation.

Deininger (2001) explains that MLAR advocates the redistribution of land from large to smaller owners via market transactions in order to achieve the two objectives of social equity and economic efficiency – the latter through the assumption of an inverse relationship between farm size and productivity. It anticipates that the new family farmers will be drawn into increasingly liberalised markets for land, for commodities, and for agricultural services such as the provision of grants and loans to enable them to enter the market, and to encourage landlords to sell off unwanted land or under-used land with compensation at the full market price.

Deininger (2001), describe the package of reforms proposed by MLAR as follows:

> MLAR, rely heavily on voluntary land transactions via the market, embedded within the wider neoliberal agenda for the restructuring and reorientation of the agricultural sector. A vibrant land market is assumed to allow the most efficient use of land resources by the most efficient users. One of its conditions is to remove all kinds of distortions in agricultural land prices, inputs and output subsidies

and complete abolition of prohibitions on land sales and rentals, in order to allow for a more fluid land market.

Moreover, the MLAR policy approach is designed around private transactions between willing sellers and willing buyers, and is thus a decentralised method of implementing reform, aimed at achieving speedy transactions as well as transparency and accountability (Binswanger 2007).

The role of the state, and especially of national government, is thus greatly reduced, and does not extend to direct involvement in every land transaction (van Zyl et al, in Lahiff et al. 2007: 1424). However, it is in this context that an MLAR approach requires the involvement of local government for land purchase mediation and tax collection (although the land taxation advocated as part of MLAR has not always materialised). Local government is thought to be nearer to the people, and hence more responsive to the actual needs of local communities. The MLAR model also emphasises the implementation roles of other players: both NGOs (particularly in the area of community facilitation) and the private sector (particularly in the provision of post-settlement support services).

The speed with which beneficiaries get access to land then depends on the level of annual appropriations, rather than on drawn-out expropriation proceedings for specific farms, and the scale of such appropriations would itself be set in response to popular demand (Binswanger 2007).

In this model of land reform, land prices are expected to be reduced, mainly because of the method of cash payment to landlords, who are expected to reduce transaction costs incurred under previous systems, which offered a mix of cash and bonds over a longer period. Because it is a voluntary process between sellers and willing buyers, it should be largely free of the political and legal complexities and problems which slowed down the processes of more conventional land reform, ensuring a relatively swift and conflict-free programme of implementation (Deininger 2001: 12).

Problems associated with MLAR

Many analysts agree that, in countries with highly unequal land ownership, land markets are no panacea for addressing the structural inequalities which reduce land productivity and hold back development (World Bank 2007: 142). Lahiff et al. (2007) highlight some emerging evidence from across the developing world which suggests that such policies are incapable of challenging the political and economic power of large landowners, and so are unlikely to meet the land needs of the rural poor and landless.[4]

Firstly, the basic, and highly debatable, assumption of the MLAR approach is that land is simply an economic factor of production. This ignores its numerous social, political, cultural, religious (as well as spiritual) and environmental dimensions, as well as class, gender and ethnicity-based relationships.

Secondly, neoliberal reforms have benefited existing landowners and other elites through formal registration of property, thus increasing the marketability and value of land and, in some cases, through the effective privatisation of former communal resources. For example, experience from land reform programmes in Egypt shows that relatively few poor people (whether landless peasants or rural labourers) have benefited from land transfer or from subsequent support services. In many cases, the benefits and the support services were directed mainly at commercial and better-off producers (Bush 2007: 1599–615).

Thirdly, although proponents of MLAR continue to assert that such policies are complementary to existing state-led reforms, in practice MLAR is more often a deliberate effort to counter any such alternatives which continue to enjoy widespread popular and legislative support. In Brazil, for example, MLAR constitutes a direct challenge to the constitutional provisions on land reform that grant fundamental rights to land seekers and limit compensation to landowners. In the Philippines MLAR has contributed to the undermining of progress made under the state-driven land reform programme. In El Salvador, despite the fact that agrarian reform was an integral part of the peace settlement between the revolutionary land reform movement and the Salvadoran government, it was subordinated to voluntary agreements with landowners, making it 'instantly more difficult to implement and land became harder to acquire and to finance' (Lahiff et al. 2007: 1431).

Fourthly, in South Africa a constitutional commitment to land reform which includes provision for expropriation at below market prices 'in the public interest' has been subordinated to market processes under a 'willing buyer, willing seller' approach. Lahiff terms this 'the landowner veto' – without any clear legal basis (Lahiff et al. 2007: 1577–97). It was expected that 30 per cent of agricultural land would be redistributed or resituated to the original owners by 2014. The achievement of this target has been delayed by a shortage of funds, and by the new owners' inadequate farming skills and under-capitalisation, while many of them are seriously indebted. Thus, the acquisition programme's worthy objective of overcoming the land poverty and inequality of the apartheid years does not necessarily make good policy sense.

Moreover, the case studies presented in the special issue of *Third World Quarterly* entitled 'Market-led agrarian reform: policies, performance and prospects' indicates clearly that the advantages of MLAR to landowners can be considerable, and generally leads only to the disposal of limited portions of their land, which cannot translate into large-scale redistribution to the rural poor and landless. It shows how landowners as a class are a politically well-organised group within highly unequal agrarian societies, who would not accept the erosion of the material basis of their power and wealth through a large-scale redistribution of land to peasants and the landless (Lahiff et al. 2007).

In countries with new and often fragile democracies, the decision to postpone land reform can mean that the problems of landlessness are eventually resolved under radically different, and much less favourable, political and economic circumstances, and often with grievous consequences, as in Zimbabwe during the 1990s.

However, Zimbabwe's land issue has generated unprecedented debates both within and outside the country according to Mkodzongi (2010). The debates, which followed the dramatic occupations of white farms by rural peasants in the late 1990s, are generally polarised between those who support radical land reform and those who support market-led reforms. The former stand accused of supporting Mugabe's regime while the latter are generally maligned as neocolonialists running a smear campaign against Zanu PF. An unfortunate outcome of these polarities has been the trivialisation of the land issue. Land occupations have been depicted as simple acts of political gimmickry, and landless peasants who occupied these farms have been branded as agents of agrarian and environmental destruction, and are often considered to be in the service of Robert Mugabe's regime.

Focusing on the politics of emerging rural movements and on processes of illegal land occupation or squatting, Manji (in Moyo 2008: 41) believes that:

> The dominance of external financial and development aid institutions in Africa's policy making processes and market are organic to most of the emergent land conflicts. Pressures for growing marketisation of land reflect both external interests in economic liberalisation and foreign access to land and natural

resources, as well as the increasing internal class struggles over primitive accumulation by a broadening African indigenous capitalist class. New land policies justify these tendencies of unequal land control, but generate growing conflicts over land allocation and use across class, gender, nationality and ethnic lines.

STEPS TOWARDS SUCCESSFUL LAND REFORM

Successful land reform in any given country is intended to improve access to land, and requires the implementation of various strategies by the state, the choice of which will depend on the specifics of that country's situation: levels of poverty; existing land tenure arrangements; population growth rates; and the number of people who are economically active and likely to be engaged in agricultural production. The World Bank (2007: 138–42) suggests the following ten steps to bring about improved access to land in developing countries:

1. Carrying out surveys to clarify land records and the provision of finance for compensation;
2. Enabling land rental markets and strengthening the land sales market (which entails political commitments);
3. Decentralising the process of land reform, and promoting the participation of potential beneficiaries in its design and implementation;
4. Making complementary investments in infrastructure and services;
5. Building the capacity of the relevant legal institutions and providing legal aid to those who need it most;
6. Promoting the role of the private sector in providing the services which are most needed – supply of inputs, marketing, credit and insurance and advisory services;
7. Recognising customary tenure by formalising customary laws in ways that are participatory and reflect the diversity of the ethnic, historical, and social construction of land. For example, during the decade since 2000 many African countries adopted new land laws which recognised customary tenure, made lesser (oral) forms of evidence on land rights admissible, strengthened women's land rights, and established decentralised land institutions (Alden, in World Bank 2007);
8. Delineating legally valid boundaries, identifying existing rights that may overlap or be of a seasonal nature (such as between

herders and sedentary agriculturalists), and registering them as appropriate;

9. Vesting day-to-day management decisions in an accountable and transparent body, for example a legally incorporated user group, with clear rules for conflict resolution which are respected by all involved; and

10. Making the evolution to more formal types of tenure possible through a well-defined and transparent process, documenting land rights and modernising land administration.

GENDER AND LAND REFORM

It is well established fact that women are responsible for 60 to 80 per cent of food production in almost all low-income agriculture-based countries, especially on small farms. If they are to use land more efficiently, and thereby make a greater contribution to food security, they need access to land and security of tenure to provide them with some control over land-based resources and economic incentives.

However, since the 1910s until the present, women's access to land has been largely gender-blind (Manji 2006). In fact, land reform, whether state- or market-led, is insensitive to gender and/or has a male bias.

In the process of reform, women have frequently lost long-established land access rights, and their traditional rights of inheritance have been ignored in the design of new land laws, thus depriving them of access to resources. Land and tenancy reform often results in new holdings/lease contracts being drawn up in men's names as owners or tenants, while assets are typically allocated to the male head of household, on the assumption that this would benefit all members equitably. In particular, this approach ignores the well-being of women and their dependents in the event of household dissolution by divorce, separation or widowhood (Manji 2006).

Women's access to land is generally based on their status within the family, and may involve only a right of use. In Asia, for example, inheritance laws favour male inheritance over female, so where a woman formally holds property rights it may be for her life only, so they revert at her death to the male line. In Africa, custom rather than religious practices generally excludes women from land ownership, with property held in a man's name and passed on patrilineally – hence a widow's right to remain on the land is not secure.

Recently, most developing countries have recognised the adverse consequences of discrimination against women in this area. In some countries this has led to changes in constitutional provisions and more specific legislation to require general equality of men and women, mandate issuance of joint titles, modify inheritance legislation, and ensure female representation on land administration institutions (see, Deere and Doss 2001; World Bank 2007).

LAND GRABBING: A NEW CHALLENGE

Rising hunger and concerns about food security and energy security worldwide have driven wealthy investors, companies and countries to buy large-scale real estate with irrigation potential in developing countries during the last decade. Significant evidence from countries such as Ethiopia, Ghana, Madagascar, Mali, and Sudan (Cotula and Vermeulen 2009: 334–6) shows that over 2.5 million hectares of land has been approved for rental or sale, in some cases through negotiation between national and regional governments and investors.

The size of single acquisitions tends to be very large, while varying considerably from one country to another. Approved land allocations include: a 452,500 hectare biofuel project in Madagascar; a 100,000 hectare irrigation project in Mali; a 150,000 hectare livestock project in Ethiopia and 300,000 hectares – an area larger than Luxembourg – allocated for 50 years at an annual rate of 20 birr (US$1.12) per hectare to farm crops including maize, wheat, and rice (Fitzgerald 2010). Private sector deals are more common than government-to-government ones, though governments are using a range of tools to support private deals indirectly, and levels of government-owned investments are significant and growing.

Evidence from a study by Toulmin (2005: 2) has revealed a 'new tragedy of the commons' in which:

Across the continent, a land grab is under way. Governments take small farmers' land to create enterprise zones. Customary chiefs reap fortunes from urban sprawl by getting rid of tenants to make way for residential development. In Côte d'Ivoire local people seize land back from migrant farmers, who thought they had bought it. Land held in Commons, whether grazing lands, woodlands, or wetlands, are being eaten away by enclosure, depriving the poorest people of their final resort when times are tough.

Cotula and Vermeulen (2009: 334–6) highlight some of the advantages (or opportunities) and disadvantages (or risks) of this new trend in land ownership. For example, increased investment may bring macro-level benefits (in terms of GDP growth, and greater government revenue), in addition to creating opportunities for raising local living standards. Investors may bring capital, know-how, infrastructure, employment opportunities and market access, and may play an important role in catalysing economic development in rural areas.

On the downside, there is a risk that, as outside interest increases and as governments or markets makes land available to prospecting investors, land acquisitions may result in local people losing access to the resources on which they depend – primarily land, but also water, wood and grazing. Large-scale land allocation may still result in displacement as demand focuses on higher-value land (for instance those with greater irrigation potential or closer proximity to markets). The position of local people may be undermined by many factors, such as: insecure use rights on state-owned land; inaccessible registration procedures; vaguely defined productive use requirements; legislative gaps; and compensation only for loss of improvements such as crops and trees, with no compensation in most cases for loss of land. Moreover, those investors who aim for good practice have to operate clear procedures and guidelines set by government (ibid).

This new trend reflects significant global economic and social transformations, with profound implications for the future of world agriculture, people's livelihoods and food security. According to Cotula and Vermeulen (ibid), hard questions must be asked by host governments in relation to the investor's capacity to deliver, and commitments in terms of level of investment, job creation, infrastructure development, public revenues, environmental protection, and safeguards in land takings. Some recipient countries whose land is being leased or bought are themselves food insecure, and workable arrangements must be put in place to protect local food security, particularly in times of crises.

Host governments need to create incentives to promote inclusive business models that integrate rural smallholders and family farms. Efforts must be stepped up to secure local land rights, including customary rights, using collective land registration where appropriate and ensuring the principle of free, prior and informed consent, robust compensation regimes, the provision of legal aid, and good governance in land tenure and administration (ibid).

In conclusion, resolving these agrarian questions is fundamental to alleviating rural poverty and promoting livelihood security in low-income, agriculture-based, developing countries. Pressure for land reform may seem to be a much lower priority for state action in developing countries in the twenty-first century than was the case four decades ago (Ellis 1992: 211). However, there are rising demands for agricultural and food production due to population pressures and increasing inequalities within and between countries, and the growing assertiveness of local and transnational rural social movements for 'an alternative rural world'. All these issues require a broader understanding of the multidimensional nature of rural livelihoods (Lahiff et al. 2007: 1433).

Peasants' movements are often the driving force of land reforms, even if they are not the only or even the main beneficiaries of the reforms as they are fully implemented (Ellis 1992: 212). However, peasants are revolting against the oppressions and constrictions of the newly emerging and powerful land-based elite following neoliberal and market-oriented policies in developing countries (for example, the land movement in Brazil and La Via Campesina Peasants International Movement).

Redistributive land reform is a necessary but not a sufficient condition to eradicate poverty and inequality in rural areas. Lahiff et al. (2007) proposed three broadly distinct but related factors required to achieve a successful outcome of land reform: (1) the ability of the rural poor to build their own independent movements and create sustained political pressure for change; (2) the creation of pro-poor national political coalitions that can use state power to implement development policies including land reform and 'growth with equity'; and (3) large-scale public investment in infrastructure and support services to ensure that land reform enhances productivity. Only through more equitable distribution of assets can the highly inequitable and anti-poor effects of today's global market forces be effectively contested locally, nationally and internationally.

The next chapter deals with the determinants of rural labour markets in agriculture-based countries.

6
Rural Labour Markets

Access to land, to water and to capital (both fixed and working capital), along with greater participation of rural people in agricultural and non-agricultural labour markets, are the most important components of any strategy aimed at reducing poverty and improving food security. However, these goals cannot be achieved in isolation from the overall political, economic and social development of any given country.

Growth in agriculture and in the rural non-farm economy will be essential for providing employment opportunities for the estimated further 106 million rural people in developing countries who were predicted to become economically active between 2005 and 2015 (ILO 2003). As agriculture intensifies and diversifies, and economies develop, two of the main challenges in relation to reducing poverty and diminishing rural–urban income disparities will be the achievement of both well-functioning rural labour markets and well-managed rural–urban migration.

However, according to the World Bank (2007), there has been minimal policy focus on the structure, conduct and performance of rural labour markets and how they might contribute to poverty reduction and food security. Thus, they have remained peripheral to policy discussions on growth, employment and poverty reduction in developing countries, and particularly in sub-Saharan Africa (World Bank 2007: 312; Cramer et al. 2008).

This chapter examines rural labour markets in agriculture-based countries and the factors affecting labour supply and demand in rural areas and beyond. It goes on to identify the specific characteristics of rural labour markets, and then provides an analysis of the complexity and the diversity of these markets. It also offers suggestions on public policy, and on the most needed supports for promoting an employment-centred development strategy which can achieve income growth and substantially reduce poverty.

RURAL LABOUR MARKETS: AN OVERVIEW

Data from 1997 to 2007 indicates that labour employment in the agricultural sector has been declining for both men and women in almost all regions of the world (Table 6.1) and, although men are migrating out of agriculture faster in some areas, the overall decline in women's agricultural employment is also significant (World Bank, FAO and IFAD, 2009: 318). The one notable exception is women's employment in agriculture in the Middle East and North Africa. Data also shows that the service sector is leading in terms of percentage share of the labour force for both men and women. Figures for employment in industry indicate positive growth for both men and women, with the highest figures being recorded for Latin America and the Caribbean. The reasons for the declining labour share in agriculture include growth in the services and industry sectors, and in large-scale farming with high levels of mechanisation in the agricultural sector.

However, rural households who are engaged in agriculture in most agriculture-based countries are confronted by many challenges and constraints in their attempts to build a secure livelihood. The majority choose agricultural entrepreneurship as their route out of poverty; others aim to achieve it through the rural labour market and the rural non-farm economy; still others choose to migrate to towns, cities or to other countries. Further, there are 'diversified households' which combine income from farming with income from off-farm labour and from migration. These three pathways are complementary: non-farm incomes can enhance the potential of farming as a pathway out of poverty, and agriculture can facilitate both the labour market and migration pathways (World Bank 2007: 75).

In these countries, agriculture is still the single largest source of employment in rural areas, where labour represents between half and almost all the value of non-land resources used in agriculture-based regions of developing countries. In those regions, a low uptake of technology, combined with low levels of education and skills, in addition to other factors, constrains higher labour productivity and better job opportunities (Wiggins and Deshingkar 2007; World Bank 2007; IFAD 2011).

Research evidence suggests that non-farm activities are becoming increasingly important. These comprise a highly diverse range of activities: from manufacturing (usually artisan), to trading, to the provision of services of all kinds, combined with diverse farming activities such as food and or export crops, livestock production and processing (Wiggins and Deshingkar 2007). Furthermore, the World Bank (2007: 288) states:

Table 6.1 Men's and women's shares in overall employment by sector, 1997 and 2007

	Employment in agriculture (%)		Employment in industry (%)		Employment in services (%)	
	1997	2007	1997	2007	1997	2007
Women						
World	43.5	36.1	16.8	17.6	39.6	46.3
Central and Southern Europe (non-EU) and CIS*	26.9	19.2	22.2	17.9	50.8	62.8
Developed economies and European Union	5.3	3.2	16.7	12.5	78.1	84.3
East Asia	51.9	41.0	22.8	25.5	25.3	33.5
Latin America and the Caribbean	14.6	10.7	13.6	14.5	71.9	74.8
Middle East	28.4	31.0	20.0	18.8	51.5	50.2
North Africa	31.2	32.6	19.1	15.2	49.7	52.2
South Asia	74.0	60.5	11.2	18.4	14.7	21.1
South East Asia and the Pacific	50.3	43.4	13.9	16.3	35.8	40.3
Sub-Saharan Africa	74.8	67.9	5.9	5.8	19.2	26.4
Men						
World	40.0	34.0	24.0	25.6	36.1	40.4
Central and Southern Europe (non-EU) and CIS	27.0	19.8	33.2	32.6	39.8	47.6
Developed economies and European Union	6.7	4.6	37.1	34.3	56.1	61.1
East Asia	44.6	36.3	25.6	28.0	29.8	35.7
Latin America and the Caribbean	28.6	24.7	24.8	27.1	46.5	48.2
Middle East	19.6	12.5	27.2	28.0	53.3	59.4
North Africa	36.6	32.9	20.1	22.3	43.3	44.8
South Asia	53.5	42.9	17.0	23.0	29.5	34.1
South East Asia and the Pacific	47.7	44.3	19.4	21.0	32.9	34.7
Sub-Saharan Africa	70.0	62.4	10.4	12.4	19.6	25.2

CIS: Commonwealth of Independent States.

Sources: ILO (2006) and World Bank, IFAD and FAO (2009).

The diversity of activities in rural areas leads to a corresponding diversification in income sources. For example, in these regions, non-agricultural activities account for an average of 30 per cent to 50 per cent of household incomes. This does not necessarily mean that individual households have diverse sources of income; only that households differ in those sources.

Wiggins and Deshingkar (2007: 1) indicate that, despite this heterogeneity, some features of rural work are common across different sectors and locations. Most rural workers are self-employed, whether on their own farms or in the small enterprises typical of rural non-farm activities.

Hired workers are in the minority: one estimate put the number of farm workers at 450 million out of a total agricultural labour force of 1,100 billion (see, Hurst et al. 2005; Wiggins and Deshingkar 2007). Most recent research indicates that between 50 and 60 per cent of rural households are participating in the rural non-farm economy in Asia and Latin America, while between 25 and 50 per cent are participating in sub-Saharan Africa. In most Latin American and Asian countries, including China (FAO 2009g), non-farm income sources make up a higher proportion of total rural incomes than agriculture (Valdé et al. 2008). However, for a majority of rural households, participation in the non-farm economy is either part-time or seasonal, serving to manage risk and diversify income sources (IFAD 2011: 185).

Moreover, in many situations the rural non-farm economy is of substantial importance for women, and although men have the greater share of non-farm employment, women make up between 10 and 40 per cent of those employed in the rural non-farm economy, with the highest shares in sub-Saharan Africa and Latin America (see, Wiggins and Hazell 2008; IFAD 2011: 185). Off-farm work is important for both adult men and women in rural areas, but there are variations depending on the local traditions and prevalent value systems.[1] According to the World Bank (2007) 'the supply of female labour (and that of other adult members of the households) is both a household decision and a determinant of the household's balance of power, and is necessary to "smooth" income and consumption over a period of time in order to achieve food security'. No doubt a household's decision to participate in the rural labour market depends on the personal, social and economic characteristics of the household itself and on employment opportunities in the rural, peri-urban and urban markets.

THE ECONOMICS OF THE HOUSEHOLD LABOUR ALLOCATION MODEL

The concept of a household's labour allocation can be traced back to the work of T. W. Schultz (1953), Becker (1981), Barnum and Morse (1979), Bryceson (2000), and Osmani (2003), and most recently the work of Mendola (2007), Cramer et al. (2008), and Ligon (2008).

Mendola (2007: 49) points out that 'farm households are located in a larger dominant economic and political system that could affect their production behaviour, but fundamentally they are characterised by partial engagement in markets, which are often imperfect or incomplete'. The members of peasant households typically have to work with markets that function sporadically and somewhat disconnectedly across various locations and times. However, Hunt (in Mendola 2007) identifies the peasant's household as both a production and consumption unit: a proportion of produce is sold to meet their cash requirements and financial obligations, and a part is consumed by them. These units involve a variety of markets and non-markets tasks such as agriculture; pastoralist; fishing; crafts; and gathering (fruits, nuts, fuel-wood, water and so on).

Because agricultural production is significantly dependent on the performance of farmers and, at the same time, poverty is disproportionately concentrated among them, a primary concern for any poverty alleviation strategy has to be an understanding of the determinants of their modes of production and of the household's decision-making on labour allocation.

Mendola (2007: 52) explores the similarities and differences among various theoretical models of household labour allocation. There are three alternative economic theories of peasant household behaviour: Schultz (1964), the 'profit maximising peasant'; Becker (1981), 'the neoclassical agricultural household model'; and Lipton (1968), Walker and Jodha (1986) and Ellis (2000), the 'risk-averse peasant'. Each theory assumes that peasant households have an objective function to maximise profit, with a set of constraints. Moreover, these theories are based on a set of assumptions about the workings of the wider economy within which peasant production takes place. Not all of these assumptions are shared by all theories, but all adopt the same theoretical method to explain farm household behaviour.

In one theoretical approach Schultz (1964) developed the concept of the 'profit maximising' peasant, explaining that farm households in developing countries are usually 'poor but efficient'. He is referring explicitly to a household's efficiency in allocating labour and resources, and implicitly to their technical efficiency, but his main caveat is that profit maximisation has both a behavioural content (the motivation of the household) and a technical-economic content (the economic performance of the farm as a business enterprise). This model has also been criticised on the grounds that it overlooks both the dimension of consumption and the role of leisure (time off) in peasant households' decision-making processes (Mendola 2007: 52).

The 'neoclassical agricultural household model' typically incorporates the notion of full household income (see, Becker 1981; Mendola 2007: 52) and conceives of the household as a production unit which converts purchased goods and services, as well as its own resources, into use values or utilities when consumed. Thus, both the production and consumption goals of farm households are included (Chayanov, in Mendola 2007: 52).

In the absence of a perfect rural labour market, factors such as family size and structure influence a farm household's subjective evaluation of labour allocation decisions (Chayanov, in Mendola 2007). Thus, farm households will maximise utility through the consumption of all available goods (that is, home-produced goods, market-purchased goods and leisure time), subject to full income constraints. This model shows that if all markets exist, and all goods are tradable, then prices are exogenous and production decisions are taken independently of consumption.

Moreover, Lipton (1968), Walker and Jodha (1986), and Ellis (1992) describe the theory of 'a risk-averse peasant', where the objective function of risk-averse behaviour among farm households in rural areas is to secure survival by avoiding risk. According to Ellis, as Mendola (2007: 53) puts it:

> Small farmers produce under very high levels of uncertainty induced by natural hazards, market fluctuations; and social uncertainty and insecurity associated with the control over resources, such as land tenure and state interventions, and war.

These conditions pose risks to their production, and make farmers very cautious in their decision making (Walker and Jodha 1986; Mendola 2007). Their criticism of the profit approach seeks to show how the existence of uncertainty and risk erodes the theoretical basis of the profit-maximising model. They argue that small farmers are, of necessity, risk averse, because they have to secure their household needs from their current production or face starvation, which leaves them no room to aim for higher income levels by taking risky decisions (see, Lipton 1968; Mendola 2007: 53). Morduch (1995) and Mendola (2007: 55) agree with Ellis (1992: 83-101):

> There are two ways of conceptualising farm household's risk-aversion: the standard expected utility theory and the disaster

avoidance approach. According to the former approach, farm households make choices from available risky alternatives, based on what appeals most to their given preferences in relation to outcomes and their beliefs about the probability of their occurrence. A risk-averse household prefers a smooth consumption stream to a fluctuating one, which in contexts of incomplete capital markets or under-developed institutional arrangements entails a low risk portfolio choice of productive activities.

Studies by Barnum and Morse (1979) and Stevens and Jabara (1988: 177) shed further light on rural households' decision-making processes in relation to allocating their labour to various types of farm and non-farm activities. Their model of household labour allocation assumes that rural households make economically rational decisions about the allocation of their labour and other resources, given the constraints of their knowledge and their social and institutional environment.

They explored the use of such a model by focusing on three sets of essential household decisions: (1) the allocation of labour to various economic opportunities; (2) farm and household production; and (3) household consumption. Then, household labour allocation decisions were modelled by allocating all of a household's labour to one of four activities: on-farm agricultural production; household production activities usually carried out by women; off-farm work; and leisure.

Barnum and Morse (1979) state that: 'To maximise overall family utility production theory indicates that the greatest net income for a household is obtained when the marginal return from each of the four income sources is equated.' Thus, for example, if marginal returns to off-farm labour increased significantly due to a rise in off-farm wages, some family labour time would be shifted to off-farm work and away from farm production. To take another example, a household's labour would be reallocated if a new and profitable investment in tailoring technology were introduced, leading to women's time being shifted from farm production to household production (Stevens and Jabara 1988: 177).

Household consumption decisions depend on how each individual seeks equal marginal satisfaction from three consumption possibilities: goods and services produced by the family; goods and services purchased from others; and leisure.

The household labour allocation model has been criticised by recent research which has highlighted the fact that the heterogeneity of household strategies reflects differences in the returns on the various activities of individuals and rural households. The economic activities and sources of income themselves also differ substantially across regions, between poor and rich households, between households with different asset endowments, and between men and women (World Bank 2007).

Indeed, most of the recent evidence indicates a great diversity and complexity of labour activities in rural areas, such that the use of standard labour market models fail to capture this reality in countries in sub-Saharan Africa, as well as in other developing countries (Taylor and Adelman 2003; World Bank 2007; Ligon 2008).

A paper by Taylor and Adelman (2003: 29–32), 'Agricultural household models: genesis, evolution and extensions', explores such limitations in detail. They state that:

> All household-farm models assume that preferences and incomes are shared by all household members. These assumptions are convenient, permitting researchers to treat the household as though it were an individual engaged in production and consumption activities, but they obviously represent a simplification of the real world, in which interests of individual household members may diverge and all incomes may not enter into 'a common pot'.

Reardon (1998: 2–3) also sheds light on the decisions made by rural households concerning the form and extent of their involvement in rural non-farm activities (referred to as RNA) – either starting enterprises or entering the wage labour market. These generally depend on two main factors: first, the incentives offered, such as the relative profitability and risks of farm and RNA activities; and, second, the household's capacity (determined by education, income and assets, access to credit, and so on) to undertake such activities. He contends that when households opt to undertake RNA activities they may be motivated by 'pull' factors, such as better returns in the non-farm sector relative to the farm sector, and 'push' factors, which include in particular:

- An inadequate farm output, resulting either from temporary events (for example, a drought) or longer-term problems (for example land constraints);
- The absence, or incomplete availability, of crop insurance and consumption credit markets (to use as ex-post measures for anticipating harvest shortfalls);

- The risks of farming, which induce households to manage income and consumption uncertainties by diversifying and undertaking activities with returns that have a low or negative correlation with returns from farming activities; and
- An absence or failure of farm input markets or input credit markets, which compel households to pay for farm inputs from their own cash resources.

However, as Taylor and Adelman (2003: 29–32) put it:

> The limitations of these models highlight the importance of moving beyond a microeconomic focus on households and analysing household-farms' behaviour in the context of both internal conflicts over resource use as well as external market and non-market relationships in which agricultural households are embedded.

To understand the factors that influence households' decisions in allocating their human resources to various economic activities within the constraints of the rural labour markets and beyond, the following two sections will explore the factors affecting labour supply and demand.

FACTORS AFFECTING LABOUR SUPPLY

Increases or decreases in labour supply depend on a number of factors, these are as follows.

Population growth rate

Data from Table 6.2 show that in the least developed agriculture-based countries, mostly in sub-Saharan Africa, the projected increase in total population is estimated at 939.8 million, with an average growth rate of 2.3 per cent. In these countries rural population continues to dominate over the period 2010 to 2050. Figures for less developed regions show an estimated increase of 2,441.3 billion by 2050 with an average growth rate of 1.3 per cent. As these figures are averages for each region, variations do exist between individual countries in terms of the rural–urban divide (for example, in most sub-Saharan African countries the percentage of people still living in rural areas ranges from 88 per cent of the total population in Uganda to 48 per cent in Botswana).

Table 6.2   World population and percentage of rural population 2007–2050

Region	Total population (million) 2010	Projection of total population (million) 2050	Average projected population growth (1–10%) 2011–2015	Rural population % of total 2010
World total	6,615.9	9,075.9	1.1	50
More developed	1,217.5	1,236.2	0.2	25
Less developed	5,398.4	7,839.7	1.3	56
Least developed	795.6	1,735.4	2.3	72

Source: UN Population Fund (2007).

Changes in the land tenure system

As market-led land reforms continue to evolve in most developing countries, there is no doubt that the losers in the process will exert pressure for policy change, in terms of providing incentives and investment in the rural non-farm sector so as to provide alternative livelihood choices for surplus labourers.

Opportunities within and outside rural areas

Provided by development taking place in the service and industry sectors, through backward and forward linkages, this will have an impact on levels of employment and wages.

Rates of net out migration

A number of economic models have shown that young unmarried people are more likely to migrate than other labourers because they can expect to earn more from urban wages, they are mobile and they have weaker family ties. Those who migrate are typically not the poorest (Beegle et al. 2008), and being able to migrate may for many be conditional on having links with an existing network of migrants. Migration may also involve upfront costs, such as payments to labour contractors, and for many there are factors that hinder migration, such as disabilities or duties of caring for children, older people or the sick – duties which are mostly borne by women (IFAD 2011: 207).

Large-scale migration

Large-scale migration for agricultural work across national borders has long been an important factor affecting both the supply and demand for rural labour in certain regions of developing countries.

Migration, and migrants' remittances, can contribute to poverty reduction both directly, for immigrant households themselves, and indirectly, for the local economy, since it can improve health, education and nutrition. For example, in sub-Saharan Africa remittances often play an essential role in supporting food security in many poor rural households, helping them face adversities such as low agricultural yields and other inherent risks of farming. For some households, remittances may be the only source of income.

IFAD (2011: 208) indicates that in South and South East Asia, each migrant has created an average of three jobs (whether on-farm or off-farm) in his or her area of origin, as a result of their remittances. Moreover, in Mexico remittances have been found to create opportunities for earning second-round incomes that favour poor people, both inside and outside the rural economy, through the diversification of income sources. However, there is no doubt that migration has its costs for the migrants and for the family left behind in terms of cultural, social and economic loss and the difficulties migrants face in the process of integration in their new host country.[2]

HIV/AIDS

The impact of HIV/AIDS – on the prime age of adult labour supply in many of the high prevalence countries in Southern Africa – is well documented. Ngom and Clark (2003) predicted that less than 40 per cent of those who were surviving to the age of 15 would celebrate their sixtieth birthdays. Throughout sub-Saharan Africa, young women (aged 15–24 years) are twice as likely as young men to be living with HIV/AIDS, according to the United Nations Save the Children Fund (UNICEF 2007), while recent South African data indicate even greater gender disparities, with females in this age group being three times more likely to be infected than males (Bradshaw et al. 2004: 140). A smaller survey in Kenya found that over 27 per cent of girls aged 15–19 were infected with HIV compared to 4.6 per cent of boys in the same age group (Glynn et al. 2001). The death of large number of relatively young adult females has important short- and medium-term implications for the age composition of the female labour supply, and for the care-giving obligations of older women, who will devote years of labour to washing, feeding and nursing the chronically ill (Steinberg et al. 2002: 15).

An article in *The Economist* (4 June 2011), entitled 'The end of AIDS?', reports that since 1981 a total of 25 million people have died from AIDS, and another 34 million have become infected. However, the rate of death from AIDS is dropping: a decade ago, half of the people in several Southern African countries were expected to die of AIDS. In 2009, for which data are available, the number of deaths in Southern Africa was 1.8 million, compared with 2.5 million in 2005. Some 5 million lives have already been saved through drug treatment, while in 33 of the worst affected countries the rate of new infections is down by 25 per cent or more from its peak. Even more hopeful is the outcome of a recent study which suggests that the drugs currently used to treat AIDS may also stop its transmission. However, achieving the goal of eliminating the disease by this means will require further research to be funded.

War

Wars can affect directly the level of labour supply. In a conflict situation, young men are conscripted into the military or become rebel fighters, depriving families of their labour and income. Conflicts may also cause farmers to reduce their production to subsistence levels, as there is no incentive to invest in production due to major disruption of agricultural markets and distraction of and diversion of infrastructure to other military use including communications and so on.

However, it is imperative at this stage to examine the numbers and percentages of people engaged in agriculture, and the percentage growth in agricultural employment compared with per capita arable land available for future growth of the agricultural labour force. Table 6.3 shows that agricultural employment as a percentage of total employment in Asia and the Pacific (43.5 per cent), and sub-Saharan Africa (46.1 per cent), is higher than that of Latin America (11.7 per cent) and the Middle East (21.7 per cent). Moreover, the countries with the highest percentage of growth in agricultural employment in sub-Saharan Africa are East Africa with 39.9 per cent and Middle Africa with 35.4 per cent. The highest growth figures for the Asia and Pacific regions shows Oceania with 34.8 per cent and South Asia with 26.6 per cent.

Corresponding figures for the percentage change of arable land available per head from 1988 to 2007 show no changes in the amount of arable land per head in all regions of Asia and the Pacific, while there was a clear decline in arable land per head in East and Central Africa (partly due to land partitioning among heirs as part of the communal and customary law which governs people's access to land, and a lack of opportunities outside farming), no change in Western Africa, and only slight increases in parts of Southern Africa (due to

Table 6.3 Numbers, percentages, growth rates and arable land per head of agricultural population in developing countries

Variable	Agricultural employment (millions)	Growth in agricultural employment (%)	Agricultural employment (% of total)	Growth in agricultural labour productivity (%)	Agricultural land (000s of hectares)	Arable land per head of agricultural population (hectare per capita)	
Sources	WDI	FAOSTAT	FAO/WDI	WDI	FAOSTAT	FAOSTAT	
Period	Closest 2007	1981–2008	Closest 2007	1981–2008	Closest 2007	1988	Closest 2007
Asia and the Pacific	1,034.26	16.5	43.5	57.1	980,070	0.2	0.2
East Asia	512.31	7.1	53.1	81.6	559,378	0.2	0.2
Oceania	2.38	34.8	50.9	16.9	1,733	0.1	0.1
South Asia	377.86	26.6	36.7	30.1	309,124	0.3	0.3
South East Asia	141.72	22.8	37.6	37.0	109,835	0.3	0.3
Sub-Saharan Africa	192.45	36.5	46.1	15.3	770,405	0.5	0.4
Eastern Africa	105.55	39.9	62.5	12.0	293,103	0.3	0.2
Southern Africa	2.29	-3.6	6.6	43.2	43,524	1.6	1.9
Middle Africa	28.68	35.4	45.0	5.4	160,086	0.5	0.3
Western Africa	55.94	31.3	35.5	26.2	273,691	0.6	0.6
Latin America and the Caribbean	42.64	-1.8	11.7	59.9	719,871	1.1	1.5
Caribbean	3.84	1.9	20.0	41.1	12,355	0.5	0.6
Central America	13.02	6.2	14.0	33.7	127,395	0.8	0.9
South America	25.79	-6.4	10.3	73.4	580,121	1.3	2.1
Middle East and North Africa	45.94	22.1	21.7	32.8	298,063	0.7	0.8
Middle East	20.97	24.3	24.3	9.7	86,161	1.1	1.0
North Africa	24.97	20.3	19.9	51.7	211,902	0.5	0.6

Source: Adapted from IFAD (2011).

large-scale farming and land consolidation by large farmers). Figures for almost all countries in Latin America and the Caribbean indicate a slight increase in arable land per head, especially in countries where small farmers are no longer able to sustain a living in rural areas and thus might sell their land to more progressive farmers and switch from farming to non-farm employment.

In summary, increases in the supply of agricultural labour can be expected for many years to come in the agriculture-based countries of Africa and Asia. With an increase in the agricultural population in these countries farm size is likely to decline, as has happened in East and Central Africa. This as it happens led to increasing numbers of small farmers and landlessness in these countries. However, there is need to promote growth in both the industrial and service sectors to absorb the anticipated growth rate of surplus agricultural labour. Moreover, it is important to emphasise that the continued existence of large numbers of small farms in developing countries has significant implications for the existing types of agricultural technology in terms of scale and innovation and for agricultural institutions in terms of research, extension and development.

FACTORS AFFECTING DEMAND FOR LABOUR

Investments in new knowledge and in technological changes to promote farm and non-farm linkages at macro and micro levels are likely to induce changes in relevant agricultural institutions such as research programmes, extension services and market-related infrastructures. These changes in turn influence the demand for rural labour in many ways, particularly by increasing direct demand for labour on farms and indirect demand for labour off-farm. Growth generated from upstream and downstream production linkages between the farming and non-farm sectors will also increase demand for the production of goods and services in rural areas. According to IFAD (1992: 165–8), demand for rural labour depends on factors such as: seasonal fluctuations in demand for labour; large-scale migration, both across national borders and intra-rural migration; the integration of rural and urban labour markets; and other interlocking factors in rural labour markets. These are explained below.

Seasonal fluctuations in demand for labour

Demand for rural labour in agricultural production is influenced by the annual farming cycle, with its peak periods of activity such as land preparation, weeding and harvesting. At peak periods, temporary and casual labourers can work for higher wages, depending on their skills, the type of work available, and labour shortages in the area. However, as IFAD (1992: 165) points out:

> Problems arise when contractual and employment relations for non-permanent labour force prove exploitative, when these workers are deprived of the benefits guaranteed by existing labour laws or when the growth in their numbers tends to depress agricultural wages below the level necessary for an adequate livelihood.

A decline in agricultural wages can come about in various ways. First, there can be a fluctuation in demand for labour without corresponding changes in labour supply. Second, this is often reflected in fluctuations in real wage rates between seasons, because of readily available labour from urban areas and from forward rural labour contracts (IFAD 1992; 2001).

Third, another set of triggers to wage decline arises because agricultural production is subject to drought, floods, pests, and to price fluctuations. These shocks (even if insured against) affect labour demand and supply in ways that exacerbate each other. On the one hand the demand for labour declines, while on the other the supply of labour from small-farm households increases to compensate for the shortfall in on-farm profit (Kochar 1997; World Bank 2007: 292). Consequently, wages vary sharply with weather conditions and other agricultural risks (World Bank 2007: 293).

Fourth, agriculture, by its very nature, makes labour supervision difficult. To overcome this problem, various contractual arrangements have been suggested which can create appropriate work incentives for labourers. One is to offer piece-rate wages rather than daily wages (Foster and Rosenzweig 1994; World Bank 2007: 293). However, piece-rate wages also mean that wage incomes vary from one worker to another based on their ability to supply work effort, so that workers who are less strong and healthy will earn less (World Bank 2007: 293).

The findings of a study by Cramer et al. (2008) in Mozambique showed that employers of waged labour in rural areas were able to exercise considerable discretion in setting wages and establishing working conditions, for the following reasons: (1) they were operating in conditions of widespread poverty; (2) there was a marked absence of trade unions and/or government inspectors; (3)

workers had low levels of literacy and education; and (4) there was a significant excess labour supply.

It has been suggested that seasonal variations in wage rates can be reduced by: (1) technological innovation, land distribution or renting, along with improvements in labourers' skills; (2) diversification into crops with different peak periods; and (3) intra-rural migration and integration of rural urban labour markets (IFAD 1992; 2011).

Agricultural wage workers face significant occupational, safety and environmental hazards rarely covered under international labour protection of farm works (Foster and Rosenzweig 1994; World Bank 2008: 293). They are also poorly protected by national labour laws. Agriculture is often excluded from labour legislation, as most labour laws target industrial employment. Even when laws are on the books, low levels of employer and worker familiarity and poor enforcement undermine compliance in rural areas (World Bank 2007: 293).

The International Labour Organisation (ILO 2011) indicates that agriculture is one of the three most dangerous occupations of all, along with mining and construction. About half the estimated 355,000 annual on-the-job fatalities occur in agriculture (Hurst et al. 2005; World Bank 2007: 293). Agricultural wage workers face exposure to toxic pesticides, livestock-transmitted diseases, and dangerous machinery, and often lack adequate training and protective equipment (World Bank 2007: 293).

To address all of these issues, labour regulations need to be adapted to ensure the inclusion of larger numbers of workers in appropriate employment which provides better worker protection, pension rights, and health security. It should also improve workers' connections to credit markets, and foster long-term investment by farms and companies in their workers through on-the-job training.

Enforcing labour standards requires innovative forms of collaboration among governments, the private sector, trade unions, NGOs and organisations of poor rural people aimed at setting up binding minimum wage levels for every sector of the economy, providing there is some flexibility, except perhaps in relation to state employment (Ureta 2002; World Bank 2007: 294). Such minimum wage levels have a clear role to play in the reduction of poverty (Devereux 2005; Field and Kanbur 2005; Heintz et al. 2008). Moreover, labour standards need to be designed to avoid discrimination between permanent and casual workers (IFAD 2011: 206).

Intra-rural migration

In addition to high levels of rural–urban migration, and migration across national borders, there is an increasing incidence of migration between rural areas in the form of seasonal labour markets, a process documented in many Latin American countries as well as in several Asian and sub-Saharan African countries. Seasonal labour markets are a result of regional disparities and advanced commercialised agriculture in some places, which require large numbers of casual workers for short periods of time. Such labour markets draw on pools of landless labourers and those smallholders who can afford to stay away from their plots for a short period of time (IFAD 1992: 196).

However, problems arise when those economically active members of the households migrate, as the elderly and disadvantaged who are left behind by migration may require additional forms of income support (Levy, in World Bank 2007: 310). For example, Brazil, Bolivia and South Africa have rural non-contributory pension schemes which create welfare benefits for recipients and have spillover effects on the education and nutrition of family members (see, Edmonds and Pavcnink 2005; World Bank 2007: 310).

However, it is not only the elderly and disadvantaged in need of financial support. Alderman and Haque (2006) argue that safety nets in a form of cash for work can also target those with few assets, including household labourers who are unable to sustain their livelihoods or find suitable employment in rural areas. Safety nets also have an insurance function as they help households to secure their basic needs and invest to improve their assets, especially during dearth seasons. They suggest a safety net that is flexible, quick and efficient, and, in addition to responsive financing, the identification of beneficiaries and the disbursement of funds must be rapid if these interventions are to remain effective. To ensure the smooth operation of safety nets when needs rapidly increase, a programme should be in place before a shock occurs (World Bank 2007: 310–11).

Integration of rural and urban labour markets

The integration of rural and urban markets has meant that rural wages have to some extent caught up with urban wages. But a rapid decline in permanent, as opposed to temporary, employment, associated in some cases with land consolidation, has led to a proportion of agricultural workers being reallocated to urban areas.

They compete with those located in rural areas for scarce temporary employment in agriculture, but because they are easier to recruit on a short-term basis they may be preferred by employers. Research evidence from developing countries indicates that permanent labour is losing ground with the growing pace of modernisation. For example, in some cases, in countries where new agricultural labour laws are aimed at protecting labourers' rights, resident workers have been expelled from large farms and relocated to urban areas where they become tenants or squatters (IFAD 1992: 167–8).

Interlocking factors in labour markets

In many developing countries, particularly in Asia and the Near East, there are important interlocking factors in rural labour markets. The best known example is when landowners and tenants enter into several transactions – such as land rental, hiring of waged labour, credit arrangements for production and consumption, cost sharing of purchased inputs, and joint marketing of output – all as part of a contract encompassing several markets (IFAD 1992: 168).

These interlinkages reinforce the impact of the imperfections in each market and often undermine the returns to rural labour, as, for example, in 'labour tying' arrangements, which are associated with the unequal distribution of land and high levels of unemployment and landlessness in rural areas. IFAD (1992) outlines how, in order to save on recruitment costs during the peak season and to ensure that labour is available during peak operations, the landowner enters into explicit or implicit labour tying contracts under which the potential employer provides consumption credit to the labourer. During the lean season this acceptance of consumption credit becomes a binding obligation on the labourer to work for the creditor on terms dictated by him or her. In general, the higher the demand for labourers relative to labour supply the larger the proportional importance of tied labour, while the higher the unemployment levels the smaller the relative importance of tied labour IFAD (1992).

It is also important to refer to the impact that food price increases have on labour employment and wages, and on large numbers of agricultural households simultaneously. Higher food prices will increase the demand for hired labour and reduce its availability to other producers and activities, both on-farm and off-farm. While having a positive impact on producers of surplus food, food price increases are likely to have a significant negative impact on the real incomes of non-food producers, whether rural or urban, and higher wages may or may not compensate for the higher food prices faced by workers (IFAD 2003: 29–32).

EMPLOYMENT, UNEMPLOYMENT AND UNDEREMPLOYMENT

There are a range of theoretical and empirical problems associated with defining and estimating levels of employment/unemployment in rural area, including: (1) problems with the timeframe of data collection; (2) the difficulty of defining productivity; (3) the influence of values and social rules on the definition and measurement of employment; and (4) the different methods used for classifying employment status and their varied criteria for the range of age groups to be included IFAD (1992).

Assessing the correct number of paid workers in agriculture is difficult because in many contexts agricultural wages complement self-employment, and labour force surveys and population census data which classify workers by their main activity typically miss large numbers of casual wage earners (IFAD 2011).

Furthermore, to overcome the problem associated with measuring unemployment and underemployment in rural areas it is imperative to identify indicators that can capture all the economic activities that people engage in, including farming and non-farming and all the informal and formal employment in agriculture as well as the variety of paid and unpaid work which is usually carried out by women.

Moreover, factors affecting the supply of, and demand for, labour determine levels of employment, unemployment and underemployment. In defining underemployment, the elements of part-time work, seasonal and short-term employment and lower than average earnings due to poor productivity, all have to be considered. Both unemployment and underemployment are closely associated with poverty and with a lack of productive opportunities within and outside agriculture, so new recruits to the labour force have to choose between unemployment or taking low-paid jobs outside rural areas, neither of which will enable them to sustain an adequate standard of living (IFAD 1992: 169).

However, Cramer et al. (2008) show that access to employment is not a sufficient condition for poverty reduction if poor people cannot earn enough to lift their families out of poverty. Therefore, improvements in both the quality and quantity of employment are required, which economic growth alone cannot be relied on to generate (Osmani 2006).

Reviewing evidence from the Gambia, Heintz et al. (2008) indicate that the growth pattern of that country has not benefited the poor, as improvements in the rate of growth appear at best to have halted the spread of poverty. This situation is partly explained by weak productivity performance, as well as by the poor quality of available employment.

Many studies indicate that rural people who are economically active are moving into the informal sector – rural or urban – even when it is clear that opportunities for employment in the informal sector are few. However, the wide range of potential jobs in this sector could be made use of to alleviate rural poverty. IFAD (1992: 196) states that:

> There must be a substantial increase in public sector investment to develop technical skills and supportive infrastructure. But such investments must serve as a catalyst for private initiatives, which should assume the key responsibility for development within a supportive policy framework. It is clear that the informal sector lacks technological skill and reinvestment of surplus; poverty alleviation would require a balanced growth of productive employment opportunities, both short term and long term, therefore support to the informal sector warrants high priority in development programmes [and support to social protection programme].

Moreover, Farrington et al. (2007) define social protection as 'the public actions taken in response to levels of vulnerability, risk and deprivation which are deemed socially unacceptable within a given society'. They propose a two-way link between agriculture and social protection (see Table 6.4).

In conclusion, in order to help create a context in which inclusive labour market policies for both urban and rural areas can be developed and implemented there is need for a more coherent approach which provides appropriate criteria for the purpose of targeting investment intervention for poverty reduction in rural areas. Public policy should prioritise spending on creating more employment opportunities through backward and forward linkages with industry and services. For example, provision of credit may help the poor to utilise more of their own labour (for self employment), increasing overall economic activity, increasing the demand for labour, and possibly affecting wage levels. Moreover, provision of credit may reduce migration to urban areas and reduce the demand for land, and would also affect the land-rent market. Chapter 7 examines the vital role of credit provision and poverty reduction in low-income countries.

Table 6.4 Examples of the two-way links between agriculture and social protection

	Social protection oriented outside agriculture, but impacting on it	Policies within agriculture to make it more socially protecting for producers and labourers	The social protection impacts of agriculture on consumers and others
International	Promotion of workers' rights; 'decent work' agenda; foreign aid distributed to households in cash and kind (including food aid, in emergencies only).	International crop and livestock disease prevention and control; international research into pro-poor crops such as cassava (and other locally acceptable food).	Smoothly functioning world market, combined with surpluses generated by agricultural innovation, keep supplies steady and prices low. This requires political will and commitments from major producers.
National	Cash transfers as a stimulus to local market demand. If poorly timed, food transfers can undermine local markets. Improve human capacities through health and education; improve health and life insurance; schemes to improve security of access to and ownership of assets by poor households (both men and women).	Crop and asset insurance, investment in irrigation, soil and water conservation. Public works on irrigation, drainage, feeder roads and communications. Creation of other community assets such as improved woodlots and grazing land. Provide incentives for backward and forward linkages with industries and services.	New technology (new varieties of plant and livestock with improved nutritional value, improved pest resistance and drought/flood tolerance) keeps supplies steady and prices low even in areas with limited access to markets. Establish and manage a buffer stock at national level.

Source: Adapted from Farrington et al. (2007).

7
Rural Financial Services and the Issue of Sustainability

Despite the rapid development of financial services, and impressive growth in microfinance institutions (MFIs) and industry in the last two decades, the majority of smallholders worldwide remain without access to the services they need in order to invest in their enterprises and improve their livelihoods. It has been estimated that there are over 1 billion economically active rural poor people (or 200 million households) in the world operating micro-enterprises and small businesses without access to adequate financial services (Remenyi 1997; World Bank 2007).

This limited access to financial services in the developing world is one of the main obstacles to income generation and social protection. It is estimated that over 4 billion people in both rural and urban areas lack access to basic financial services such as credit, savings, money transfers, leases and insurance (Ghalib and Hailu 2008).

Financial constraints are more pervasive in agriculture and related activities than in many other sectors, reflecting both the nature of agricultural activities and the average size of farms, as well as farmers' lack of collateral against which to borrow. Financial services in rural areas involve higher transaction costs and risks than those in urban areas because of the greater spatial dispersion of production, lower population densities, greater number of frequent small transactions, lower quality of infrastructure, and the seasonality and great diversity of rural production activities. As a result, banks and other traditional for-profit financial intermediaries tend to limit their activities to urban and densely populated areas, to larger enterprises and wealthier clients, and to the more commercial areas of the rural economy (Remenyi 1997: 1; World Bank 2007; Ghalib and Hailu 2008).

Clearly, the quality and extent of coverage of an economy's financial services will determine the ability of agricultural enterprises and rural households to invest for the long term in sustainable livelihoods and food security, and to make calculated decisions in relation to the risks associated with various sources of income flows.

This chapter describes rural credit markets and highlights their main characteristics. It starts by defining credit and credit products, and moves on to discuss the various providers of rural credit markets, including both formal and informal institutions. The issue of gender and access to microfinance will also be discussed. Then it explores the question of building sustainable banking services for poor rural households.

RURAL CREDIT MARKETS

Credit provision has been one of the most popular types of state intervention in the agricultural sector, as well as being the largest agricultural sector recipient of aid funds from external aid donors (see, World Bank 1975; Ellis 1992: 152). Credit as a concept is defined as: 'a sum of money in favour of the person to whom control over it is transferred. It also involves a price for the transfer of control over money, which is the interest rate charged by the lender to the borrower'. Put simply, 'neoclassical economics treats the market for credit like any other market: it contains a demand schedule, a supply schedule, and a price: the interest rate that adjusts to bring demand and supply into balance' (Ellis 1992: 152).

The lender in any credit transaction is an individual who is willing to postpone some of his/her consumption needs, so that a borrower can borrow to consume or to invest. Lenders, referred to as financial intermediaries, include institutions such as banks, cooperatives, credit unions or NGOs which supply credit to potential borrowers (Ellis 1992: 152), along with a range of money management and banking services. 'Credit provision may be from informal or formal, private, or state banks. Informal credit services refer to the financial services provided by moneylenders (rich farmers, traders, and others in the rural economy who lend money on the basis of personal knowledge of each transaction)'. Formal credit services are those bound by the legal regulations of a country, and they include private banks, state banks, registered cooperatives, and a host of others (Ellis 1992: 154; Remenyi 1997). Their services can be grouped into four basic 'product types' (Remenyi 1997: 1):

- *Credit*: a reliable source of working capital, disbursed against 'collateral' such as security of land tenure, a herd of animals, the households' own house, a viable enterprise and so on. In cases of lack of collateral, and with the provision of credit through microfinance, 'collateral substitutes' are used, such as an individual's standing in the community, a group guarantee or compulsory savings.

- *Deposit services*: designed to offer poor households alternative savings options to the hoarding of cash or other stores of value. 'The saver is a person, or household, or institution that is prepared to supply funds to be held by a financial institution in return for an income flow in the shape of interest payments' (Ellis 1992: 153).
- *Insurance products*: including insurance against loan default due to misadventure, illness, death, natural disasters or unanticipated economic crisis, plus anticipated savings goals related to life-cycle, such as preparation for weddings, funerals or other socio-cultural obligations.
- *Financial advisory services*: whereby the views and needs of the borrowers are discussed, and advice is given on the most relevant products available. For example, where microfinance is involved, the views of the poor are given a voice and brought to the attention of policymakers, regulators and those with the authority to influence the environment in which poor households and informal sector institutions have to operate.

The borrower in a credit transaction is the person or enterprise who has a demand for credit in order to: (1) achieve a short-term loan for consumption; (2) even out fluctuations in the availability of cash, in order to buy recurrent farm inputs; or (3) make an investment in order to realise future increases in income (Ellis 1992: 153).

Thus, in the processes of saving, lending and borrowing, debt claims by savers over lenders are converted into debt claims by lenders over borrowers. The institutions that enable this to take place by bringing together savers and borrowers with differing needs in space and time are called financial intermediaries (Ellis 1992: 153).

CREDIT FOR AGRICULTURAL DEVELOPMENT AND POVERTY REDUCTION

Credit has always had a special place in mainstream thinking on agricultural development and poverty reduction in developing countries. Credit policy is defined as 'policies related mainly, but not exclusively, to the provision of working capital for the purchase of variable inputs used in farm production' (Ellis 1992: 155). IFAD (1992: 193) outlines its role thus:

Provision of credit to rural people through formal and informal institutions has important effects on land, labour and product markets which operate directly or partly through backward and forward linkages. Its total effect on the land market depends on factors such as the total land available, the land tenure system, and employment opportunities in rural areas.

For example, in countries with a surplus of land, credit and land reform should increase the intensity of land use. Also, land settlement schemes cannot succeed without credit, services and complementary inputs (HYV seeds, organic and or non-organic fertiliser, and water).

Moreover, provision of credit to rural households has an effect on both supply of and demand for labour, with consequent effects on wages, as it can enable the poor to achieve higher disposable incomes through the following well-known effects, which are specific to investment and savings activities (Ellis 1992; IFAD 1992: 193–9; Remenyi 1997: 4):

- Access to credit in the form of working capital may help the poor to utilise more of their own labour in self employment and help to break down patterns of bonded labour;
- Increased overall activity will raise the demand for hired labour, and hence wages;
- The availability of credit affects the urban market by reducing migration to urban areas;
- Increases in self-employment in non-land-based activities may reduce the demand for land and thus reduce rents;
- Credit availability strengthens the bargaining positions of labourers vis-à-vis their employers;
- Access to credit promotes investments in upgrading existing productive assets or acquisition of additional productive assets;
- Credit availability facilitates higher returns for goods and services marketed through access to new or higher valued markets; and
- Access to credit may lower production costs as a result of technology transfer, leading to lower-cost loans and better access to cheaper basic goods and services.

THE EVOLUTION OF RURAL CREDIT MARKETS

Historically, during the 1950s and early 1960s, donors placed most emphasis on market-oriented farmers and on commercial agricultural enterprises such as plantations and large estates, with aid going mostly to progressive farmers – those with large farm size and greater use of modern technology in farming (Ellis 1992: 152–6).

Then, from the mid-1960s to the late 1970s, poor farmers became the chief target of credit interventions by government and donors through subsidised direct credit schemes and farm projects. There were several reasons for these interventions, in particular: (1) the perceived efficiency of small farmers; (2) their output potential, based on the use of the new Green Revolution technology; (3) their lack of collateral for loans; (4) the exploitative or monopolistic behaviour of money lenders; and (5) small farmers' lack of cash at critical periods in the crop or livestock season. It was considered especially important to replace the fragmented and incomplete private rural credit market and to offset the disincentive effects of low output prices and high exchange rates, as well as to replace costly inputs and subsidies (Ellis 1992: 155).

Between the mid-1980s and 1995 a new paradigm, in the form of microfinance institutions (MFIs) or micro-credit, evolved during the era of liberalisation and structural adjustment and reinforced belief in the virtue of markets. It had been preceded by years of heavily subsidised and generally ineffective government- and donor-financed credit programmes, which had frequently failed to benefit the poor to any significant extent, but which had also dismantled many of the financial institutions that were forced to deliver them, along with the natural 'credit culture' of the poor (Harper 2003).[1]

Ellis (1992: 160–3) highlights the fact that since the 1970s there has been a considerable volume of critical literature concerning states' credit policy in developing countries (see, McKinnon 1973; Shaw 1973; Donald 1976; Fry 1982; Adams et al. 1984). Ellis lists some of the central components of these critiques, as follows:

- *Fungibility*: exists in all tiers of the credit system, from farmers, to the financial intermediary, to the central bank. The fungibility of money makes it difficult for lenders to ensure that borrowers use the loan funds in the way lenders wish; one way they try to get round 'misuse of funds' is to lend in kind, especially in rural area (Ellis 1992: 152–6).
- *Subsidised interest rates*: create several negative effects for the long-run viability of rural financial institutions, as well as of borrowers and savers. A negative real rate of interest makes the loan a gift from the lender to the borrower. Moreover,

low interest rates to borrowers make it impossible to offer attractive interest rates to savers, and impossible for the lending institution to cover the transaction costs. It also brings about an excess of demand for credit over supply of credit, resulting in formal and informal credit rationing, which favours large and wealthy borrowers over those who are small and poor (ibid).

- *Transaction costs*: the cost of administration, of information gathering and of processing of loans can increase threatening the viability of all financial institutions, whether private or state. According to Adam and de Sahonero (1989) and Sarap (1990) lending to large numbers of small borrowers costs more per unit of money than lending to small numbers of large borrowers, especially in the context of externally funded credit schemes.
- *Loan recovery*: occurs when farmers default on repaying their loans due to crop failure or being unwilling to repay because they viewed the loan as a grant. The incentive to default is high where borrowers have no stake in the lending institution (that is, they are not savers) and where they can see that credit availability is of limited duration (as in many fixed-period donor-funded projects).
- *Savings failure*: Ellis argues that, since rural credit agencies fail to encourage rural saving, they also fail to amass funds that can make them independent of central or external funding. Thus they are incapable of surviving as self-sustaining institutions in the long run. Moreover, it is always more costly to provide financial services in rural areas than in towns, for several reasons: the nature of rural areas in terms of outreach coverage; staffing requirements; costs per transaction due to frequent small transactions and greater use of staff time; smaller levels of borrowing, savings and deposits; illiteracy levels among small farmers; and lack of access to information and communication technology (Ghalib and Hailu 2008: 4).

The above-mentioned problems of traditional rural credit schemes and approaches, whether provided by government or aid agencies during the 1950s and 1960s, have forced many countries and donors to rethink the methods of operation, viability and sustainability of their credit systems. The transition from the old credit systems to a new one meant that the new challenge and critical new objective of credit policy should therefore aim for the creation of a self-sustaining rural financial system, not reliant on subsidies to cover losses and not dependent on injections of external funds from foreign aid donors or the central bank (Ellis 1992: 164).

However, many approaches have been used during the transition from the old credit systems (1950–1970s) to the new one (1980s to the present time), including the downscaling of commercial banks and the creation of start-up, for profit, microfinance institutions. One approach, which has proved successful in many cases around the world, is through the transformation of non-governmental microfinance providers into regular deposit-taking financial institutions (Ledgerwood and White 2006).

It should be noted that the old and new paradigms are not mutually exclusive. While the new paradigm is emerging as the dominant model, the old one remains entrenched in many places, while in many countries microfinance programmes based on the old paradigm are operating alongside other programmes based on the new paradigm (Frasier and Bne Saad 2003).

DO MICROFINANCE INSTITUTIONS HELP THE POOR?

Over the last three decades there has been a transition from the old paradigm of subsidised credit delivery to the new paradigm of market-based microfinance. The latter emphasises the idea that, given enabling macroeconomic political, legal, regulatory and demographic conditions, MFIs can be developed to provide financial services to the poor and can deliver services at the local level without subsidy and with wide coverage and outreach (Robinson 2001).

Remenyi (1997: 4) suggests that:

> Microfinance may not be a panacea for poverty but is a component of the fight against poverty. Persistent poverty cannot be overcome unless investment by the poor in the poor is increased. Investment by the poor is low not because poor people do not save, nor is it because they have few investment opportunities, are lazy or know no better. However, MFIs can make significant contributions to the economic welfare and the capacity for self-reliance of poor rural households.

According to Ellis (1992: 164–8) four new approaches characterise the new paradigm:

1. Reorienting formal credit markets by decentralising their operations to work better with poor rural people;

2. Shifting from branch-based to village-based lending;
3. Utilising a mobile credit officer scheme with both male and female staff, who visit potential clients in their villages to process loan applications; and
4. Setting up village development funds, which are community-managed credit and savings associations established to improve members' access to financial services, build community self-help groups, and help members accumulate savings (Ellis 1992).

However, the key elements of microfinance are the solidarity group, village banking and individual lending.

The first MFIs were established in South Asia almost 30 years ago and were based on the solidarity group approach (Hulme and Mosley 1996). The most successful examples are Grameen Bank (GB) and the Bangladesh Rural Advancement Committee (BRAC), both established in the 1970s as pilot projects. During the 1980s GB became a private sector bank with a limited licence, and the BRAC became a non-governmental organisation. These two institutions have had a global influence, and have been replicated successfully in many other countries in Latin America, South East Asia, Africa, China, the South Pacific, Central Asia, and even in the US in the form of new schemes targeting low-income families who are encouraged to have their own stake in self-sufficiency.

GB tried, in its provision of credit, to address three problems: to identify the poor and bring microfinance services to the areas in which they live; to mobilise saving by the poor, both for their own benefit and to help support the credit side of the operation; and to provide loans in such a way that, while they meet the credit needs of the poor, they also encourage a high rate of repayment and thus promote the sustainability of the scheme (Yunus 2009).

These challenges, it was discovered, can be met by:

1. Eliminating the exploitation of the poor by moneylenders;
2. Encouraging self-employment for income-generating activities, and housing for the poor, as opposed to credit for consumption; and
3. Creating an institution that the poor can relate to, and in which they can find socio-political support in addition to economic incentives (Yunus 2009).

Remenyi (1997: 1) lists five key lessons learned from the operations of microfinance institutions in their outreach to the poor: how to accommodate collateral substitutes as an effective basis for client selection; how to use self interest to manage risk and maintain high on-time repayment rates; how to minimise the cash costs of making small loans and collecting small savings; how to mobilise peer pressure and social mores to enforce contractual obligations; and how to segment the market so as to remain focused on the poor yet target the well motivated.

Thus, microfinance providers have come to understand that banking with the poor can be profitable but only if costs are contained, risks are managed, and clients treated as active partners in the conduct of the business of the enterprise.

Studies show that microfinance institutions do benefit the poor. A study by Hulme and Mosley (1996: 14) concluded that well-designed credit schemes can raise the incomes of significant numbers of poor people. However, this study also emphasised that improving the operation of financial institutions is not enough for sustained poverty reduction.

Most writers agree that an environment of economic growth is essential for poverty reduction. In a 1996 study of 114 poverty reduction and structural adjustment programmes supported by the World Bank and implemented between 1980 and 1993, it was reported that 'in no country where growth was negative did poverty decrease' (Jayarajah et al., in Remenyi 1997: 2).

Remenyi (1997: 2) argues that:

> The process of economic growth and development must involve increasing rates of investment in people's education, in access to technology, decent infrastructure and institutions, and improved access to market outlets. In contrast, the poverty 'trap' is characterised as a situation wherein poor people invest very little and have little to invest. The non-availability of microfinance is one important reason why this trap persists.

However, as development proceeds and average income levels increase, the imperfections of rural credit markets diminish. Growth of real income should reduce the probability of default and the risk of high premiums, which in turn will reduce interest rates (Ellis 1992).

SECOND GENERATION MFIs

Wegner (2006: 2) suggests that:

> MFIs in fact have developed beyond being purely a poverty-alleviation tool to financing economic development. They have

done so through their proximity to local entrepreneurs. Their successful uptake is due to a flexible formula offered to small entrepreneurs, bypassing stringent regulatory and collateral requirements. For example, Novobanco, active in Africa and Latin America, provides credit to small and medium-sized companies based on no fee accounts with no minimum balance, informal guarantees (house assets and a guarantor) and a continued relationship with loan officers.

Remenyi (1997: 4) argues that MFIs will always remain marginal to the big picture, while Ghalib and Hailu (2008: 3) emphasise the fact that in many developing countries it will be a long time before commercial lending can attend to the poor's financing needs. Until then, policy will have to include a mix of measures designed to ensure that the poor have access to the financial services that could lift them out of poverty. Wegner (2006: 2) agrees that:

Despite their adequacy to local needs, however, MFIs remain small and fragile. They often lack the skills to assess project proposals or to adopt and develop innovative financial tools. MFIs struggle to follow their clients as they grow, since they suffer from lack of medium to long-term saving to transform into long-term lending. Furthermore, the refinancing of MFIs through the formal banking sector is limited by lack of collateral and high cost of financing, unlike commercial banks, MFIs have no access to central bank refinancing at low costs and do not qualify for refinancing through venture capital as they are not formally financial institutions. They thus are forced to rely on aid.

Wegner (2006: 1) also points out that:

In order for MFIs to reach more poor people they should become an integral part of the financial sector, and develop as sound domestic intermediaries. They should go commercial, broadening their client basis and scaling up their loans to small enterprises.

Wegner questions whether MFIs lose their soul if they become an integral part of the financial sector. She believes that in fact 'no, on the contrary they will inject more soul into formal banking practices' (2006: 1-2).

Ghalib and Hailu (2008: 3) support the forming of synergies between MFIs and commercial banks to provide greater access to financial services. Commercial banks have the network capability to facilitate this process, and thus each party could benefit from the expertise of the other. Consequently, target groups and an intended beneficiary could have greater access to both credit and non-credit services such as insurance, money transfer and so on.

Wegner gives, as a good example of a mutually beneficial outcome, the cooperation in Benin between Association pour l'Appui et la Promotion des Petites et Moyennes Enterprises and the Bank of Africa based on transfer of clients from the association to the bank as their financing needs increased. Linking informal financial organisations and formal institutions can help the former move closer to formality and expand services such as saving accounts and insurance (Wegner 2006: 2).

Moreover, specific legal provisions may help MFIs to extend their lending activities to small- and medium-sized enterprises (SMEs), mainly by increasing the maximum loan amount and by extending the loan maturity date. Following such changes many MFIs have developed into fully fledged rural banks and are able to finance medium-sized enterprises. Muhammad Yunus, the founder of the first MFI and the Grameen Bank in Bangladesh, saw the potential of going further with second-generation microfinance. Grameen II is a 'diversified conglomerate' with operations in solar energy, mobile phones, health and house insurance, and industry (Wegner 2006: 2).

The World Bank and USAID began the process of commercialising microfinance in the 1990s for the purpose of transforming the sector and thus facilitating poverty reduction strategies. However, among other commentators, Bateman (2010: 1) argues that the reality has not measured up to the ambition, a topic debated at an Overseas Development Institute (ODI) seminar in London called Microfinance in the Era of Neo-liberalism:

> Commercialised microfinance is increasingly associated not with sustainable poverty reduction, but with speculative excess and, in many cases with poverty and insecurity.

He emphasises that commercialised microfinance has damaged local economies in the countries where it should have been helping, giving an example from India:

> Studies show that the very poorest subsistence farmers have become trapped in 'micro-loan bicycling', taking new micro-loans to repay old ones. There has been little impact on agricultural

production and, with interest rates typically between 30 per cent and 45 per cent, the money earned on any extra produce was largely eaten up by interest payments.

Bateman (2010: 2-3) indicates that the channelling of scarce financial resources into least productive of small land plots in Andhra Pradesh, and away from more productive larger family farms, is seen as responsible for the 20 per cent fall in rural incomes between 1993 and 2003.

NON-GOVERNMENTAL DEVELOPMENT ORGANISATIONS AND MFIS: THE DILEMMAS

According to Remenyi (2006: 250) 'most development NGOs, among them Oxfam, World Vision, Care, Caritas and Plan International are not convinced that they should sacrifice their social development goals for the financial imperatives of profit-driven institutional sustainability'.

However, specialist MFIs have adopted the path of profit-driven specialisation in order to sustain their operation as 'banks to the poor'. In making this choice MFIs have been supported by donors and multilateral agencies, such as the Consultative Group to Assist the Poorest (CGAP) and the United Nations Development Programme (UNDP), which have made institutional financial viability, not impact on poverty, the key of MFI performance indicator. Remenyi argues that this difference in focus and philosophy has established an unintended and unnecessary 'firewall' between MFIs and non-governmental development organisations (NGDOs) involved in microfinance, which must be dismantled if strategic alliances between specialist MFIs and NGDOs are to be encouraged and facilitated.

He continues, 'to date, experience has shown that NGDOs typically do not succeed in transforming themselves into financially sustainable providers of financial intermediation services', that is, profitable entities independent of donor subsidies.

The reasons for these differences are complex (see also Yaron 1994; Remenyi and Quinons 2000). Remenyi (2006: 250) sheds light on the differences between NGDOs and more financially viable MFIs:

For the most part, the main international NGDOs and their indigenous partners engage in microfinance on the basis of grant income. If cost recovery is achieved, it is often serendipitous or intended to result in partial rather than full-cost recovery. Most NGDOs tend to be limited to credit services, provided on a welfare basis and grounded in subsidised interest rates. NGDO-based microfinance programme costs are generally funded from ongoing external sources of donations in contrast to cost-recovery pricing strategies of specialist and financially viable MFIs.

Remenyi's article (2006: 247–65), 'Globalising credit: prospects for microfinance institutions and non-governmental development organisations' strategic alliances', concludes by highlighting the fact that MFIs have an opportunity to accelerate their outreach to poor households by wholesaling access to microfinance through strategic partnerships with NGDOs.

However, NGDOs need to be attracted into strategic partnerships with MFIs as long as MFIs demonstrate that they are able to respect the holistic goals of development NGOs. Remenyi proposed the following ten critical factors in microfinance wholesaling a sustainable partnership with NGDOs: (1) know your market; (2) lead with saving; (3) concentrate on your best clients; (4) follow the principle of subsidiarity; (5) keep it small; (6) keep it frequent; (7) honesty and integrity demonstrated through transparent procedures; (8) targeting poverty; (9) commercially efficient management and participatory risk management are essential; and (10) the poor do not need charity, they need good products and services.

Remenyi believes that regulators can significantly enhance partnerships between MFIs and NGDOs if the regulatory regimes they administer facilitate the ability of MFI providers to abide by these success factors (Remenyi 2006: 247–65).

THE SUSTAINABILITY OF MICROFINANCE OPERATIONS

Economic and social policies influence both the ability of MFIs to provide financial services effectively and the types of activities micro-enterprises undertake (Ledgerwood 1999). For example, economic policies that affect the rate of inflation in a country, the growth of the economy, or the degree of openness to market forces, will influence the required interest rate on loans as well as the ability of micro-entrepreneurs to successfully operate their businesses and thus utilise financial services. A government's investment in infrastructure development, the scale and depth of poverty in a country, and access to social services, all affect the ways in which micro-entrepreneurs are able, or not, to reach markets, be food secure, access health care services, or send their children to school. All of their activities are affected by their ability to access credit and so too is their use of financial services (World Bank 2007).

Alamgir (in IFAD 1992: 58) sums up the factors affecting rural savings and investment:

> Rural savings and investments can be influenced by: income, wealth, land tenure systems, external resources and support, taxation, demography, price levels, rural market structure, technology and last but not least, rural credit. However, the relative importance of these factors may vary according to the situation of each case study.

The volatility of markets affects the risks taken, and hence the choices made, by business owners and financial institutions. So in general the stability of financial and other markets makes micro-enterprises, and consequently microfinance services, more viable (Yaron et al. 2007).

Progressing from charity to sustainability, the pioneers of microfinance, both in the 1980s and well into the second decade of the twenty-first century, were and are motivated by a desire to help the poor rather than to make money. Jackelen and Rhyne (1991) point out that microfinance seems to have squared the circle, proving itself to be an intervention that can not only alleviate poverty, but that can and should also pay for itself, be 'sustainable', and even make profits. Only in that way, they argue, can it reach the millions who need it.

The questions are: what needs to be done to make microfinance more effective as a tool for economic growth and development? What are the essential criteria for providing sustainable financial services to the poor without neglecting the poorest? How can MFIs expand their outreach and target clients so as to cover medium-sized enterprises?

Common elements of sustainability and growth in MFIs

Sustainability refers to the extent to which a microfinance scheme can cover all its overhead costs without subsidies, and the extent to which the coverage of the scheme (in terms of clients served) can be expanded. There is a clear consensus among academics and practitioners (see, Chizdero et al. 1998; Robinson 2001; Frasier and Bne Saad 2003; Remenyi 2006) on the requirements for the sustainable growth of MFIs. Thus, to build the base for a sustainable rural credit operation the following conditions are proposed:

1. Mobilising savings is one of the conditions under consideration by credit providers. A strong savings base reduces reliance on external funding, as in any given urban or rural setting savers and borrowers are often the same people at different points in time, which reduces the 'information costs' of transactions. Moreover, when people are involved with an institution for both saving and borrowing they are less likely to default on loans. Also, farmers with savings can often self-finance small outlays, so that loans become orientated to bigger outlays with lower transaction costs per unit of money (Ellis 1992: 164; Besley 1994: 27–47; Yaron 1994: 49–70).

2. The interest rate level has to be sufficient to cover the following three components: (i) the interest rate paid to savers; (ii) the average cost of making transactions; and (iii) a risk margin to cover the probability of default.

3. Loan recovery can be improved by tougher recovery discipline, for example: allowing no new loans until old loans are paid; setting more realistic interest rates; and establishing more joint saving and borrowing operations. It is important to identify the reasons for default, especially those that are unavoidable, such as natural calamities (flood, drought and so on). These are time- and location-specific, so borrowers can normally repay when the situation improves. Other defaults may be due to inaccurate rainfall predictions, a failure to conduct soil tests, or specific state policies (for example, low output prices), and in these cases failure lies less with the borrower and more with the lending agencies (Ellis 1992: 164).

4. MFIs can play an additional role in risk management, according to the World Bank (2007), by reducing the costs of insurance on the assets purchased when a loan is taken out – for example, to insure against the loss of a cow. They may require clients to insure themselves against external factors that could interfere with the borrower's ability to repay on schedule, or they might offer loan-protection insurance to ensure that debts are not passed on to survivors. MFIs in the process of developing into providers of a broader range of financial services, can take advantage of their ability to collect small amounts regularly, for example in setting up savings accounts. In addition, since the marginal costs of collecting payments are reduced when staff

networks are already in place, this opens up the possibility of providing death and disability insurance as well as health and crop insurance.

The above conditions can be achieved with good financial management that draws on the financial principles of cost recovery and growth where savings form an important element. Furthermore, the common components needed for the sustainability of MFIs can be grouped into seven broad categories: leadership and mission; knowledge of the MFI sector; organisational and institutional structure; sound financial management; institutional ownership; human resources; and outreach (Chizdero et al. 1998; Robinson 2001; Frasier and Bne Saad 2003):

1. Leadership and mission. No doubt for an institution to move along the difficult path to sustainability it needs strong leadership and vision. This may include knowledge of the clients and their household coping mechanisms, and financial expertise including portfolio management, financial controls, reporting, and management information systems (MIS).
2. Knowledge of the MFI sector and its clients. This includes: knowledge of the social, economic, political and legal environment of the area; understanding the dynamics of local markets, both formal and informal, in a variety of sectors and how these activities fit into wider networks; and an in-depth understanding of the types of microfinance products demanded.
3. Organisational and institutional structure. Putting in place appropriate MIS and administrative procedures that are transparent and ensuring staff are trained in these areas; ensuring high-quality supervision and internal controls and establishing effective governance arrangements; and management of the institution's portfolio with clear policies on loan loss provision and on write-offs.
4. Sound financial management. This may include providing products and services in demand by low-income households and priced for institutional sustainability, and working to achieve high on-time loan repayment rates with built-in insurance to protect against default. This needs to be based on the setting of realistic interest rates and fees to reflect the cost of doing business including inflation, likely loan losses and the opportunity cost of funds.

5. Institutional ownership. This is achieved through having a clearly defined organisational mission and mandate, along with the setting of interest rates and fees that cover fully all non-subsidised financial costs, operating and risks and audit.
6. Human resources. These can be strengthened by developing management and staff training programmes that are specifically designed for microfinance and by the provision of appropriate incentives for staff motivation at all levels of the MFIs.
7. Outreach. MFIs should aim to achieve economies of scale (that is including more clients with wider area coverage) and hence greater levels of financial sustainability. Key indicators of outreach are the number of active clients and low default rate.

Governments and donors are increasingly concerned with creating an enabling environment and supporting best practice in microfinance rather than providing ongoing funding. Table 7.1 shows four levels of time-bound operations proposed towards financial sustainability (Castello et al. 1991; Johnson and Rogaly 1997: 61).

Table 7.1   Steps to achieving sustainability of microfinance institutions and services

Level I	Subsidy-dependent	Operating expenses and the capitalisation of the loan fund are covered by grants or very soft loans (long-term loans with very low-interest payments).
Level II	Partial operational efficiency	Revenues generated from interest income and a fee cover the cost of the borrowed money and a portion of operating expenses. Grants are still required to finance some aspects of operations. The loan fund is capitalised by grants and loans, some of which are on terms that begin to approach market rates.
Level III	Approaching self-sufficiency	Operating expenses may be covered by interest income and fees, but expatriate advisers or the cost of inflation might require external funds. Most subsidies are eliminated. Loans used to capitalise the portfolio are usually below but approaching market interest rates.
Level IV	Fully self-sufficient or profitable	All subsidies are eliminated. Operating expenses and all costs are covered by interest income and fees. The loan fund is fully capitalised from savings of clients and funds raised at commercial interest rates.

Sources: Johnson and Rogaly (1997) and Castello et al. (1991). Adapted by Frasier and Bne Saad (2003).

GENDER AND CREDIT POLICY

Ninety-seven per cent of GB clients are women, and the known repayment rate on its micro-loans has been close to 95 per cent. Many feminist writers have debated the role of credit in women's empowerment by asking whether credit in fact empowers women or whether it merely increases women's work burdens. Other commentators have accused MFI providers of creating a 'feminisation of debt', just like the 'feminisation of food production' in developing countries. It has often been the case that MFIs have overlooked the dynamic of the decision-making process within the household, and failed to address questions such as: who decides to apply for a loan? For what purpose is the loan application being made? How is it going to be repaid? Who is responsible for the repayment? And what level of collective responsibility for repaying the loan exists among members of the household?

Rural credit policy, like other agricultural and rural development policies, can have unintended negative impacts as well as positive outcomes. For example, traditionally poor women were denied access to formal credit markets because of their lack of collateral, a situation closely linked to the ownership structure of land and other assets in a given society. One clearly negative result of credit being made available for labour-saving equipment and machines may be that these displace more women than men in both farm and non-farm operations. Moreover, the availability of credit for export crop production, in which men rather than women tend to be engaged, can result in conflict between men and women about land and labour use (Ellis 1992).

Positive results from women's access to credit were demonstrated by research carried out by Todd (1996), who studied the effects of rural Bangladeshi women's use of credit by comparing women in two GB centres comprising 40 women (who had been members of Grameen centres for at least 8–10 years) with a control group of 22 non-Grameen members. Her research findings indicated that the women with access to credit showed flexibility in relation to their conformity with gendered norms, and used their access to credit to negotiate social rules (for example rules about *purdah*).[2] She found that these women did not usually exercise absolute control over credit, yet through a combination of this credit, their management skills and knowledge of extended social networks they wielded a significant amount of power both within the household and in the local community.

Most of these women were buying land, making loans, or engaging in a variety of leasehold relationships for land that was then farmed by their male kin. Todd discovered that the issue of joint activities within the household was in fact more important than control over separate earnings.

With regard to the household's socioeconomic situation, over two-thirds of the women with access to credit were able to earn more than 50 per cent of the household's income without increasing their work burden. Typically, the men actually worked longer hours while the loans taken out by the women were used to safeguard men's income through own-farm production – by increasing the productivity of their own farms rather than through shareholding arrangements. In this way the GB members became themselves the bankers and 'managing directors' within their households.

However, Todd also found that some women had relinquished control of their loans to their husbands, which in some cases resulted in default and a worsening of their own situation, which became one of greater dependency. She argues that, in these cases, bank staff should have exercised more control to make sure that loans were used for their intended purposes.

Also, for some women, chronic illness acted as a drain on resources, especially during the lean season, taking its toll on members' incomes over the lifespan and resulting in a very precarious position for them later in life. This shows the importance of such banks diversifying and offering other MFI products, such as health insurance programmes, for members and non-members alike (Ranck 1997).

Other significant findings from her research related to children as GB members, showing that they were less likely to be involved in child labour contracts with landlords than non-members.

MFIs AND THE GLOBAL FINANCIAL CRISIS

The global financial crisis (GFC) is considered by many economists to be the worst financial crisis since the Great Depression of the 1930s. It resulted in the collapse of large financial institutions, the bailout of banks by national governments and downturns in stock markets around the world. In many areas the housing market also suffered resulting in numerous evictions, foreclosures and prolonged unemployment. It contributed to the failure of key businesses, declines in consumer wealth estimated to be in the trillions of US dollars, and a significant decline in economic activity, leading to a severe global economic recession in 2008 (Wikipedia 2012). There is clear evidence that this global financial meltdown is affecting the livelihoods of almost everyone in an increasingly interconnected world.

The Secretary General of the UN, Ban Ki-moon (2009), sums up the UN responses to this crisis:

> The world is currently faced with the worst recession since the 1930s, which resulted from an unsustainable growth pattern as well as systemic weaknesses in the global economy. Though the crisis did not originate there, developing countries are being severely hit through weaker trade, tighter global financing conditions and lower remittances. Poverty and hunger are increasing and major reversals in hard-won gains towards the millennium development goals (MDGs) will likely be seen. Children, women, the working poor, migrants and people already at disadvantage will be hit first. There is an increased risk of accelerated environmental degradation and social tensions are on the increase.

To consider closely the impacts that the financial crisis has had on MFIs lending to the poor, an *Economist* article (14 August 2009) entitled 'Microfinance: sub-par but not subprime' records the views of the leaders of the big microfinance companies (among them Muhammad Yunus, the founder of Grameen Bank, for which he won the Nobel Peace Prize in 2006) who express their belief that business remains unscathed. Yunus says that:

> we have not been touched in any way by the financial crisis and that is because we are rooted to the real economy – we are not paper-based, paper chasing banking. When we give loans of US$100 behind the US$100 there are chickens, there are cows. It is not something imaginary.

Proponents of MFIs argue that any similarity with subprime lending is misleading. However, some MFIs do not enjoy the same insulation that their borrowers do because many of them are funded internationally. According to CGAP, foreign capital flows into microfinance tripled between 2004 and 2006, and about half the industry's funding comes from the World Bank's private arm, the International Financial Corporation (IFC), which gave 55 per cent more each year to microfinance lenders between 2004 and 2007.

Furthermore, foreign currency borrowers may have to cope with exchange rate fluctuations (*The Economist* 14 August 2009).

In conclusion, financial constraints are more pervasive in agriculture and related activities than in many other sectors, reflecting both the nature of agricultural activities and the average size of farms in low income agriculture-based countries as well as farmers' lack of collateral against which to borrow. The limited access to financial services in the developing world is one of the main obstacles to diversifying income generation activities and achieving food security. It is estimated that over 4 billion people in both rural and urban areas lack access to basic financial services such as credit, savings, money transfers, leases and insurance. The success of GB and BRAC in Bangladesh, in their outreach, coverage, principles and provision of various financial products, can be sustained by enhancing their work towards poverty reduction, but they need to be able to pay for themselves, be 'sustainable' and even make profits. Only in that way can microfinance reach the millions who need it.

Moreover, most writers agree that the sustainability of microfinance lending depends on working closely with the formal banks. They believe that successful MFIs will inject more 'soul' into formal banking practices rather than the MFI sector losing its own soul.

8
Water for Livelihoods

Throughout history, human progress has depended on access to clean water and on the ability of societies to harness the potential of water as a productive resource. Water for life in the household, and water for livelihoods through production are two of the foundations for human development, but for a large section of humanity these foundations are not in place. (UNDP 2006: v)

UNDP defines water for life as:

a basic human need and a fundamental human right. Yet more than one billion people have no access to clean water, and 2.6 billion people lack access to adequate sanitation. These lacks, combined with malnutrition, result in producing 1.8 million deaths among children every year through diarrhoea and other diseases. (UNDP 2006: 5)

Water for livelihood poses a different set of challenges. Water security in agriculture affects all aspects of human development, while land and water are the two key assets on which poor people depend for their livelihoods. Water cannot be considered in isolation from wider capabilities such as health and education, or from access to other productive assets including land, labour and capital (both fixed capital and working capital). Water insecurity represents a powerful risk factor for both poverty and vulnerability among smallholder agricultural producers and other micro-enterprise operators in the rural areas of developing countries (ibid: 174).

Further challenges arise from competition for water supplies, which varies from one country to another. Globally, about 15 to 35 per cent of total withdrawals are estimated to be unsustainable because the use of water exceeds the renewable supply (Millennium Ecosystem Assessment 2005; World Bank 2007: 182). Two broad trends are discernable. First, as urban centres and industry increase their demands for water agriculture is losing out and will continue to do so. Second, within the agricultural sector competition for water is intensifying. On both fronts there is a danger that agriculture in general, and poor rural households in particular, will suffer in the inevitable adjustment (UNDP 2006: 175), which would have grave implications for global poverty reduction and for efforts to improve food security.

Other challenges to global water security are already arising from climate change and global warming. The *Framework Convention on Climate Change* adopted in 1992 warned governments that 'where there are risks of serious and irreversible damage, lack of full scientific certainty should not be used as a reason for postponing action' (UNDP 2006: 15).

This chapter explores key issues in regard to rural households' access to water for livelihood, focusing on the link between food production and access to, availability of and utilisation of water in developing countries. It examines the political and legal dimensions of transboundary water regulation and elaborates on the socio-economic and environmental constraints associated with most irrigation schemes. It then highlights the issue of institutional arrangements in the management of large-scale irrigation systems, exploring questions of resource allocation and market failures, water charges and farmers' participation. It also describes some innovative, cost-effective and appropriate methods of irrigation technology for small farmers in developing countries.

WORLD WATERS: AN OVERVIEW

> Among the many things I learnt as a president, was the centrality of water in the social, political and economic affairs of the country, the continent and the world. (Nelson Mandela at the World Summit on Sustainable Development 2002, in UNDP 2006: 172)

Agriculture uses 85 per cent of the water supply in developing countries, despite the fact that irrigated farming accounts for only about 18 per cent of the cultivated area and produces about 40 per cent of the value of agricultural output (Hazell and Wood 2007; Sebastian 2007; World Bank 2007: 182).

Water, according to UNDP (2006: 175–204), 'is underpinning all aspects of human society, from ecology to agriculture to industry'. 'It is also an integral part of the production systems that generate wealth and well-being'. Globally, agriculture and industry are adjusting to tightening hydrological constraints, although scarcity in the large majority of cases is as a result of institutional and political factors rather than a matter of deficient supply. Moreover, in many countries 'scarcity is the product of public policies which have encouraged the over-use of water through subsidies and under-pricing, which in turn has exaggerated inequalities between large and small farmers, and between men and women, in rural areas' (UNDP 2006: 173). According to Webb et al. (2005: 2):

> Like food, water availability is not matched by equal access for all regions or all people. Fresh water is unevenly distributed geographically and temporally, resulting in surpluses for some people and a threat of severe water insecurity for others. For example, Canada has 120,000 m³ per capita per year of renewable water resources, compared with Jordan's 300 m³. Similarly, while India has a national average of 2,500 m³ per capita, some states, like Rajastan, have only 550 m³.

International water basins – catchments or watersheds, including lakes and shallow groundwater, that are shared by more than one country – cover almost half of the Earth's land surface. Two in every five people in the world today live in these basins, which also account for 60 per cent of global river flows. The number of shared basins has been growing, largely because of the break-up of the former Soviet Union and former Yugoslavia. 'In 1978 there were 214 international basins. In 2006, there are 263' (UNDP 2006: 205).

According to Briscoe (in UNDP 2006: 205) 'the depth of inter-dependence implied by these figures is revealed by the number of countries in shared basins – 145, accounting for more than 90 per cent of the world's population'. More than 30 countries are located entirely within transboundary basins and for some 39 countries, with a population of 800 million people, at least half of their water resources originate beyond their borders (Giordano, in UNDP 2006: 205–11).

There are many examples of shared water resources: Iraq and Syria rely for most of their water on the Tigris and Euphrates rivers flowing out of Turkey, while Bangladesh depends on flows from India for 91 per cent of its water for crop irrigation and replenishment of aquifers. Egypt depends almost entirely on external water sources delivered through the Nile which originates in Ethiopia.

Lakes are less renewable than rivers and are more sensitive to pollution and water withdrawal, adding to competitive pressures. Aquifers, on the other hand, are invisible, but they are repositories for more than 90 per cent of the world's fresh water and, like rivers and lakes, they also span borders (see, Puri and Arnold 2002; UNDP 2006: 209).

The intensive use of ground water for irrigation is rapidly expanding in some countries with the adoption of tube well and mechanical pump technology. In the Indian subcontinent, ground water withdrawals have surged from less than 20 cubic kilometres to more than 250 cubic kilometres per year since the 1950s. China and India are the largest users of underground water irrigation and are expected to increase water consumption almost three-fold by 2020, as a result of expansion and intensification of irrigation combined with macroeconomic and industrial growth. Growth in the last two areas provides the resources for investment in further irrigation, while also underpinning increased demand for food[1] (Webb et al. 2005).

Reliance on ground water is highest in the Middle East and South Asia (Shah et al. 2003; World Bank 2007). In these regions water has contributed more than any other input factor to regional food production which is by far the largest user, taking nearly 90 per cent of the total (Bazza 2005: 3). Water use in such arid developing countries is increasing rapidly and, according to FAO estimates in 2004, their growing farming, industrial and urban needs are likely to result in a 40 per cent increase in demand for water by 2030.

National water governance is about striking a balance among these competing users. While countries may legislate individually for water as a national asset, the resource itself (in the form of rivers, lakes and aquifers) crosses political boundaries and extends hydrological interdependence across national frontiers (UNDP 2006: 203). UNDP points to the fact that:

> Cross border waters almost always create some tension between the societies they bind. These tensions cannot be considered in isolation. They are tied up in wider factors than relations between states, including concerns over national security, economic opportunities, environmental sustainability and fairness. Managing shared water can be a force for peace or conflict, but it is politics that will decide which course is chosen.

As the costs of non-cooperation are conflicts, environmental deterioration, poverty and food insecurity, there is clearly a profound need for cooperation (UNDP 2006: 204).

SHARED WATER RESOURCES: THE POLITICAL AND
LEGAL DIMENSIONS

Competition among political and economic interests in the management of scarce water resources at the national level has profound implications for poverty, for the distribution of opportunity and for human development. Its effects are no less profound beyond national frontiers (UNDP 2006: 209). Governments, and most members of the public, tend to think of the water that flows through their countries as a national resource and, according to UNDP (2006: 209), that perception may be accurate. However, much of what is perceived as 'national water' is in fact shared water.

At the national level water is governed and managed through laws, norms and institutions developed through historical and political processes, influenced by a country's particular political system and development agenda. However, the laws, institutions and norms for governing water which crosses borders are less well defined. At the international level the *Harmon Doctrine* (1895) advocates that, in the absence of contrary legislation, states should be free to use the water resources in their jurisdiction without regard to effects beyond their borders, but in practice most governments accept that this absolutist approach to water rights is not a helpful guide to policy design (UNDP 2006: 217).

After decades of consideration, principles for sharing water were codified in the 1997 *UN Convention on the Law of the Non-navigational Uses of International Watercourses*, which built on the 1966 *Helsinki Rules on the Uses of the Waters of International Rivers*. The core principles are: 'equitable and reasonable utilisation', 'no significant harm' and 'prior notification of works'. The guiding principle is that governance of international watercourses should be developed by taking into account: (1) the availability of alternative water sources, (2) the size of the population affected, (3) the social and economic needs of the watercourse states concerned, and (4) the conservation, protection and development of the watercourse itself (UNDP 2006: 215–18).

Research evidence suggests that concern over national sovereignty and the absence of practical enforcement mechanisms, and of tools for resolving competing claims, has undermined the adoption and implementation of the UN Convention. The 1992 UN Economic Commission for Europe's *Convention on the Protection and Use of Trans-boundary Watercourses and International Lakes* (ECPUTW) focuses on water quality, considering a river basin as a single ecological unit. This Convention also emphasises member states' responsibilities, and is based on current water needs rather than historical water use (UNDP 2006: 218).

Moreover, as knowledge of water scarcity has increased, the notion of integrated water resources management (IWRM) has attained prominence in the debates about water management (Global Water Partnership 2000; Jonker, in Movik and Mehta 2009). The Global Water Partnership (2000) defined IWRM as 'a process, which promotes the coordinated development and management of water, land and related resources in order to maximize the resultant economic and social welfare in an equitable manner without compromising the sustainability of vital ecosystems'.

IWRM, and the associated concept of integrated river basin management (IRBM), are themes of many policies and water legislations and feature the guiding philosophies of the international donor community's approach to water (Lankford and Hepworth, in Movik and Mehta 2009: 6). Establishing IWRM is a big challenge for governments and institutions, as it can generally only be realised through a long process of implementation with numerous elements including: restructuring legal and institutional frameworks; investing in infrastructure; enhancing stakeholder participation in decision making; capacity building; and establishing efficient monitoring and information systems (Global Water Partnership 2000).

Critics of the IWRM approach highlight the fact that it tends to be technocratic, focusing on the implementation of particular requirements and thresholds which are to guide water allocation and management in river basins (Movik and Mehta 2009: 6). They state that:

> The hierarchical structures of basin management, with an apex body that oversees and regulates formal water rights, tend towards rigidity and technocratisation, that seldom work well in the vast basins in developing countries that are often prone to high variability and unpredictability, due to a dearth of capacity, lengthy, costly and complex litigation processes and patchy frameworks.

This IWRM approach has been challenged by emerging research in developing countries by Warner et al. (2008), which highlights the uncritical adoption of IWRM as it becomes another arena for the state and other authorities to assert territorial control over water resources despite their claims of consultation and participation (see, Movik and Mehta 2009: 6; Sitorus 2009).

Moreover, with regards to cooperation, the UN Economic and Social Commission for West Asia (ESCWA) (in Bazza 2005: 11) has stated that:

> In the ESCWA region, there have been a limited number of successful experiments in creating organisational frameworks for transboundary water resources. In general, these have consisted of little more than setting up institutional frameworks for some boundary-straddling aquifers. Cooperation has been essentially driven by projects funded from external assistance and loans; it has no firm institutional roots, and may well come to an end once the projects in question have been completed.

Another example of cooperation involves Vietnam, Cambodia, Laos, Burma and Thailand, whose national governments established a commission in 1995 to regulate the use of the Mekong River. They pledged to: notify each other about any big projects; exchange data on water flow; put a system in place to monitor activities; and fix the minimum amount of water each country must discharge downstream[2] (UNDP 2006).

In Africa a revised protocol of the Southern African Development Community (SADC), signed in 2000 by the member states, gave greater influence to downstream states and to environmental needs. Its objective was to promote the SADC agenda of regional integration and poverty alleviation. The member states adopted a watercourse agreement – 'the South African Water Act of 1998' – setting up joint institutions, encouraging coordination and harmonisation of legislation and policies and joint data collection, and they agreed to promote the exchange of information and research findings. They also established formal procedures for notification, negotiation and conflict resolution, supported in national legislation.

Africa boasts the largest watercourses and natural storage reservoirs in the world, but many areas still suffer from acute 'water and economic stresses' due to financial and technical constraints preventing them from fully utilising this resource. Agriculture uses 85 per cent of all water in the continent, although this varies hugely from one country to another (African Ministerial Conference on the Environment (AMCEN), 2002). In 2005 the Commission for Africa, concerned about its lagging agricultural performance, pointed out the need to ensure more sustained and stable agricultural production in order to improve food availability and foster development.

However, in light of more recent developments, there can be no doubt that demand for irrigation water will be increased as a result of the push by external investors to utilise African resources, especially land and water, for food and biofuel production.

The AMCEN (2002) report focused on the challenges of increasing spending on physical irrigation infrastructure and extending the area under irrigation to twice the current coverage. Movik and Mheta (2009: 6), highlighting the fact that 'Just seven per cent of Africa's arable area is under irrigation compared to 33 per cent for Asia', and asking the question 'does Africa need a "blue revolution"'? However, the Commission's report was largely focused on creating new infrastructure as opposed to looking at the social and institutional aspects of water management, or indeed enhancing the potential of dry land agriculture. Often, extending irrigation infrastructure tends to mean building large dams with associated massive canal networks (Movik and Mheta 2009: 6).

STATE COOPERATION

The case for cooperation, according to UNDP (2006), along with the mechanisms for achieving it will inevitably vary across international shared water systems. At its most basic level, cooperation implies acting in a manner that minimises the adverse consequences of competing claims while maximising the potential benefits of shared solutions. Taking the principle that states seek to pursue rational and legitimate self-interest as a starting point, 'cooperation will occur only if the anticipated benefits exceed the costs of non-cooperation. Enlightened self-interest can help identify and broaden the range of potential benefits'. Sadoff and David (2002) proposed a useful framework and identified four layers of potential gains from cooperation over shared river water:

- Benefits to the rivers: this refers to conserving, protecting and developing rivers to generate benefits for all users;
- Benefits from the rivers: this refers to the promotion of efficient techniques for water storage and distribution, and for expanding irrigation acreage. It also refers to the provision of hydroelectric power to meet the needs of industry, services and households;
- Benefits because of the rivers: this refers to the costs avoided by reducing tensions and disputes between neighbours. Strained interstate relations linked to water management can inhibit

regional cooperation on a broader front, including trade, transport, telecommunications and labour markets;
• Benefits beyond the river: this refers to the ways in which increasing the benefits from the river, and decreasing the costs arising because of the river, can unlock a wider potential for human development, economic growth and regional cooperation (UNDP 2006: 218–21).

According to UNDP (2006: 228) 'States, civil societies and international organisations can create the conditions for initial cooperation and move towards wider benefit-sharing systems'.

The following steps according to UNDP (2006: 228) can eliminate socio-economic constraints experienced by countries sharing water resources: (1) assessing human development needs and goals; (2) building trust, increasing legitimacy, enhancing the legal aspect of water use between countries and so on; (3) strengthening institutional capacity; and (4) financing transboundary water management.

WATER FOR LIVELIHOODS: SOCIAL, ECONOMIC AND ENVIRONMENTAL CONSTRAINTS

The links between rural livelihoods, access to water, and poverty reduction efforts and food security are well known. UNDP (2006: 174) highlight the fact that:

The majority of small farmers in developing countries depend on agriculture for their livelihoods, primarily by producing staple food crops and a few livestock on small farms (of less than two hectares). Most of them also depend on rainfall and lack access to a stable supply of water. Variation in rainfall, or disruptions in water supply, can make a difference between adequate nutrition and hunger, health and sickness and ultimately life and death.

Webb et al. (2005) define water for life and livelihood as 'access and usage by all individuals at all times to sufficient, safe water for a healthy and productive life and sustainable livelihood'. This definition, which is an adaptation of the food security definition (World Bank 1986, see Chapter 1 of this book), incorporates elements including not only water availability, but also access to water, water usages in terms of quality (maximum thresholds of purity or absence of contaminants/pollutants), and the minimisation of water-related risks to health and livelihoods. Webb et al. (2005: 3) elaborate further on these three elements:

- *Water availability*: is a function of supply and distribution, and it is dependent on ecological, legal, political, socio-economic and institutional factors. However, risks to water supply can arise from disruption of the supply lines by upstream users deliberately curtailing water flow to downstream users, or due to lack of maintenance. Ultimately the absence of legally binding contracts committing users to share information on projects or diversion of water sources, and from climate-related factors such as drought or flood, would worsen the situation for downstream users.
- *Water access*: refers to a household's control of water as a commodity and/or as a public good, for domestic use and for farming. This level of control is partly determined by distribution policy (national policies and investment priorities play important roles), and partly by effective demand – that is, how much a household can actually 'take home' (to kitchen and farm). The latter depends on income, location in relation to distribution channels, and sometimes on a household's economic status. In areas where people have to pay for the water they use for farming and household needs, a household's loss of income may lead to a reduction in water consumption, while a loss of access failure may also result from sickness or death of adults in the household.
- *Water usage*: relates to individual physiological entitlements and depends on quantity of water consumed, its quality (safety), opportunity costs (price), and knowledge (of hygiene, sanitation, consumption and disease control). Lack of information on best practice, or health constraints that reduce the potential benefits of access to adequate water, are risks that can impact on water utilisation for life and livelihoods.

However, regulating access to water is mediated by government policies and forms an important part of government development strategy, which in some countries also involves donors and NGOs. Government macroeconomic policies, including their fiscal, monetary and trade policies, can directly and indirectly affect both demand for and investment in water-related activities such as irrigation, flood control and dams (Webb et al. 2005: 4). So what is irrigation policy?

Irrigation policy

Irrigation policy is defined by Ellis (1992: 254) as 'the use of human technology and or mechanical technology to increase and control the supply of water for crop production'. Ellis provides another definition: 'policies concerned with the provision of water as a resource in farm production, often involving large-scale public investment in the infrastructures of farm production'. It stipulates the role of the state in promoting or providing irrigation facilities, and involves policy choices that are made with respect to alternative irrigation technologies, the management of large-scale irrigation schemes, and alternative methods for recouping from farmers the cost of providing them with irrigation.

Water for irrigation is a variable input that exhibits a high degree of complementarity with other variable inputs such as seeds, fertilisers and pesticides. Moreover, Ellis (1992: 255) provides some examples of the link between irrigation and other complementary policies regarding farm production:

- Credit policy, due to the increased demand of irrigated crop production for working capital;
- Mechanisation policy, because it involves some of the same issues of technology choice;
- Land reform, because irrigation schemes often involve changes in land tenure or land resettlement;
- Marketing policy, since a workable market infrastructure must exist to handle the sale of produce from an irrigation scheme;
- Pricing policy, since irrigation may make farmers more responsive to price changes; and
- Research policy, since the priorities of research are likely to be predicated in part on the overall proportion of irrigated farmland and on future irrigation plans.

However, 'economic policy-makers tend to confront policy issues one at a time, stating policy objectives in single dimensional terms' (Bahatia and Falkenmark 1993; Webb et al. 2005: 4). And 'far less attention has been focused on cross-sectoral relationships in household's water use and competition for community based water resources, or on alternative policy and institutional options to address equity concerns' (Webb et al. 2005: 4).

According to Movik and Mehta (2009: 14) there is an emerging understanding that access to water for life and livelihoods is a cross-cutting issue, and should be a key framework for future innovation and research which must go beyond the often narrow focus on the particular purpose and use of water and associated policies. Thus, access to a stable supply of water for life and livelihoods should be considered a cross-cutting resource and policy matter, and must take into account the vulnerabilities and risk factors affecting rural households.

Ellis (1992: 256) states that the overall objectives of irrigation policy are to achieve equity in income distribution, to reduce poverty and vulnerability, to increase food security at micro and macroeconomic levels, and to achieve long-term sustainability. Table 8.1 shows the key dimensions and impacts of secure access to irrigation water.

Table 8.1 Impacts of secure access to irrigation water on poverty and vulnerability in rural areas

| Production | Key dimensions of secure access to water | | | |
| | Income and consumption | Employment | Vulnerability and food security | Other assets |
		Key impacts		
Increased:	Increased:	Increased:	Enhanced food availability:	Other effects:
Crop areas	Income from production	On-farm employment opportunities	Increased opportunity to produce and retain food for home consumption	Reduced indebtedness
Cropping intensity	Stabilisation of farm family income	Off-farm employment opportunities		Increased resources for health and education
Crop diversification	Family consumption of food	Stabilisation of employment opportunities	Lower level of consumption shortfall	Improved overall resource base
Adoption of high-value crops	Reduced food prices	Rural wages	Reduced risk of crop failure	Increased demand for credit
Opportunity for year round cropping			Reduced seasonality effects on production	Increased research activities
				Improvement of market's infrastructures, roads and communications
				Increased demands for inputs
				Conditions created for backward and forward linkages

Source: Adapted from UNDP (2006).

The degree to which irrigation can achieve higher farm output by means of these effects will be determined by both technical and socio-economic constraints, especially in resource-poor environments (Ellis 1992: 254–7). The following section deals with these constraints.

Socioeconomic and environmental constraints

Most recent discussions on issues concerning irrigation policy centre around three policy issues. These are: first, the choice of technology in irrigation, especially the relative type of technology-to-labour cost; second, the issue of institutional structure in the management of large-scale irrigation schemes; and third, the issue of charging farmers for irrigation water, which is linked to the economic problem of resource allocation in a context of market failure (Ellis 1992: 254–5). In relation to the economic costs of irrigation, Ellis (1992: 254-5) notes that:

> Irrigation represents a classic example of market failure, so that state involvement of one kind or another has been virtually axiomatic in most types of irrigation development. Market failure may be understood in this context as the inability to define private ownership rights to water as a resource, resulting in (1) the non-formation of a market price for water, (2) the existence of externalities caused by the impact of individual user behaviour on the collective access to water of users as a group, and (3) a divergence between the private marginal costs and social marginal costs of water provision for irrigation.

To explore the issue of whether irrigation water is a public good or a commodity it is necessary to define these terms. A public good, according to Ellis (1992: 262–3), is 'One which once made available, cannot exclude individuals from its use, and therefore cannot charge them a price for its use'. Goods are considered to be public when 'the extent of their utilisation by individuals cannot be measured, and their use cannot therefore be priced'. Ellis (1992: 262–3), gives canal irrigation as an example:

> Canal irrigation can be characterised in part as a public good. Once the canal system is installed, it would cost too much in practice to regulate the amount of water consumed by the individual farmer, and it is often not possible to prevent farmers

at the periphery of irrigation schemes from making use of water made available by the scheme.

He goes on to point out:

> Irrigation schemes are state financed and no attempt is made to charge farmers for the water they consume, although a land tax may sometimes be used in order to recoup some of the capital or running costs of schemes. (Ibid: 263)

However, Bazza (2005) highlights the fact that between the late 1950s and the 1980s most countries in the Near East invested heavily in irrigation developments such as dams, irrigation canals and distribution networks. The irrigated area expanded by an average of 1 per cent per year during the early 1960s, reaching a maximum annual rate of increase of 2.3 per cent from 1972 to 1975. Subsequently, the financial crises of the second half of the 1990s adversely affected investment in irrigation, and since then it has lagged behind output and trade growth. The declining investment not only affected the expansion of irrigation but also the operation and maintenance of old irrigation schemes, which in turn has affected both efficiency and productivity.

In Mexico during the 1990s subsidies paid to operate and maintain water systems (excluding capital investment costs) amounted to 0.5 per cent of GDP (see, Rosegrant et al. 2001; Webb et al. 2005: 8). For the same period, in India about 30 per cent of all public investment has gone into establishing irrigation systems, for which water was then supplied almost without cost to the users (Bahatia and Falkenmark 1993; Webb et al. 2005: 8). This approach can prove problematic, as Ellis (1992: 263) points out:

> Equity in water distribution in canal irrigation can be undermined when demand for an essentially 'free' service at peak time outstrips the capacity available. Due to the absence of a market price to reflect this congestion, non-market mechanisms take over the allocation of scarce resources. These include bribery of irrigation officials, meddling with gates, blocking channels, breaking canal banks and taking water out of turn.

Within irrigation systems unequal access to water is often a corollary of unequal access to land. In Pakistan the largest 2.5 per cent of farms (those of more than 50 hectares) account for 34 per cent of cultivated land, while the smallest 55 per cent of farms (those of less than 5 hectares) account for 12 per cent (World Bank 2005). In relation to China, the analyses of a number of authors (Hussain and Wijerathna 2004; Lipton 2004; UNDP 2006) show that equality of land distribution played an important role in promoting equality of access for most farmers to irrigation water. This is in marked contrast to Pakistan, which is the least efficient in this matter. However, it is likely that other factors – such as water regulation systems, monitoring mechanisms, and farmers' participation in operation and maintenance – also play their part.

However, the debates over water policy and management should differentiate between the two types of water use, namely water for life and water for livelihood. Webb et al. (2005: 8–9) argue in favour of removing water policy and management from the public sector for two reasons:

> On the one hand, government control of water distribution has typically involved public subsidies with a view to 'making water affordable', yet, subsidies have already rarely benefited the poor simply because they tend to be physically removed from piped [for domestic use] water services or irrigation perimeters [for agricultural production].

Shifting control of water management and distribution to the private sector is seen by Webb et al. (2005) as a way of both increasing efficiency and reducing political distortions in relation to the benefits of access to water. However, it has been clearly documented that poor households already pay relatively more for water than wealthier households, and would be willing to pay more for a good service (see studies by Whittington et al. 1991 on Nigeria; Altaf et al. 1993 on Pakistan; Cestii 1993 on Indonesia; and Cestii 1995 on Cairo).

Movik and Mehta (2009: 9–10) argue that since the turn of the century privatisation controversies have charged water debates worldwide. This is often associated with notions concerning the 'inefficiency' of the public sector and the need to inject new capital into the sector. While private corporations' engagement in the provision of water for life is far from unproblematic, and the issue of whether water supply services should be a public or private responsibility is still hotly debated, discussions are often muddled by misconceptions in terms of what is actually at stake. In particular, there has been a protracted and rather polarised debate around whether water should be perceived as a human right or an economic good (see, for example, Perry et al. 1997; McNeill 1998; Briscoe 2003), when it would be better to explore ways to reconcile these views through regulatory action and concentrate on how to secure poor people's access to water through technological innovations and regulatory measures.

In canal irrigation 'viable policy solutions to the management problems lie somewhere in the middle ground between the pure public good approach and the flawed private ownership proposal' (Boyce 1988: A-13). Ellis (1992: 269), indicates, any such solution must accept that:

> Volumetric water pricing to farmers is not economically viable even where it is technically feasible, and that other types of levy must therefore be devised in order to give farmers the necessary access to water. Any solution must also take into account the externalities and common property aspects of irrigation provision, which means that methods of cooperation and trust must be built into proposed solutions.

Externalities

Problems of water quantity are exacerbated by the problems of water quality (Bazza 2005: 5), and irrigation 'is rife with externalities' (Ellis 1992: 263). Three types of externality exist in relation to water quantity and quality, some of which relate to transboundary water arrangements between countries, while others are scheme-wide externalities within countries. The third type relates to farmer-induced externalities, including issues concerning the use of ground water as an 'open access' resource.

However, in relation to the extent of the impact of externalities on water quantity and quality, and on the hydrological interdependence of water resources between countries which share rivers, lakes and groundwater, UNDP (2006: 204–5) indicates that:

- There is competition for a finite supply of water. Across borders, transboundary water links people and their environment to sustain livelihoods and generate growth. However, an important aspect of externality of water for livelihoods is that use in one place may restrict availability in another. For example, the retention of water upstream for irrigation or power generation in one country restricts flows downstream for farmers and the environment.

- There are impacts on water quality. The way an upstream country uses water affects the environment and quality of water that arrives in a downstream country. Uncoordinated dam development can cause silting in reservoirs, preventing the rich sediment from reaching low-lying plains. Similarly, industrial or human pollution can be transported through rivers to people in other countries.
- There are effects on the timing of water flow. Upstream users, acting in their own economic interest, may control the volume of water released to downstream users, which can have crucial implications for agricultural users, especially in water-scarce environments.

Moreover, public debates about dams are polarised by, on the one hand, governments that are trying to meet the growing demands for water and energy needs and, on the other hand, NGOs that are more concerned about ecosystems and environmental impacts (Alhassan 2009). However, 'The World Commission Report on Dams in 2000', in a pragmatic but critical way, succeeded in raising questions regarding the notion of the large dam as the panacea for addressing water scarcity. The report's conclusions were openly rejected by dam-building nations such as China, India and Turkey, and to some extent by the World Bank, which had played a key role over the two-year period of the Commission's work. However, while Western countries now balk at the prospect of investing in risky dam projects, China willingly makes low-interest loans and concessions available for the construction of large dams and other infrastructure projects in Africa and countries in the global South (see, Wild and Mepham 2006; Kaplinsky et al. 2007; Alhassan 2009: 148; Movik and Mehta 2009: 12).

However, low-income countries which depend on aid to finance their development programmes need to explore alternative methods and more cost-effective technologies such as rainwater harvesting, irrigation by drips, and the use of solar-generated electricity, rather than borrowing significant amounts of money to finance the capital cost of dams and related infrastructure, including canal irrigation schemes.

Lipton and Lichfield (2003) examined the World Bank review of 192 supported irrigation projects implemented between 1950 and the mid-1990s and found that more than two-thirds of these projects performed satisfactorily, with an average rate of return of 15 per cent of agricultural production. Most of these were large schemes benefiting larger landowners (for example, in northern India). However, some secondary benefits to less wealthy farmers were observed, including increased employment opportunities (Webb et al. 2005). However, these potential gains were, as Webb et al. (2005: 8) put it, rarely spread far beyond the immediate hinterland of irrigation schemes because of market constraints, price controls, or simply transport infrastructure deficiencies.

Kaosa-ard and Rerkasem (2000) argue that long-term equity concerns in the distribution of water resources between farmers in South East Asia had led to dangerous social conflicts and even violence arising over the use of water resources, which could compromise the social fabric of some communities. Considering another world region, El Kady (in Webb et al. 2005: 8) suggests that in many Middle Eastern countries 'there is a relationship between injustice and water scarcity' which is mediated through governmental inability to manage water resources efficiently, or to ensure that the poor not only have access to water but are also protected from pollutants reaching them from upstream via industrial and agricultural waste products.

Open access resources

> Open access resources are most commonly associated with ground water use for irrigation, and sometimes confused with common property resources, the key difference being the existence of social mechanisms for controlling the level of access by individuals in the latter case, and the absence of such mechanisms in the former. (Ellis 1992: 264)

As a resource, ground water is renewable, but can only replenish itself at a certain rate (for tube-well irrigation the replenishment rate is known as the 'recharge rate' of the water-holding aquifer). Thus, where ground water use is most intensive the aquifer recharge rate is often too low to sustain it (Comprehensive Assessment of Water Management in Agriculture 2007, in World Bank 2007). The difficulty of monitoring and measuring excessive withdrawal rates from aquifers, which occur due to high demand by private users during peak periods, can lead to a 'tragedy of the commons' in the form of the over-exploitation of a common resource past the point of sustainability (Ellis 1992: 255; UNDP 2006: 209).

This feature of open-access nature, in most cases where over exploitation occurs, is leading to: depletion; contamination by municipal, industrial and agricultural users; and saline water intrusion. Some argue that ground water offers a buffer to ameliorate the impacts of climate change, but viable technologies for utilising such fossil resources in a sustainable manner still need to be developed (Movik and Mehta 2009: 6).

THE ENVIRONMENTAL COSTS OF INTENSIVE AND EXTENSIVE FARMING

The world's population is estimated to reach 9 billion by the year 2050, so the world's water will have to support agricultural systems that feed and create livelihoods for an additional 2.7 billion people. To increase food production and achieve food self-sufficiency, agricultural producers have only two options: intensification or extensification of agricultural production.

There are strong arguments for intensification based on the success of the adoption of Green Revolution technology by both small and large farmers in developing countries. The use of certified HYV seeds, complemented by a stable supply of water and fertilisers in areas well endowed with water, succeeded in doubling cereal production with no significant expansion of the total land area cultivated. Such intensification of agriculture has to some extent met the world's demand for food and reduced hunger while preserving forests, wetlands, biodiversity and to some extent the ecosystem and the benefits they provide (World Bank 1992; Nelson and Maredia 2007).

However, both intensification and extensification have created adverse environmental effects. In intensive cropping systems the excessive and inappropriate use of agricultural chemicals such as fertilisers and pesticides has polluted waterways, poisoned people, and in some cases upset ecosystems. Wasteful irrigation has contributed to the growing scarcity of water, the unsustainable pumping of groundwater, and degradation of prime agricultural land. More intensive livestock systems also present environmental and health problems. Meanwhile, extensive use of the land area available has led, in many places, to the degradation and loss of forests, wetlands, soils and pastures (World Bank 1992).

During the 1960s and 1970s most developing countries sought to achieve self-sufficiency in basic food crops, irrespective of the natural resource base of the country. This policy, especially in arid and semi-arid regions, ignored the likely economic and environmental costs. But with economic stagnation, growing water scarcity, broader policy reforms, and new and changing global trade policies, the old paradigm of self-sufficiency in food is being replaced by concepts of self-reliance and competitiveness (Bazza 2005: 7).

As food-deficit countries become more dependent on food imports, Bazza has argued that importing food is the equivalent of importing water in a condensed form, which he terms 'virtual water'. The principle behind this concept of virtual water relates to the need for countries or regions to diversify their production, based on the comparative advantages they have. In this way they can earn foreign exchange to buy food imports instead of growing low-value, high-water-consuming crops. Virtual water can be considered the simplest and least costly form of water transport and trade between regions. An FAO survey of irrigation and water resources estimated that 86.5 cubic kilometres of water would have been needed to grow the food that was imported into the Near East region in the early to mid-1990s – more than the annual flow into the region of the Nile River. In this region, for example, Egypt, Saudi Arabia, Algeria and Iran import 44 cubic kilometres of water equivalent in food, while Turkey is the only country in the region that is a net exporter of cereals (Bazza 2005: 7).

Bazza argues that virtual water has potential benefits for importing countries as well as for global water management, for two reasons. Firstly, cereals are one of the main food imports in most regions of the world, and these can be produced with less costly water in countries with high water availability and productivity. Secondly, the bulk of the imported grain is produced under rain-fed, temperate conditions, and is therefore only consuming soil moisture and not surface and ground water that might be allocated to other uses.

This argument is sound in cases where food prices are stable and affordable by low-income food deficit countries, and in situations where investing in high value crops can guarantee the income required to buy the food that is most needed on the international markets. These conditions, however, are not always likely to be satisfied: since global food prices are notoriously volatile and, depending on world markets for food, can be dangerous, especially when exporting countries prioritise their own political and economic interests.

CHOICES IN IRRIGATION TECHNOLOGY: SHAPING THE FUTURE

Looking to the future, prospects for extending irrigation is limited while pressures from industry and domestic water users are rising. Secure rights to water can expand opportunities for poor people to escape poverty, while the absence of secure rights leaves them open to the risk that they will be unable to assert their claims in the face of competition (Ellis 1992; UNDP 2006). In arid and semi-arid regions irrigation is an important component of increasing agricultural productivity. This chapter has already discussed some of the key issues with respect to the impacts of dams, and shown how unevenly the benefits and costs (social, economic, environmental and health related) have been distributed. The next step is to consider possible future pathways in the form of technological innovations and choices that are cost effective, relevant and appropriate to the environmental, social and economic constraints facing small farmers in developing countries (see, Lovell et al. 1996; UNDP 2006: 195–8; Movik and Mehta 2009: 9).[3]

As the UNDP report (2006: 200) on the 'global water crisis' indicates, it is time to abandon the age-old dichotomy between large-scale and small-scale approaches. There is a wide range of technological options that could be adopted to increasing agricultural productivity by getting 'more crops by drop, rather than more water for the fields', in both large-scale and small-scale agriculture. This issue is becoming the central concern in public policy debates, as increasing water productivity is one obvious response to water scarcity. This can be achieved, for example, by: supplementing rain-fed agriculture with simple treadle pumps; rainwater harvesting; small-scale watershed development; use of 'bucket and drop' kits; irrigation by drips; sprinkler irrigation; collector wells; and desalinisation of sea water.

Other options include enhancing cropping techniques, such as that developed for the system of rice intensification (SRI)[4] in India, China and Madagascar, which may have great potential (Prasad et al., in Movik and Mehta 2009: 9). In parts of Africa, substantial results could be achieved by the more effective utilisation of floodplains, along with improved agronomic practices, such as mulching and zero tilling, spacing and plant management systems, and increasing the drought resistance of crops by developing those which are more tolerant of saline and/or poor-quality water (IWMI 2004, in Movik and Mehta 2009).

It is noteworthy that, for the last 20 years, funding for irrigation has been reduced to a trickle due to disappointing results and poor returns on huge investments, and the term 'irrigation' has almost disappeared from development debates (Lankford, in Movik and Mehta 2009: 9). As with any other farm production technology, it is important to move away from a preoccupation with technological solutions per se and instead look at the contextual factors that determine their appropriateness. It is also essential to ensure that the end users – the farmers, peasants and smallholders – ultimately determine the choice of the most appropriate options from the wide range of available technological innovations (ibid: 9).

GOVERNANCE IN IRRIGATION SYSTEMS

An issue with important implications for human development and global poverty reduction is how to manage water resources to meet rising food needs while protecting the access of poor and vulnerable people to the water that sustains their livelihoods.

People's legal rights count for little if the institutions charged with protecting them are inaccessible or unresponsive. It is important that the public policy objectives of social justice and ecological sustainability are not subordinated to the pursuit of private gain (UNDP 2006). Policy issues of management and resource use efficiency apply especially to large-scale public canal irrigation schemes – however, all types of irrigation, including private tube wells, display features related to externality and common property.

Ellis (1992: 267) identifies a number of governance-related problems, which vary according to different types of administrative structure, and which include corruption and income seeking on the part of officials, and preferences by government agencies for funding new capital construction rather than the recurrent costs of operation and maintenance. In addition, the top-down bureaucratic mode of operation of such agencies, coupled with their central financing, is ill suited to the involvement of farmers in the management of canal systems. Also, farmers themselves have little incentive to contain their water demands, to comply with rules, or to contribute to scheme maintenance.[5]

Ellis (1992: 269) outlines a number of practical solutions to improve water governance, such as: (1) encourage farmers' participation from the outset to regulate water flow and to contribute to its operation and maintenance; (2) separate the function of dam and canal construction from the function of operation and maintenance to insure efficiency of operation; (3) establish efficient systems of cost-recovery linked to the benefits from irrigation systems which would help to rationalise the use of water and to finance maintenance (UNDP 2006: 199). Recurrent operation and maintenance costs can be met by an irrigation service fee. From an economic viewpoint it would be more effective to make the income of the local operation and maintenance service agency dependent on the collection of fees from farmers, thus creating the necessary link between payment and quality of services which has often been missing because of government inability to put a price on water.

IRRIGATION POLICY AND GENDER

According to UNDP (2006: 194), in many countries women have rights to use irrigation water but highly restricted rights of control. Gender inequalities are deeply entrenched as a result of the formal and informal rules that mute women's voices. Moreover, control rights are often linked to wider property rights, which are highly unequal between men and women:

> Lacking rights to land, millions of women in South Asia and sub-Saharan Africa are denied formal membership rights to participate in water association meetings. Meanwhile, in many traditional communal irrigation systems people earn the right to use water by working on maintenance. However, cultural norms often preclude women from engaging in this activity. Moreover, even when they do, water rights do not automatically follow, as research from Kenya and Nepal documented. (Meinzen-Dick et al. and van Koppen, in UNDP 2006: 194)

However, women are responsible for two-thirds of food production in developing countries. Thus, failure to consult women systematically is not just bad for social justice and equity, it is also bad for efficiency. As producers, women have skills and knowledge vital to soil conservation, water management, food production and household food security.

IRRIGATION IN A RESOURCE-POOR ENVIRONMENT

Ellis (1992) identifies the following problems associated with irrigation schemes in a resource-poor environment:

- In some cases large-scale irrigation schemes with intensive capital investments in projects such as dam building can, in resource-poor environments, fail to increase the output of food crops because cash crops are then substituted for food crops. In this way, such schemes can widen the divergence between farm household goals and state goals.

- Irrigation projects may fail to achieve the desired output gains simply because of a shortage of labour at peak periods.
- The operation and maintenance of an irrigation project may prove unsustainable in the face of a collapse of supply lines, or a lack of foreign exchange, while other deficits in relation to fuel, transport, spare parts, cement and so on can also lead to failure.
- Finally, other problems affecting the productivity of farms involved in an irrigation scheme – such as lack of essential purchased inputs and approved seeds, difficulties over crop marketing or poor prices for output – can also undermine the success of a scheme.

The UNDP report (2006: 199) *Beyond Scarcity: Power, Poverty and the Global Water Crisis* concludes that:

> as concern over global water supply and food availability increases, governments should look beyond water scarcity issue, to a wider human development. Giving equity and human development more prominence in the governance of irrigation water management frameworks is a starting point.

The report proposes three main requirements for addressing the challenge at national levels:

1. Prepare a transparent national strategy setting out how water resources will be allocated in the years ahead to provide predictability;
2. Integrate that framework into national poverty reduction strategies and policies to ensure that water policy is aligned with wider human development goals; and
3. Recognise the right to water of poor households with customary entitlements, and enforce the provision of rights by creating institutions which empower the poor. Protecting and extending the water rights of women farmers should be a central priority in all countries.

One of the challenges, according to UNDP (2006: 199), is:

> To develop legal systems that clarify and strengthen existing rights rather than introducing sweeping tradable private property rights. This would provide a basis for the development of equitable

transfer mechanisms. Such mechanisms, used voluntarily and with provisions for compensation, are better for enhancing water security than arbitrary administrative transfers or imperfect markets.

Moreover, public spending on irrigation and water management in many countries has fallen below levels needed to maintain infrastructure (UNDP 2006: 200). 'Current national spending on irrigation financing is estimated at US$30–US$35 billion but is on a steep downward trend' (Cleaver and Gonzalez, in UNDP 2006: 201). 'The same trend applies to development assistance. Although international statistics are unreliable, lending for irrigation and drainage by multilateral agencies fell from US$3 billion annually in the mid-1980s to about US$2 billion in the mid-1990s, with no recovery since (ibid 200). No doubt the global financial crisis put further pressure on donors to provide assistance in this regard.

'In view of the growing pressure on water systems and the threats of global climate change, it is important to reverse this trend. Private finance and public spending by governments will have to provide the primary impetuses. But aid also has a role. The World Bank estimates that donor support over the next 20 years will need to double, to around US$4 billion annually'(World Bank, in UNDP 2006: 200). Moreover, UNDP (2006: 200) emphasizes that aid to low-income agriculture-based countries in sub-Saharan Africa should be a priority for donor support as part of a wider set of measures to support small-scale agriculture and rural development.

As governments develop water management strategies for dealing with water scarcity it is important that pro-poor technologies and other interventions – such as promoting micro-irrigation technology, support to microfinance and public investment in infrastructure – should figure prominently.

Progress towards household water security for all requires a fuller understanding of the multiple characteristics and functions of water as a natural resource to be managed, but also as an economic commodity to be optimised and a human entitlement to be fulfilled (Webb et al. 2005: 15). Webb et al. (2005: 15) state that:

Water and food are two of the necessities of life, and the two are inextricably linked. Just as food security cannot be achieved for all simply by making food available, enhancing the supply of water to under-served countries will not suffice where household's water security is concerned. On the one hand, targeting the needs of least served households is essential since these hundreds of millions of people bear the brunt of the economic, nutritional, and health deprivations that go along with low water consumption. This is a development priority of the highest order that involves enhancing access to clean water but also enhancing access to water for smallholder agriculture (rain-fed and ground water management as well as smaller-scale irrigation).

Moreover, the achievement of good water quality is 'crucial not only to reducing the huge global burden of water-related diseases, but also to maintaining the ecological integrity of fragile, as well as presently highly-productive ecosystems' (Webb et al. 2005: 15). Chapter 9 further examines the topic of gender and food security.

9
Gender[1] and Food Security: Invisibility Revisited

Almost all the literature on the issue of gender and food security is in agreement that in most countries women's contribution to agricultural and rural development, and to food security, is not considered in the formulation and implementation of agricultural policies (see, Ellis 1992; Deere 2005; Lastarria 2006; World Bank, FAO and IFAD 2009). This is despite the fact that they cultivate more than half of all the food grown worldwide. For example, in South Asia women provide up to 90 per cent of the labour for rice cultivation; in sub-Saharan Africa they produce up to 80 per cent of food production, both for household consumption and for sale. They perform 25 to 45 per cent of agricultural field tasks in Colombia, Peru and the Caribbean and in these countries produce up to 80 per cent of basic foodstuffs. In Egypt, women constitute 53 per cent of the agricultural labour force (Karl 2009).

The productivity of women farmers is constrained by the same factors that affect small agricultural producers in general, but it is compounded by gender-specific factors in relation to inequality in access to land, to other farm resources and services, to markets, inputs, and to formal credit services. In addition they experience their own specific constraints as they try to juggle their productive and reproductive roles[2] (FAO 2007c; IFAD 2009; World Bank, FAO and IFAD 2009).

Women's contribution to agricultural production varies from country to country, from crop to crop, and from task to task. It also varies in relation to farm size, levels of technology used, and levels of engagement with local, regional or international markets. Often women and men share or divide tasks in the production of certain crops, but sometimes they have distinct tasks or responsibilities for different crops or livestock (Karl 2009: 14).

In general, women play an important and multi-faceted role in food security: they are food producers, keepers and transmitters of traditional farming knowledge, food processors, and food providers for their families (see, ILO 1981; Dixon-Mueller 1985;

Becker 2000; Karl 2009). They also suffer disproportionately from food insecurity. The World Food Programme Report (WFP 2009: 4) reveals that 'gender inequality is a major cause and effect of hunger and poverty, it is estimated that 60 per cent of chronically hungry people are women and girls and 20 per cent are children under five'.

> Gender-based inequalities[3] occur all along the food production chain, 'from farm to plate', impeding the attainment of food and nutritional security. Thus, maximising the impact of agricultural development on food security entails enhancing women's roles as agricultural producers as well as the primary care takers of their families. (World Bank, FAO and IFAD 2009: 2)

Unfortunately, there is a shortage of gender-specific statistics identifying women's and men's specific situations, and quantifying their respective economic and social contributions (especially in the agricultural sector), and this is a major constraint in relation to policy development and resource allocation. Despite their acknowledged contribution to food production, women's work remains largely undervalued and underestimated in national income accounts (Scanlan 2004: 1809).

This chapter addresses two central concerns: first, how do women contribute to agricultural development and food security? Second, what are the implications of agricultural policies on women's contribution to food security? The chapter deals with rural women's invisibility in the context of the legal, social and economic forces that determine national development and agricultural policies, which results in the undervaluing of women's contribution in national income. It also examines the extent of feminisation of agricultural production both in non-traditional agricultural crops and in smallholder agriculture. It goes on to explore attempts made by international development agencies to integrate women or to mainstream women's concerns in development processes. Finally, it outlines issues relating to gender and food security and highlights the resulting policy implications.

INVISIBLE RURAL WOMEN

Policymakers must be mindful of the major aspects of socially ascribed gender functions as well as the specific needs of men and women. If development policies are to be sustainable, they must consider existing gender disparities in employment, time allocation, poverty, family life, health, nutrition, education and the environment. In addition, rural women's unequal participation to decision-making processes and institutions – within the household, and at district, regional and national levels – has to be taken into account. As Karl (2009) states:

> It is generally accepted that misguided agricultural and trade policies have contributed to the current food crisis, and these have included a failure to recognise women's roles in agricultural production and household food security.

Despite some improvements in the status of the world's women, gender inequality remains extremely significant in the context of development (Scanlan 2004: 1807). Their unequal status leads to huge contrasts between their enormous contributions to human development, and their small share of its benefits (see, UN 1995; Scanlan 2004: 1809).

Studies show that there are strong links between female empowerment in the family, household food security and family welfare, underlining the importance of pursuing policies that recognise women's rights and acknowledge their contributions to societal well-being (Scanlan 2004: 1809).

Large gender gaps exist in access to education, health and nutrition as well as to public institutions. Women continue to be denied equal opportunities for political and economic participation, and in the laws of many countries women do not enjoy the same protections and rights as men. Discriminatory legislation in many countries limits women's access to land, to credit, and to membership of agricultural cooperatives. Even where legislation does not limit women's rights to land titles and membership in cooperatives, tradition itself may do so (Karl 2009: 17).

According to the FAO (1997: 3–5) rural women in many developing countries have to face many challenges, for example:

- Constitutional challenges: such as recognition of their existence as adults, having equal rights as citizens, the capacity to bring legal actions, and the rights to vote and to be elected;
- Economic challenges: such as equal inheritance rights, the capacity to engage in business, equality of access to land as owners or through guaranteed rights of use, and access to sources of finance; and

- Social challenges: such as equality of access to employment, equality in relation to tasks and wages, equal access to subsidies, welfare and family allowances, and recognition of their multiple roles and status as parents, producers and workers.

Many writers (such as Meillassoux 1997; Droy 1990 and Le Magadoux 1995: 3), agree that women's weak legal status, or their total lack of recognised legal status, can be partially explained in terms of the mechanisms of rural society, which is made up of family groups organised into production units under the supervision and authority of a family head. Since the availability of labour is of primary importance, the survival of the unit is dependent on its members' reproductive capacities. So women of reproductive age are invested with value in this context and become subject, as though they were property, to the law of exchange rather than being recognised as independent and equal citizens.

It is imperative to mention that even when making the assumption that rural households are production units there is a need to assess the detrimental effects of this assumption on food security in terms of intra-household distribution of food and other basic needs, since income earned by the male head of household may not benefit everyone, or enable the household to purchase sufficient food for everyone's needs. In many cases, income is not pooled, yet women remain responsible for supplying the household's food (Karl 2009: 13).

As Le Magadoux (1995: 3) points out:

for women, this situation is manifested in their weak or non-existent legal capacity. It is an exception for women to have authority over management, decision-making and control of resources and property (which, in any case, can only rarely belong to them).

The most critical factor in women's lack of rights concerns land access, ownership and use. Rural women are often excluded from owning this primary production factor through either inheritance systems or land tenure regulations. Land succession rules favour men, and land reforms and laws inadvertently exclude women from rights of access to the land. Usually land ownership and/or land use are awarded to the family head, and in most cases is a man. Although rural women often fulfil this function in the absence of men (through migration, death or divorce) they are still not eligible to hold land, since the law does not recognise their status as family heads in most of sub-Saharan Africa (Ellis 1992; Le Magadoux 1995: 3; FAO 1997).

However, legal recognition of women's rights to land has been increasing. At least 115 countries (UN 2011: 39) now specifically recognise women's land rights and treat them on equal terms with men's rights. Such laws are in place in almost all the countries of Central and Eastern Europe, Central Asia, Latin America and the Caribbean, but in other regions laws that explicitly discriminate against women remain in place. Furthermore:

> even in those countries with laws in place, women's actual control over land is limited. Property laws that guarantee equal rights may have unequal outcomes because they interact with discrimination built into other aspects of the legal framework, particularly on divorce and inheritance. (UN 2011: 39)

Villarreal (in UN 2011: 39) argues that:

> The factors determining who controls land typically involve a complex interplay of different legal systems, state, customary and religious and cultural norms. In some countries in sub-Saharan Africa and Asia, despite constitutional guarantees of women's land rights, customary law is recognised as taking precedence on issues of inheritance and marriage. This means that in the event of marital breakdown or widowhood, the control of marital property rests with husbands and their families.

Le Magadoux (1995: 3) points to the contradiction that all countries set goals of self-sufficiency and food security based on rising food production and productivity, which are in practice the responsibility of women. She asks the question: if women neither have access to land nor are guaranteed rights to its use why should they invest in increasing its productivity?

Women's production responds primarily to the basic demands of individual and family consumption, and not to the food security requirements of the country as a whole. Land is subject to rules on purchase, access and use. Acquisition of capital is subject to rules on guarantees and capacities to enter into trade agreements (Le Magadoux 1995: 4).

DATA DEFICIENCIES: MAINTAINING RURAL WOMEN INVISIBILITY

As mentioned earlier, most studies have acknowledged women's contribution to agricultural production as self-employed producers, unpaid family workers, and as waged workers in both the traditional and non-traditional agricultural sectors. However, official statistics based on census returns and household budget surveys continue to underestimate women's work and their contribution to national wealth.

Research from Latin America indicates that data regarding women's work in agriculture are deficient, inadequate and even conflicting (see, Deere 2005; Lastarria 2006: 15). Whitehead (2008), studying sub-Saharan Africa, identified a number of contributory factors in the persistent undercounting and under-reporting of women's work, including:

- The problem of the definition of work: census officials generally define work in monetary terms, thus excluding unpaid family (mostly women's and children's labour), which results in underestimating women's earning potential and undercalculating their contribution to national income;
- In many countries, a woman's identity card may indicate her status simply as 'housewife', not a producer in their own right. In addition, as noted by Whitehead (2008) and Lastarria (2006: 16), some women are reluctant to report their contribution to the household's agricultural production or role in decision-making processes (except in the case of female-headed households);
- Data on 'work' may be limited to work in the fields, thus ignoring home garden work, small animal production, post-harvest storage and processing work, and other income-generating activities usually carried out in the home;
- Finally, the timing of census data-gathering on agricultural production may be significant. Since much of women's agricultural work (both on their own farms and in waged work) is seasonal, it may not always be counted.

Moreover, national development programmes and projects are still not designed to enhance the role of rural women as producers in their own right. Rural women are rarely the beneficiaries of rural services and support.

THE FEMINISATION OF AGRICULTURE

In many countries and regions there has been a trend over several decades towards the so-called 'feminisation of agriculture', or the growing dominance of women in agricultural production and the concomitant decrease of men in the sector (FAO 1997: 10; Deere 2005: iii; Lastarria 2006: 1). This process has been driven by economic and socio-cultural forces and by demographic trends which have brought about temporary as well as permanent shifts in women's tasks and responsibilities depending on the type of women's work and duration of involvement (World Bank, FAO and IFAD 2009).

According to Lastarria (2006: 17):

> The implementation of neo-liberal economic policies [that is, stabilisation and structural adjustment lending programmes of the IMF and the World Bank] in Latin America in the early 1980s and in sub-Saharan Africa in the mid 1980s, and trade liberalisation with agricultural policies that favour export crops, promotion of high-value horticultural crops and support for agribusiness provided a growing demand for wage labour.

Moreover, studies show that the devaluation of national currencies as part of structural adjustment programmes has resulted in higher input costs, lower farm-gate prices, and significant rationing of access to credit and extension services for the smallholder sector which produces food for local and regional markets. Increasing land concentration in Latin America and the beginning of land scarcity in sub-Saharan Africa compounds the impact of these policies (Deere 2005; Lastarria 2006; Whitehead 2008). Therefore, the decline in the profitability of food production and growth of rural poverty has forced low income and low asset rural households to seek other income sources (off-farm employment) in order to maintain the household's food security and other basic needs (Deere 2005: iii; Lastarria 2006).

However, women more than men are increasingly taking responsibility for household survival and responding to economic opportunities in commercial agriculture (Deere 2005: iii). 'The labour intensive nature of horticultural production motivated the industry to hire women workers who command lower wages, particularly in the rural sector' (Lastarria 2006: 2–4).

The other set of forces that have influenced the extent of the feminisation of agriculture are gender relations and the gender division of labour.[4]

> The global market and international competition have driven product prices down, keeping wages low but more importantly, keeping the labour market flexible. Lower wage rates and flexible employment conditions for women have contributed to the growth of agribusiness production and export of high-value crops. (Lastarria 2006: 17)

For example, men's greater mobility and migration in search of lucrative employment off the farm, along with the depredations of HIV and AIDS in sub-Saharan Africa, have also encouraged this trend. In some areas the feminisation of agriculture has altered the viability of labour for producing crops, which in turn may alter cropping patterns, tasks and crop technologies that were the traditional preferences of men and women (Lastarria 2006: 18; Whitehead 2008; World Bank, FAO and IFAD 2009). However, the World Bank, FAO and IFAD (2009: 523) point out that:

> Migration can provide additional cash to invest in crop agriculture and facilitate a move from subsistence to more commercially oriented agricultural systems. These shifts can offer new opportunities for women but can also imply cultural changes and a redefinition of gender roles in crop production.

Evidence from Latin America and Africa points to the fact that women themselves are often the ones who migrate in search of employment, which again has significant consequences for crop production and should be considered when formulating agricultural policies (Deere 2005; World Bank, IFAD and FAO 2009: 523).

Differential access to assets and resources by men and women can also affect women's bargaining positions within the household and in labour markets. For example, well-endowed agricultural producers with access to assets and resources such as credit, technology and product markets are in a position to benefit from more liberalised markets. 'Women, with decreased access to resources, are not able to participate equitably in these liberalised markets, except as wage labour and unpaid family labour' (Lastarria 2006: 18).

The feminisation of non-traditional agricultural production

Lastarria (2006: 3–8) suggests that it is useful to locate women's work in agriculture within the broader agricultural context. In broad terms, export agriculture in developing countries has shifted from traditional export crops grown on plantations, such as coffee, sugar and cocoa, to more labour-intensive horticultural crops such as vegetables, fruits and flowers. She indicates that:

> Demand for women's labour in non-traditional or high value crop export production has increased but their working conditions in this sector are characterised by insecurity, long working hours, environmental health hazards, low wages, and limited opportunities for training and skill development. The competition among agri-business firms, particularly horticultural export firms, pressures them to reduce costs by hiring unskilled women as casual workers at low wages and without social benefits. Little or no advance notice is given when workers are laid off. (ibid 2006: 3–8)

Moreover, the World Bank, FAO and IFAD (2009: 344) point out that:

> Occupational segregation in plantation agriculture is standard practice. Many of the tasks are divided according to physical strength, but another division is related to the use of equipment. Men are usually accorded jobs that involve training and use of light or heavy equipment. This segregation leaves women in lower-paying positions and provides them with limited upward mobility.

Deere (2005: 30–7), reviewing numerous case studies in Latin America and Africa, came to the same conclusions as Dolan and Sutherland (2002: 29–33) and others, namely that:

- Women are employed in labour-intensive types of tasks generally earning lower wages than men and are more likely to be paid at piece rates;
- Workers, including women in packaging and processing plants, earn more than field workers and have better working conditions. Their work is nonetheless hard, often involving

long hours of standing and long work days during peak
seasons; and

- Women form a labour reserve for this type of production,
  and are the main providers of temporary, seasonal and casual
  labour, while men occupy the majority of permanent jobs, as
  well as administrative and supervisory positions.

The feminisation of smallholder production

There is also strong evidence in some countries of the feminisation
of smallholder production. National data and local case studies
from Latin America and sub-Saharan Africa indicate that women
are assuming more responsibility in agricultural production, either
as principal farmers or as unpaid family workers (see, Deere 2005;
Lastarria 2006). This trend is associated with an increase in the
proportion of rural women who are heads of households, as well
as with male migration and/or employment in off-farm work and
with the decreased viability of peasant farming under neoliberal
policies (Deere 2005: iii).

In smallholder agriculture there has been little change in the
gender division of labour within the household in regard to
reproductive household tasks. Men on the other hand are not
involved in household tasks, even though women's participation
in both on-farm and off-farm productive activities is increasing
(Lastarria 2006: 3–8).

However, various studies have indicated that the demand for
women's labour in rural areas varies according to the land tenure
system, the commodity being produced, the degree of integration of
agriculture into the market economy, and the level of male migration.
In households where agricultural production is integrated into the
market economy, women's participation tends to be relegated to
manual tasks such as weeding, cleaning and conveying crops from
fields to stores. But in an advanced economy, where farm operations
are highly mechanised, women are often engaged in the business side
of agricultural production such as paying bills or keeping records
(Bne Saad 1990).

Nevertheless, women's increased contribution to the cash income
of smallholder households does not seem to alter the gendered
division of labour. Rural women provide their unpaid time for
both food production and cash crops within the household in an
attempt to secure the household's food needs. In fact, their work
on cash crops increases their overall work burden since they are
still responsible for food production, domestic chores and bearing

and rearing children. This may have significant effects on family welfare as studies have found that women's food production is in fact reduced.

RURAL WOMEN'S PARTICIPATION IN DECISION MAKING

Research into the contribution of women to agricultural and food production and their role in decision making within the family and community indicate that there is a positive relationship between women's waged work and their status in the household. It appears that women who work off-farm as waged workers and receive their own wages directly have more control over how this income is allocated, and therefore have more power in household decision-making (Lastarria 2006: 12; World Bank, FAO and IFAD 2009: 345).

However, the 'employment versus empowerment' debate is difficult to resolve in the context of high-value agricultural industries. Employment does engender some tangible gains for women, who often obtain access to an independent income stream, increased autonomy and new social networks, and in some cases employment can also bring access to education, health care and training, all of which further bolster women's empowerment (Lastarria 2006: 12).

Bne Saad (1987) studied 200 farm households from three villages south of Baghdad which were engaged in vegetable production, a sector where women in Iraq make a substantial contribution. She found that the vast majority of farm decisions were made by the women's husbands, and their own degree of involvement in farm decision-making was very low. Those women who were involved in farm decisions were younger, educated to post-primary level, had small numbers of dependent children and were also involved in women's groups. These were the women who had an almost equal share with their husbands in the decision-making process.

In fact women in general, and rural women in particular, are rarely involved in policymaking and planning at the macro-level, intermediate level or micro-level. Rural women face barriers in access to decision making, both at household, community and national levels. There are very few, if any, represented at community committees or at national assemblies. They have little or no control over child bearing as many factors influence their decision on the number of children they can have (such as religious belief, husbands, government policy on family planning and so on), and have minimum education and training levels because of the lack of awareness in rural areas of the value of women's education. They also, as discussed in earlier chapters, experience barriers in relation to access to legal assistance and resources (land, credit, inputs, technology, advice, membership of cooperatives and associations).

Getting more women into policymaking and into research institutions is an important step towards bringing gender issues into clear focus in national strategies and policies. For example, in Uganda women are particularly visible in national politics due to affirmative action programmes, which have also contributed to their participation in regional political decision-making. Women hold four of the Ugandan representative positions in the East African Legislative Assembly (EALA) and there are two women among the five Ugandan members of the African Parliament.

In Uganda the affirmative action phase has come to an end since new enabling laws deriving from the 1995 Constitution were put in place, mainly as a result of the activism of women's groups. These are: (1) the Land Act of 1998, which provides for the protection of the land rights of the poor, the majority of whom are women; and (2) the Local Government Act of 1997, which explicitly states that women shall form one-third of the membership of all local councils at all levels. As a result, the proportion of women in local councils rose from 6 per cent in the early 1990s to 44 per cent in 2003 (Bantebya-Kyomuhendo, in World Bank, FAO and IFAD 2009: 38–9).

POLICY APPROACHES TO WOMEN IN DEVELOPMENT

There are abundant resources, frameworks and tools available which aim to 'incorporate', 'integrate' and 'mainstream gender' into the development process. Most of these resources, since the 1950s, have been designed and formulated by both bilateral and multilateral donors' development agencies based on their experience working with women in developing countries. These agencies were motivated by the fact that women make up half of the world population, and thus there is need to highlight their concerns about the impact of the development processes on their lives and attempt to integrate and enhance their contribution to the welfare of their families and societies. Caroline Moser (1989), in her article 'Gender planning in the third world: meeting practical and strategic gender needs', provides a critical analysis of these approaches from the 1950s to 1990s.

One of the earliest policy approaches to 'women in development' (WID) was the 'welfare' approach. It originated in the 1950s, in the social welfare policies of colonial administrations, and was associated with the modernisation and economic growth model of development. It aims to bring women into development as well-informed mothers and wives, as this was seen as their most important contribution to development. It recognises the reproductive role of poor women and attempts to facilitate women's practical gender needs (in food, basic literacy skills, water, health and family planning). Women are seen as passive beneficiaries of development aid as it focuses on their capacity to regenerate the household's human capital, focusing on their reproductive role (Moser 1989). It is still popular in many low-income countries and among poorer communities.

From 1975 to 1985 the next WID approach, that of 'equity', came about at the same time as the drive for modernisation through accelerated economic growth had failed to achieve any tangible progress in most developing countries. It coincided with the launch of the first UN Decade for Women in Development in Mexico City (19 June to 2 July 1975). Women in this approach are seen as active participants in development. Thus an attempt was made to promote equality between men and women through 'top-down' state interventions intended to facilitate women's participation in a country's political and economic activities. Critics argue that this approach has identified women's subordinate position in relation to men but has proved extremely challenging for developing countries to implement due to traditional attitudes and macroeconomic constraints (ibid).

The third approach to women in development, the 'anti-poverty' approach, has been less controversial. It has been linked to 'basic needs' projects, which are partly implemented by national governments and donor agencies, and focuses on poverty as a problem of underdevelopment not as a result of gender inequalities and women's subordination. From the 1970s onward, most projects implemented at the time in developing countries were intended to increase women's productivity and facilitate their involvement in small-scale income-generating activities. Unfortunately, many of these small-scale projects were under-resourced in terms of both finance and staffing, and lacked market foresight, which resulted in unsustainable outcomes (ibid).

The worldwide economic downturn in the mid-1980s, which particularly affected developing countries from sub-Saharan Africa to some countries in Latin America and South East Asia, and the implementation of economic adjustment and stabilisation policies, provided the environment for the launch of the fourth approach to women in development: the 'efficiency' approach. This has focused on improving women's capacity to increase on-farm production and off-farm contribution to supplement family's income. In this approach, women's unpaid work in agriculture and in caring for a household's welfare is seen to be crucial in securing the household's basic food needs, as well as covering its health and education costs in order to make up for government cuts in public expenditures on social services such as health and education in addition to the removal of subsidies on food and other essential items. Women themselves are seen in terms of their delivery capacity and their ability to extend their working hours (ibid).

Policies for empowering women – politically, economically and socially – have been on the agendas of developing country governments and international development agencies since the UN declaration of the three Decades for Women in Development (1975–1995). During that period, collaboration intensified between women's organisations and development agencies in order to address the limitations of the equity, efficiency and anti-poverty approaches, and their attempt to integrate women into the development process.

During the above period the 'empowerment' approach emerged, based on a new analysis of the position of women in the developing world. It focuses on women's subordination, which is seen as the result of inequality between men and women and of policies and attitudes inherited from the colonial and post-colonial (or neo-colonial) political and economic order. Women's groups and feminist writers in developing countries called for grassroots mobilisation and greater self-reliance, and they demanded equality between men and women in access to assets and resources. This approach, however, posed challenges to both governments and development agencies, including NGOs, as it implies the need for significant changes in national legislations in order to recognise women's equal rights as citizens, their capacity to bring legal actions, and their rights both to vote and to be elected. Other rights were identified as in need of recognition: the right to inherit, the capacity to engage in business, equality in access to land (as owners or through guaranteed rights of use), and access to sources of finance such as credit and to technology.

The UN Nairobi Conference in 1985 (15–26 July) launched the second 'UN Decade for Women in Development'. At this conference a group of women activists and academics from developing countries were organised into a new group of women from the South, who put forward a strategy for Development Alternatives with Women for a New Era (DAWN). They reject the idea of separating women's personal needs from the political processes that denied them their rights to equal participation in development. They emphasise the need to empower men and women through a holistic and bottom-up approach to development, incorporating social, political and cultural factors. Their work reflects the awareness of women in the South regarding a need for strategic alternative to the ongoing development theories and processes which place the drive for profits before the needs of the people.

DAWN's strategy has three main goals: (1) reclaiming the state for the benefit of the majority, and challenging the markets to be socially responsible; (2) building state institutions and strengthening civil societies; and (3) giving special attention to the role of the women's movement. They state that reducing social inequalities is dependent on restructuring existing economic, social, legal and political arrangements at both national and global levels.

DAWN emphasise the roles and needs of both genders, rather than the needs of women as a separate group, and thus provide the basis for the 'gender and development' (GAD) approach. This approach focused on designing programmes based on disaggregated data and analysing the role played by men and women in the development processes of their households and communities and on their practical and strategic needs. According to Moser (1989), the GAD approach is potentially groundbreaking for long-term development as it demands a huge reassessment of development from all angles.

The third UN World Conference on Women, Action for Equality, Development and Peace (4–15 September 1995 in Beijing, China),[5] proposed 12 Priority Areas of Concern representing an important acknowledgement of the complexity of the problems faced by women and their societies in the drive to achieve equality. These are: (1) poverty reduction; (2) promoting education and training; (3) improving access to health care and related services; (4) the elimination of violence against women; (5) special attention and policies to protect women living in situations of conflict and under foreign occupation; (6) pro-poor economic structures and policies; (7) sharing of power and decision making between citizens and the state, and between men and women; (8) provision of mechanisms including funding for the advancement of women; (9) protection of human rights; (10) improving access to communication systems; (11) improving management of natural resources; and (12) protecting the rights of female children.

Finally, as the world of both genders entered the new millennium in 2000, a further new approach was emerging: 'gender mainstreaming'. This happened in response to the slow progress on many of the UN objectives (adopted throughout the three UN Decades for Women in Development).

GENDER MAINSTREAMING

The new policy approach, gender mainstreaming (GM), has generated volumes of source books and material resources advising governments and practitioners alike. It proposes to mainstream gender concerns through a country's poverty reduction strategies, and also urges the alignment of efforts by governments and development agencies, including NGOs, in the hope of achieving greater aid effectiveness in both government development programmes and donors' development intervention efforts.

GM is defined by the UN (1997: 9) as:

> A strategy for making women's as well as men's concerns and experiences an integral dimension of the design, implementation, monitoring and evaluation of policies and programmes in all political, economic and societal spheres so that women and men benefit equally and inequality is not perpetuated. The ultimate goal is to achieve gender equality.

There is no doubt that good analytical work about the role of gender in agricultural development can lead to more and better treatment of agricultural issues in policy debates, which in turn can result in more and better projects and programmes, whether implemented by national development agencies or in partnerships involving international development agencies. However, Karl (2009: 15) contends that:

> Gender analysis, tools and [frameworks] alone are insufficient to enable women to optimise their contribution to food security. A gender perspective that is the views of both women and men must be taken into account. Women must have the opportunity to express their views and bring their perspectives into development and food security policies and programmes. There must be equitable participation of women in decision making and policy making.

Karl (2009: 15-6) also points out that:

- Feminism has brought a greater depth of understanding about gender. Gender roles and needs intersect and are intertwined with other factors such as race, class and ethnicity that affect or even determine the conditions faced by men and women, and their opportunities and choices;
- GM has sometimes had the unintended effect of marginalising women in development programmes, as in most cases resources allocated to gender programmes were miniscule, leaving women isolated in small income-generating projects tacked on to larger development programmes;
- GM by development agencies has tended to ignore the bigger and more complex realities of gender concerns within the community and in the country as a whole;
- GM overlooks the importance of taking the first step, which is to empower women to participate in decision making and policymaking, through bringing about changes in structures and attitudes, as well as new legislation. Keeping in mind the fact that women's empowerment should come from themselves, they need to organise themselves in groups to raise their knowledge and awareness, build solidarity and mobilise;
- Feminists have strongly criticised the notion of mainstreaming women into a patriarchal model of development, arguing that this could mean the drowning of women's concerns in the 'male stream'.

Karl (2009: 17) argues that 'only if women enter the mainstream in sufficient numbers and with sufficient strength and ability to challenge and change the mainstream, does it make sense to mainstream women'.

Moreover, greater attention should be paid to the factors that influence policymaking in relation to mainstreaming gender into agricultural policies and programmes in any given country, which will include: (1) the country's political system; (2) interest groups with power and authority; (3) technical experts with access to privileged information; (4) inherited policies and practices from previous years when there is need to look for innovative solutions to deal with a problem – policymakers rarely chose radically different solutions; and (5) the influence and impact of international financial institutions (IFIs) such as the policies of the World Bank and the

International Monetary Fund (IMF), which can affect gender mainstreaming efforts either positively or negatively.

Furthermore, Karl (2009: 15) calls mainstream economic models and development policies into question because they continue to promote large-scale commercial agriculture to the detriment of small food producers:

> Agriculture and trade are increasingly dominated by large agro-industrial corporations which control crop, livestock and fishery production, food processing and marketing as well as seeds, fertilisers, pesticides, and farm and fishery equipment. Transnational Companies are also taking over millions of hectares of land in developing countries for the purpose of converting them to the production of monoculture of a single crop to promote industrial biofuels. As a consequence, millions of peasants and small farmers, especially women food producers, are losing the ability to produce and provide food for their families.

GENDER AND THE MILLENNIUM DEVELOPMENT GOALS

In the year 2000, at the UN General Assembly, the heads of all states pledged their commitment to the Millennium Development Goals (MDGs), which aim by 2015 to: halve hunger and extreme poverty; achieve universal primary education; promote gender equality and empower women; reduce child mortality; improve maternal health; combat HIV/AIDs, malaria and other diseases; ensure environmental sustainability; and enhance global partnerships for development.

Much has happened since the declaration of the MDGs, including the global financial crisis, the food price crisis and the famines in Somalia. However, with three years left before 2015 the world is nowhere near achieving the targets of the World Food Summit (WFS, 13–17 November 1996) and the first MDG of halving hunger and extreme poverty. On the contrary, hunger levels are increasing around the world (see Chapter 1).

Most research points to the fact that gender inequality is a major cause and effect of hunger and poverty. To Antrobus (2003) the MDGs are major 'distraction gimmicks' – distractions from the much more important Beijing Platform for Action with its 12 Priority Areas of Concern, representing a much closer approximation to the complexity of the relationships between male and female equality and empowerment (third MDG) and the other MDGs and targets.

According to Antrobus (2003: 2) the establishment of the MDGs provided a common framework, agreed by all governments, with measurable targets and indicators of progress around which governments, UN agencies, IFIs and civil society alike could rally. They also provided 'a strategic talking point for assessing the barriers to the achievement of these goals, and ... a tool with which to hold donor agencies and governments accountable'. However, she also highlights some of their limitations: (1) their inadequate targets and indicators;[6] (2) their restriction to indicators that are quantifiable, when much of what is most important – such as women's equity and empowerment – is not easily quantifiable; (3) their omission of important goals and targets, such as violence against women and sexual reproductive rights; and (4) their silence on the contexts and institutional environments in which they are to be achieved.

Another crucial point concerning women's contributions to agricultural development, and to national and household food security, is that the MDGs fail to monitor and protect women's rights to own or co-own land and their rights of access to all available resources (including financial and technical resources), which are necessary if they are to achieve economic independence and to cope with the demands associated with their roles and responsibilities. Since food security is a cross-cutting issue, there is a need to monitor and evaluate national policies of health, education, employment and trade, and to analyse their implications for agricultural policy in general and gender roles and needs in rural areas in particular.

GENDER AND FOOD SECURITY: POLICY IMPLICATIONS

Ellis (1992: 316) highlights the fact that national food and nutrition policies are often handled by different state agencies at central government level, in addition to various international development agencies. For example, domestic agricultural production is almost always handled by the ministry of agriculture, while nutrition strategies may be located in the ministry of health. Public employment schemes or food-for-work projects may be in the domain of the ministry of labour or the ministry of public works. The effort of coordinating the food security activities of all these agencies is considerable and seldom achieved, except perhaps in food disaster situations.

This chapter is about mainstreaming rural women's concerns into agricultural and food policies. Thus it is about identifying how women's roles and needs differ from those of men so that policies are devised to take into account the different circumstances of both women and men. Kandiyoti (in Ellis 1992: 297) argues that:

> The reasons for taking the role and status of women seriously in the formulation of food policies are not just ones of moral indignation concerning the subordinate status of women or the erosion of their dignity in the development process, although many would argue that these were grounds enough. The neglect of gender sometimes results in policy outcomes that fall short of their intentions, and may even be negative in the sense that policy reduces rather than increases the living standards of those it is designed to assist.

Ellis (1992: 286–90) proposes a dual-purpose framework for organising ideas about the impacts of agricultural policies on women's roles and needs in rural areas. One purpose is to trace why similar types of policy have different impacts on women in different places, the other is to provide an organising principle for taking women into account in the design of such policies. Within this framework there are six elements by which households can be distinguished one from another:

1. *Household's social status*: which can be characterised by identifying indicators relating to whether a household is: (i) more than self-sufficient in food, (ii) less than self-sufficient in food, (iii) landless, and (iv) a household headed by women or men. The impact of agriculture policies, on households that *hire out* labour – categories (ii) and (iii) – is likely to be quite different from the impact on households that *hire in* labour. Likewise, policy impacts will vary between male-headed and female-headed households. For example, the material welfare of women if they are in food self-sufficient households may be improved by labour-saving technology, but the reverse is true for women in landless households.
2. *Time allocation patterns*: for various tasks carried out by men and women (on-farm, off-farm/productive, household reproductive role and others).
3. *Resource ownership and control*: data should be collected and disaggregated on the basis of who owns what and who controls what, in terms of resources such as land, capital (working and fixed), water and labour.

4. *Control over income and its distribution*: Ellis (1992) argues that increasing male control over cash income, often the result of the increased integration of peasant households into the market economy promoted by government policies, by no means ensures rising living standards for women and children. It is for this reason that many writers advocate the adoption of policies that seek to raise women's income directly. Gender-oblivious policies cannot be guaranteed to improve the conditions of women, even if they generate more income for the household.

5. *The gender division of labour in relation to marketing and processing*: this is an important feature determining the outcomes for women of various agricultural policies. Post-harvest processing of food in some societies is a major task for women, and is often time consuming and repetitive. Technology that reduces the drudgery of food processing can be beneficial to women by releasing time for other activities, but this technology can also reduce employment opportunities for landless women. The impact of technical changes in food processing, like so many other changes, cannot be discussed in isolation from the social conditions in a particular place.

6. *The impact of market and relative prices of inputs and outputs*: these elements are discussed below from the point of view of the impacts of food policy on various types of rural households. In analysing the impacts of agricultural policies on women one needs to investigate a number of things: how labour markets set the market wage for men and women; how output markets set the prices for crops produced by men and women or by both jointly (for example cash crops versus food crops); and how input markets determine the availability and cost of the various inputs that are most needed by both men and women or for each enterprise separately.

Ellis's framework is very useful in both the short term and long term as it is intended to facilitate data collection and analysis. On this basis the impacts of agricultural policies on women's gender roles and needs can be interpreted, and lessons can be applied in order to improve the efficiency and effectiveness of including gender in agricultural and food policies and processes.

Moreover, for the purpose of facilitating research and data collection with the objective of mainstreaming gender concerns in agricultural production and food security policies, and on which an analysis of gender issues should be based, the World Bank, FAO and IFAD (various years) propose five clusters of indicators: (1) a context matrix, which refers to the factors limiting or facilitating gender-equal participation in development processes; (2) an activity matrix, which helps identify who does what within the household and community; (3) a resources matrix, which defines women's and men's access to and control over resources and income; (4) a needs matrix, which identifies the particular needs and priorities of men and women; and (5) an action matrix, which defines mechanisms that could be introduced in project design and in order to reduce gender inequities.

RURAL WOMEN'S VOICE

Finally, a group of women farmers, peasants and indigenous women food producers from every region of the world participated in a Rural Women's Workshop, which was organised by Isis International, Via Campesina and the People-Centred Development Forum, in advance of the World Food Summit in Rome in 1996. These women, according to Karl (2009: 18-9), 'deplored their exclusion from the process of food policy deliberation and formulation and declared that food is a human right'. They drew up a statement for action and proposed seven key strategies to ensure food security. They call upon world leaders to give it due consideration in their national development strategies and policies:

1. The democratisation of access to resources, especially land, water, seeds and intellectual property;
2. Promotion of sustainable agriculture and community-based resource management;
3. Establishment of local, people-based, trading systems and infrastructure;
4. Empowerment of women through equal representation in decision-making bodies at local, regional, national and global levels;
5. Access to education for women and girls;
6. Access to credit and other financial supports for women;
7. Appropriate education, health, recreation, child care and other infrastructural support systems designed by rural communities with consideration for all genders.

In conclusion this chapter, while drawing on discussions from earlier chapters about the impacts of agricultural policies on gender, is centred on the question of how rural women and their roles can be fully acknowledged and mainstreamed within agricultural and food security policies. At the national level government policies on agriculture, health, education, employment, welfare and food security are inextricably linked. Coordination between all these policies and governmental political and economic commitments is a step towards achieving the target of zero hunger in low-income food deficit countries within a reasonable time frame.

Moreover, the agricultural sectors in each country are dependent on the available natural resources, as well as on national legislations, development strategies and policies, in addition to the institutional capacity that governs those resources. These factors influence women and men in their choice of crops and levels of potential productivity. Most countries set goals of achieving food self-sufficiency and food security, which are in practice the responsibility of women on small farms in developing countries. Policymakers need to be reminded that gender inequality is a major cause and effect of hunger and poverty.

10
Conclusion:
Food Security in Perspective

Hunger is on the increase. Rising food prices have already aggravated poor people's problems of access to food worldwide, and women and the landless in developing countries have suffered disproportionately. They are joined by millions more newly food-insecure people from the urban areas of developing countries (Karl 2009). In the first ten months of 2009 food prices rose by 9.8 per cent, prompting fears of a resumption of the surge that began in 2007 (*Economist* 19 November 2009). The vast majority of urban and rural households in developing countries rely on food purchases for most of their food needs and stand to lose from high food prices. Such high prices reduce real income and worsen the prevalence of food insecurity and malnutrition among the poor by reducing the quantity and quality of food they consume (FAO 2008).

Currently, 1 billion people cannot even satisfy their basic needs in terms of food energy. As *The Economist* (18 February 2012) reported, 'on top of one billion without enough calories, another billion are malnourished in the sense they lack micro-nutrient (this is often called "hidden hunger"). And a further one billion are malnourished in the sense that they eat too much and are obese. It is a damning record: out of a world population of 7 billion, 3 billion eat too little, too unhealthy, or too much'.

However, the 2 billion people who are malnourished and food insecure in terms of not having enough calories are living in hunger 'hot spots'. These are often ecologically fragile areas, and many of them have to cope with conditions of high population pressure and deteriorating ecosystems (FAO 2009a: 6). Much of the natural resource base already in use worldwide shows worrying signs of degradation, such as soil nutrient depletion, erosion, desertification and the depletion of water reserves, with the result that the productivity potential of land, water and genetic resources may continue to decline at an alarming rate (ibid: 8).

However, the rural populations of countries with especially low-incomes can play a vital role in ensuring the enhanced and sustainable management of natural resources. This could help improve sustainable growth and productivity, as well as raise incomes locally and generate public goods at national and international levels, if appropriate institutions and incentive systems are put in place (ibid: 9).

Food security is about the supply of and the demand for food and how food is utilised by household members. On the supply side, there are the three Ps: food and agricultural policy, crop patterns and food production. On the demand side, there are the three As: availability, access and ability to utilise food (CUTS (Consumer Unity and Trust Society) 1998).

The most comprehensive definition of food security is provided by the NGO Global Forum, and was drawn up at the United Nations Conference on Environment and Development (UNCED), Rio de Janeiro, 3–14 June 1992 (Fowler in CUTS 1998: 2):

> Food security is having the means as an individual, family, community, region or country adequately to meet nutritional needs on a daily and annual basis. It includes freedom both from famine and chronic malnutrition. Food security is best assured when food is locally produced, processed, stored and distributed, and is available on a continuous basis regardless of climatic and other variations.

To put this definition into practice, food security policy should be based on disaggregated analysis in respect of the supply of food (domestic food production, food imports and food aid if needed) and the demand for food (income, social safety net, per capita food consumption/kcal) and the utilisation of food (household feeding practices, food preparation methods, diversity of diet, clean water and sanitation, good health, and the intra-household distribution of food disaggregated by age and gender – see Chapter 1).

The political and socio-economic circumstances in any given country influence people's access to and utilisation of food. When a food policy is being designed it must be based on disaggregated indicators describing the livelihoods of various social groups, both urban and rural, especially those at risk of inadequate access to food. These groups are likely to be the unemployed or those depending on casual labour for their survival. They may be landless or own some land, but barely sufficient for family subsistence. They may be farmers in drought-prone zones who regularly confront the borderline between survival and starvation in pursuit of a livelihood. In most cases they will be amongst the poorest groups in the population (Ellis 1992: 309).

The issue of food availability has to be considered at all levels – international, national, household and individual – and should apply to all people, at all times (Ellis 1992; CUTS 1998: 3):

- At international level food availability is strongly influenced by global supply and demand, as well as by patterns of food trade between countries and volatility in world prices for staple crops. A central issue is the degree to which world food output keeps pace with world population growth. A related concern is geographical variation in food surpluses and deficits.
- At national level it is strongly influenced by stability of domestic food production and a country's ability to import food in times of shortages.
- At district level marketing and transport problems in low-income developing countries often inhibit the effective implementation of food distribution policy, as it is strongly influenced by the capacity of both the state and private sector to deliver a timely response to market demand.
- The household is the basic unit of consumption and production, especially for smallholder farmers and in rural areas generally. The distribution and utilisation of food within a household are important elements of its food security.
- It is also crucial to consider the individual level, because gender inequalities within a family often result in the food insecurity of women and children (especially girls).

In terms of global food supply, very large increases in production will be necessary to feed the future 9 billion people who will inhibit the earth in 2050 – and whose per capita income is likely to increase, particularly in the emerging economies of the developing world. It is estimated that annual cereal production will need to rise to about 3 billion tonnes from the 2.1 billion tonnes produced in 2011, and annual meat production will need to rise by over 200 million tonnes to reach 470 million tonnes (assuming current consumption patterns). The FAO report 'How to feed the world in 2050' (2009a: 2) argues that:

The required increase in food production can be achieved if the necessary investment is undertaken and policies conducive to agricultural production are put in place. However, increasing production is not sufficient to achieve food security; hunger can persist in the midst of adequate and aggregate supplies because of lack of income opportunities for the poor and the absence of effective social safety nets.

Food shortages affect entitlements primarily via increases in the market price for food, which diminish the purchasing power of the poorest groups in the population who are dependent on market purchasing of food for their survival (Ellis 1992: 308). What matters at the household or individual level is people's ability to access food, and this varies according to the nature and strength of their food entitlements (see Chapter 2). In countries with highly unequal income distribution, widespread unemployment or underemployment and extensive poverty, there can be a high incidence of inadequate nutrition despite the existence of sufficient food at the aggregate level (Ellis 1992: 309).

France, to take one example, is a high-income country with an institutionalised social security system and its agriculture is highly protected. Evidence as far back as 1994 shows that, at national level, French agriculture generated a trade surplus of US$10 billion, yet 3 million people lived in poverty and another 2 million received food aid (CUTS 1998: 4).

Moreover, the United States of America is considered the food basket of the world and yet 11.9 million Americans went hungry in 2008, including 700,000 children. These figures are more than 50 per cent higher than the previous year, and Americans on food stamps exceeded 30 million for first time. Analysts attribute the jump primarily to rising unemployment. Rising food costs are also a factor, which hit 6.5 per cent in October 2008 and was predicted to increase to 8 per cent by the end of 2009 (Black 2008). In fact, unemployment figures rose to 9 per cent in January 2012 (*Guardian* 26 January 2012).

These examples demonstrate clearly that food security and hunger are global issues: in poor countries a large number of people cannot obtain their minimum daily energy requirements, and in rich countries increasing inequality along with rising unemployment are putting more and more people at risk of social exclusion. Overcoming hunger, therefore, is not simply a matter of agricultural production: it is more a question of equitable social and economic policies, and of the political will to carry them out (CUTS 1998: 4).

Despite the fact that during the last two decades world prices for staple grains have tended to decline in real terms, the option of importing food to supplement domestic output was and has become a valid alternative to the pursuit of food self-sufficiency (Donaldson 1984; World Bank 1986: 31; Ellis 1992: 304). However, in light of the recent food crisis, importing food on a significant scale is not a viable economic option for low-income NFIDCs in sub-Saharan Africa and elsewhere, due to the fact that world food prices are highly volatile and because of the expectation – voiced by expert analysts – that food prices are now set for a period of significant and long-lasting inflation.

Moreover, in actuality the acute shortages of foreign exchange, and the logistical problems of moving imported food from points of entry to deficit zones, have instead led many of these countries to establish policies aimed at improving national food self-sufficiency following the successful examples of South and South East Asia.

ECONOMIC AND AGRICULTURAL GROWTH IN AFRICA

Agricultural reforms in agriculture-based countries followed the macroeconomic reforms of the 1980s. They were heavily supported by external donors through policy advice and conditional lending (World Bank 2007). The International Food Policy Research Institute (IFPRI) indicates that:

> a remarkable economic and agricultural recovery has taken place in Africa in the past 10–15 years. Since 2001, the growth rates for African exports – in volume as well as in value terms – have exceeded the world average. As a consequence, Africa's share in the agricultural export market, has stabilised at between 2 and 3 per cent and may even be trending upward again. (IFPRI 2008: 1)

Technical change and efficiency have been cited as significant contributory factors in the productivity growth of Ghana, Mozambique, Nigeria and Uganda, countries where the rate of poverty and the incidence of hunger have fallen significantly. The fact that countries with higher agricultural growth exhibit lower poverty rates is primarily due to higher incomes among farmers, who make up the poorest segment of the population. Moreover, higher incomes in agriculture tend to induce even higher incomes in the rural economy outside of the agricultural sector, as well as in the rest of the economy, and thus reduce poverty among broader sections of the population at large (IFPRI 2008: 2).

It is a striking fact that, over the decade to 2010, six of the world's ten fastest-growing economies were in sub-Saharan Africa. On IMF forecasts, Africa will grab seven of the top ten places in 2015. *The Economist*'s analysis of the past decade indicates that the simple unweighted average of countries' growth rates was virtually identical in Africa and Asia, and anticipates that over the next five years Africa is likely to take the lead, with growth in the average African economy outpacing its Asian counterparts (*Economist* 6 January 2011).

This is a huge achievement for the sub-Saharan African region, but the question is whether this growth can be translated into further investments, both in agriculture and in the types of non-agricultural economic activity which can generate employment opportunities for economically active people who are no longer required as labour in rural areas.

Other crucial questions are: how can this growth be sustained? How can budget allocations be channelled in a meaningful way to reduce vulnerability to the external and internal shocks which disproportionately affect the poor and the food-insecure in these countries? It is also essential to look at the base from which this growth is being generated, including the utilisation of non-renewable resources, and to ask how economic growth correlates with good governance and sound social protection policies.

The IFPRI (2008: 2) states that:

> For the foreseeable future and in the large majority of African countries, agriculture will remain the most important sector in the battle to reduce poverty and achieve food and nutrition security. However, the challenge is to sustain this growth in the medium to longer term and even accelerate it over the next few decades.

To meet the challenge of sustaining growth in the long run, developing countries need to take the initiative and make major internal structural reforms – providing capable small- and medium-sized farmers and more efficient producers and agribusinesses with essential skills, tools and infrastructures. If they can also facilitate private investments they will be better suited to meeting unprecedented threats to national food production (IFPRI 1998: 10).

Moreover, to increase food production developing countries need to increase their annual investment in agriculture by 50 per cent more than their average annual investment of US$142 billion (from public and private sources) in 2009. According to the FAO (2009a: 2), achieving this level of investment will require a major reallocation of national budgets, as well as of donors' funding programmes. However, investment policies must be complemented by policies which will enhance access to food by fighting poverty and establishing effective social safety net programmes for all vulnerable people in both rural and urban areas.

Increased investment, effective regulation and incentives are needed with regard to all three natural resources required for sustainable and stable growth in agricultural production: land, water and human resources. The aim should be to stop over-exploitation, degradation and pollution, promote efficiency gains and expand overall capacities as appropriate. Adequate regulation and incentives are also needed to provide the rural population with the relevant knowledge which can improve the sustainability of the environment, mitigate climate change and improve their incomes (FAO 2009a: 11).

On the demand side, the main social and economic factors driving increasing food demand are population growth, increasing urbanisation and rising income. Despite declining fertility rates in both developed and developing countries it is estimated that there will be 2.3 billion more people in 2050, with the vast majority of this increase taking place in developing countries.

Most estimates suggest that by 2050 more than 70 per cent of the world's population will be urban. Urbanisation, accompanied by income growth, will bring changes in lifestyles and consumption patterns. For example, a diversification of diets is likely to occur as the proportion of grains and other staples in a typical diet decline while the proportion of other food groups – vegetables, fruits, meat, dairy and fish – increase (FAO 2009a: 5-6).

'While the share of urban population is growing, however, rural areas will still be home to the majority of the poor and hungry for quite some time' (ibid: 6). Investments in promoting rural non-farm economic activities have to be part and parcel of any strategy which aims to diversify income sources in order to facilitate a gradual transition to non-farm employment.

NET FOOD IMPORTING COUNTRIES AND WORLD TRADE[1]

Most NFIDCs will continue depending on international trade to ensure their food supply. It is estimated that by 2050 NFIDCs' net imports of cereals will have more than doubled, from the 135 million metric tonnes in 2008–2009 to 300 million metric tonnes (FAO 2009g: 3).

Even so, current trends indicate that hunger will persist into the future, and trust in world grain markets is weak among developing countries and industrial countries alike. Industrialised countries share the blame for the failure to complete the Doha Round of trade talks as they continue to safeguard their national political and economic interests and to subsidise agriculture and food production in addition to biofuels, which have taken large quantities of food crops such as maize, corn and so on out of the food markets.

The collapse of confidence in the international grain market, and fear of future negative trends, has led, since 2007, to around two-thirds of developing countries undertaking some sort of non-market-based measures to support farmers, including tariffs, input subsidies, price intervention and improvements in the operation of their markets (*Economist* 19 November 2009).

Industrial countries have also put in place support policies and protection of their borders costing hundreds of billions of dollars each year, and these are clearly harming agriculture in developing countries. Such policies include price guarantees, income support measures, and input-related and crop insurance subsidies that stimulate national farm production. They also include tariffs and tariff-rate quotas (TRQs) that restrict market access for developing countries, and export subsidies that move high-priced farm products into world markets (von Braun et al. 2004). Furthermore, according to Anderson et al. (2006), 'The global welfare costs of current trade policies fall on both developed and developing countries. Recent estimates show that the global costs of trade tariffs and subsidies would reach about US$100 billion to US$300 billion a year by 2015'. Moreover, about two-thirds of the costs are estimated to come from agricultural tariffs and subsidies (World Bank 2007).

International trade is one of the most important instruments for achieving sustainable development and poverty reduction. However, while trade liberalisation can lead to economic growth, it is not a sufficient condition in itself (FAO 2003; Kirkpatrick 2006). Most writers agree that the expansion and liberalisation of international trade does not guarantee either immediate economic growth or longer-term economic development. Nor will trade necessarily contribute to sustainable development, facilitating economic, social and environmental progress in ways that meet the needs of the present without compromising the ability of future generations to meet their own needs (Kirkpatrick 2006).

The debate on the links between international trade policy and food security has been at the forefront in the development literature, and nowhere has trade liberalisation been more profoundly contested than in the case of agriculture. The question is whether further liberalisation of trade and agricultural policies will help to achieve food security in sub-Saharan Africa and South Asia, where hunger and poverty are the most severe (Matthews 2006).

Proponents of trade liberalisation in agriculture estimate that it has the potential to increase international commodity prices on average by 5.5 per cent for primary agricultural products and 1.3 per cent for processed foods (Anderson et al. 2006). They also estimate that developing countries' share of global agricultural exports will increase by 9 percentage points from 54 per cent to 65 per cent (World Bank 2007). However, not all developing countries will gain, since these are aggregate figures that hide large differences across commodities and, therefore, across countries.

Opponents of trade liberalisation, among them some NGOs, argue that the market-based model for the liberalisation of international trade is not appropriate for developing countries. They emphasise that further liberalisation of international trade by developing countries (that is, opening their borders, price liberalisation and cutting all support and subsidies) will not help them, and is more likely to prevent them from achieving their food security goals and reaching the MDG of halving hunger and extreme poverty by 2015 (Matthews 2006). They also claim that the liberalisation of agriculture has so far mainly benefited larger, more export-oriented, farmers and has led to a concentration of farms, thus marginalising smaller farmers and exacerbating unemployment and poverty levels (ibid).

However, the integration of developing countries into the world economy has increased steadily over the past three decades. Many have opened their economies to international trade and investment as part of a broader development strategy of economic liberalisation. Most developing countries are members of the World Trade Organisation (WTO) and are important stakeholders in WTO negotiations, not only to promote global economic growth, but also to support the economic development of poorer countries through policies appropriate to their needs (Kirkpatrick 2006).

During the fourth WTO Agricultural Ministerial Conference, which launched the Doha Round of multilateral negotiations in November 2001, developing countries articulated their concerns over the WTO 'Agreement on Agriculture' (AoA),[2] asserting that it was 'unbalanced with a skewed set of obligations' (Matthews 2006: 94). They argued that changes to WTO rules were necessary if they were to have the flexibility to implement policies which adequately addressed their issues in relation to food security, rural development and poverty alleviation (Matthews 2006: 94). They urged the most powerful members of the WTO to realise that countries emerging as centres of global growth, and poor countries large and small, would only buy into a rules-based world trade system if they were brought into its decision-making processes. The new 'rules of the game' must be written jointly by rich, middle income, and poor nations (Von Braun et al. 2004). Thus there is a need to move towards a global trading system that is fair and competitive, and that contributes to a dependable market for food (FAO 2009g: 3).

As a result of the argument of developing countries, the Doha Round proposed measures such as the development box, which aimed to exempt particular food security products from further tariff reductions (or indeed from tariff disciplines altogether) in addition to other, more complex, arrangements to safeguard low-income food deficit countries' potential for food security (Matthews 2006).

Global welfare, development and poverty alleviation will be well served if rules-based, multilateral liberalisation of agricultural trade can be achieved in the conclusion of the Doha Round. This would bring gains for developing countries, not just from new market opportunities created multilaterally but from trade-based investment and the technological advances these opportunities induce. Trade policy reform and international assistance to agriculture in poor countries can be complements, rather than alternatives, in the creation of benefits for the poor people who are concentrated in global agriculture (Von Braun et al. 2004).

AID TO AGRICULTURE

The eighth MDG aims to promote and enhance global partnerships for development and poverty reduction. However, if the development assistance policies of developed countries continue to neglect agriculture this will effectively mean accepting the continuation of chronic poverty in the low-income NFIDCs, especially those in sub-Saharan Africa and South Asia – for the next generation if not for longer.

World Bank and OECD data indicate that the share of agriculture in official development assistance (ODA)[3] declined sharply over the last three decades, falling from about 18 per cent in 1979 to 3.5 per cent in 2004. It also declined in absolute terms, from about US$8 billion in 1984 to US$3.4 billion in 2004, with the biggest decline relating to assistance from the multilateral financial institutions, especially the World Bank.

Figures for 2008 show that total ODA devoted to agriculture in sub-Saharan Africa is about US$1.2 billion of the US$22.5 billion overall (OECD 2009). This decline in attention to agriculture is all the more striking because it has happened in the face of rising rural poverty and hunger (World Bank 2007), and represents an inadequate response to need in view of the very high proportion of the population in these countries who depend on agriculture, and the fact that poverty there is predominantly a rural problem.

Among the many complex reasons cited by the 2007 World Bank Report for this decline are:

- Falling international commodity prices that made agriculture less profitable in developing countries, and also induced farmers' groups in donor countries to oppose aid to agriculture;
- Increased competition within ODA priorities (macroeconomic reforms, debt relief for highly indebted developing countries and associated conditions);
- The need for emergency responses to numerous crises;
- A shift to more demand-driven approaches to allocating ODA, reflecting some governments' prioritisation of industrialisation and social development; and
- Opposition from environmental groups who saw agriculture as a contributor to natural resource destruction and environmental pollution.

A more interesting reason is the failed agricultural and rural development efforts of donors in the past, which also influenced donors' expectations (World Bank 2007).

The IFPRI urges the international community to resist redistributing development assistance resources away from the medium- and long-term growth agenda in favour of short-term, high-visibility, but less productive investments (IFPRI 2008: 3). It suggests that there is a need to strike a balance between short-term 'safety-net' interventions and long-term productivity enhancing investments. They state that:

If the economic and agricultural sector performance of the past decades is to be sustained and broadened to accelerate growth and reduce poverty, African countries and their partners need to focus on boosting the supply response to the rise in international food prices during the next two to three years.

Moreover, African countries need to accelerate progress towards meeting the 2004 Maputo 'Declaration Pledge' of a 10 per cent budget allocation to agriculture, and the implementation of comprehensive, long-term sector development programmes. According to the IFPRI (2008: 4):

> Africa's chances of dealing successfully with the world food crisis are much better today than at any other time in the continent's recent past. The strong growth performance of the past 10–15 years provides a solid foundation to build upon and seize the opportunities emanating from the rise in world food prices, which is going to hold for the foreseeable future.

At their meeting in L'Aquila in July, the Group of Eight (G8) large rich economies promised to increase spending on agricultural development by US$20 billion over the next three years. They also promised to revitalise the world trade talks and agreed to conclude the Doha development round. However, it is not clear how much, if any, has been delivered. The amount also falls far short of the US$44 billion that the FAO estimates will be needed each year to end malnutrition. The IFPRI estimates that an annual US$7 billion will be the bill for developing countries to protect agriculture from the impact of climate change. And it excludes the far greater sums developing countries themselves are promising to farming.

Agriculture and food security have become the core of the international agenda, and in 2009 the World Bank increased its spending on agriculture by 50 per cent to US$6 billion. Moreover, the Islamic Development Bank is creating an agriculture department for the first time (*The Economist*, 18 February 2012: 49).

The good news is, according to *The Economist* (18 February 2012: 49), that investing in better nutrition can yield significant returns to national income:

> Fixing micro-nutrient is cheap. Vitamin supplements cost next to nothing and bring lifelong benefits. Every dollar spent promoting breastfeeding in hospital yields returns of between US$5–67. And every dollar spent giving pregnant women extra iron generates

between US$6–14. Nothing else in development policy has such high returns on investment.

However, the question still stands for developing countries' national governments and international donors: how can budget allocations be channelled in a meaningful way to reduce vulnerability to the external and internal shocks which disproportionately affect the poor and the food-insecure in these countries? How much of this new financial commitment by the international community will be channelled in the direction of combating both caloric and micro-nutrient deficiency among the 2 billion people of the world who are suffering from 'the hidden hunger'?

FUTURE CHALLENGES (1): CLIMATE CHANGE

Climate change is one of four major issues that have influenced the debate about food insecurity in developing countries. The others are high food prices, increasing oil prices and the continuing financial crisis. Climate change is broadly caused by the release of greenhouse gases (GHGs) into the atmosphere, bringing about a warming effect which could have potentially serious implications for agriculture across the globe. Among the associated physical impacts are loss of biodiversity, rising sea levels, a greater incidence of drought and flooding, an increasing spread of diseases, shifts in weather patterns, changes in freshwater supply, and an overall increase in extreme weather events. Developing countries are likely to suffer most from climate change, particularly when combined with socio-economic changes – not only are they likely to be worse hit in terms of reduced food production capacity, but they also have fewer resources to absorb shocks and deal with disruptions.

It is important to understand that the vulnerability of food systems is not determined by the nature and magnitude of environmental stress per se, but by the combination of the societal capacity to cope with, and/or recover from, environmental change, coupled with the degree of exposure to stress (Gregory et al. 2005).

Climate change has been on the international agenda since the UN Earth Summit in Rio de Janeiro (3–14 June 1992) and the Kyoto Protocol of the United Nations Framework Convention on Climate Change (UNFCCC). Two major research studies have contributed to the analysis and understanding of the impact of global warming on world agricultural production and food security: the Stern review on *The Economics of Climate Change* (2007) and the report *Climate*

Change 2007 (Pachauri and Reisinger 2007). These studies have raised the international community's awareness and facilitated the ongoing negotiations that led to the United Nations Climate Change Conference, commonly known as the Copenhagen Summit, held in Copenhagen, Denmark (December 7–18 2009).

The Economics of Climate Change states that 'on current trends, average global temperatures could rise by 2–3 per cent within the next fifty years' (Stern 2007: 18-21). This could particularly harm agricultural yields in Africa. Reduced water availability could also threaten productive capacity in some regions of the world. On balance, higher temperatures could reduce global cereal production by perhaps 5 per cent, with production shifting from developing to developed countries. Higher prices are likely to boost supply, but they also affect the purchasing power, and hence nutritional intake, of people in poorer countries (Stern 2007: 18-21).

Studies have estimated that the aggregate negative impact of climate change on African agricultural output in the period 2018–2100 could be between 15 and 30 per cent. Agriculture will have to adapt to climate change, but it can also help mitigate the effects of climate change by conserving biodiversity through reforestation and combating desertification (among other things). In any event, trade represents an important element of climate change adaptation. Already global markets continually incorporate potential and actual impacts of supply disruptions and extreme weather events (for example, El Niño and hurricanes) (ibid: 400-6).

Stern argues that because supply volatility will increase, not reduce, there is a need for well-functioning and widely traded international markets with the capacity to smooth out short-term surpluses and shortages. The incentives for stockholding would increase for traders and countries due to fear of recurrent food shortages. The Stern report is confident that the international market system can handle short-term volatility, and that it is equally well placed to adapt to gradual changes in the pattern of supply and demand over time, whether caused by climate change or other significant demographic and economic developments.

However, although one would wish to share Stern's view and confidence in world trade systems and food markets, so far the evidence does not support it – especially when energy security is competing with food security. Increasing oil prices and investments in the production of biofuel are already putting pressure on food and feed availability worldwide and on existing resources available for food production (that is, land and water) in both developed and developing countries. This is in addition to both the political and economic interests of major producers and countries in deciding their domestic agricultural policies and priorities.

FUTURE CHALLENGES (2): BIOFUELS

Worldwide, rising oil prices and the increasing use of food crops as biofuel have increased anxieties in developing countries that a continuation of such trends will reduce food availability and create instability in world food markets.

In reality, biofuel production based on agricultural commodities increased more than threefold from 2000–2008. In 2007–2008 the total usage of coarse grains for the production of ethanol reached 110 million tonnes, about 10 per cent of global production (FAO 2009a: 3). Looking ahead, the FAO has estimated that demand for biofuels will grow by 170 per cent in the next three years to 2015, a trend strongly reinforced by climate change arising from our use of fossil fuels. As Lester Brown, President of the Worldwatch Institute in Washington, told The Guardian (8 September 2007): 'the competition for grain between the world's 800 million motorists, who want to maintain their mobility, and its two billion poorest people, who are simply trying to survive, is emerging as an epic issue'.

The most dramatic changes in comparative demand are seen in the US Corn Belt, following the government's decision to increase its targeted output of biofuels from 7.5 billion gallons in 2012 to 35 billion in 2017. In 2007, 40 per cent of the highly subsidised US maize crop was sold as fuel rather than food or feed, increasing in price by 50 per cent, while the price of soybeans increased by 30 per cent. The OECD (2006) has indicated that replacing 10 per cent of US motor oil with biofuels would require the cultivation of about one-third of the total cropland currently devoted to cereals, oilseed and sugar crops.[4]

A study by Doornbosch and Steenblik (2007: 10–41), 'Biofuels: is the cure worse than the disease?', outlines the many concerns which are raised by the development of biofuel technology: (1) without subsidies, most biofuels cannot compete on price with petroleum products in most regions of the world; (2) the amount of land they require is substantial, and its use for this purpose has put pressure on food and water prices; (3) food prices are now set for a period of significant and long-lasting inflation as a result of land being diverted to grow energy crops; (4) the current push to expand the use of biofuels is creating unsustainable tensions that will disrupt markets without generating significant environmental benefits (OECD 2006); (5) biofuels could cut energy-related emissions by 3 per cent at most, a benefit achieved at a huge cost which is likely to be unpopular with taxpayers (ibid).

The study also suggests that the cultivation and use of biofuels could cause significant damage to the environment. As long as environmental values are not adequately priced into the market there will be powerful incentives to replace natural ecosystems such as forests, wetlands and pasture with dedicated bioenergy crops. Moreover, the Bioenergy Pact (15 October 2007) between Europe and Africa aims to use the potential for the production of bioenergy in the developing world, and most notably in sub-Saharan Africa, as a lever to create a new development paradigm in which access to energy, energy security and sustainability play key roles. The question is: at what cost (see Chapter 6 on land grabbing)? Enabling Africa to reduce its dependence on foreign oil and bringing carbon emissions down are two different things (OECD 2006).

Research on the impacts of biofuels on the reduction of GHG emissions is progressing but is far from conclusive. The complexity of the assessment is related to many different elements that must be included in the analysis: (1) the type of crop grown; (2) the amount and type of energy embedded in the fertiliser used to grow the crop and in the water used; (3) emissions from fertiliser production; (4) the resulting crop yield and the energy used in gathering and transporting the feedstock to the biorefinery; and (5) alternative land uses and the energy intensity and fuel types used in the conversion process Doornbosch and Steenblik (2007: 10–41). Doornbosch and Steenblik (2007: 10–41) state that, 'we need to wait for second and third-generation technology before judgments are made. But as the transition is made, there is no denying the potentially huge consequences for the world's poorest people as food and fuel compete with one another'.

CONCLUSION

In light of the above discussions, food security must be considered as a multidimensional process with at least three levels: global, national and individual.[5]

At the global level, new trade rules should permit NFIDCs the right to selected trade tariffs and import quotas to regulate imports of food and to prevent dumping of highly supported and subsidised agricultural commodities, including food crops. It has been calculated that all the development aid provided by donors – who are also effectively involved in protecting their own countries' agricultural industries and farmers' interests – is of less value to developing countries than their potential gains from a truly fair world trading system. Thus, 'trade not aid' and 'aid for trade' are what most smallholders in developing countries seek to achieve from the conclusion of the Doha Round.

At the national level, food security is a complex and cross-cutting issue. It affects people's health, performance in school and productivity in work, and can lead to great losses of potential national income. Food security policies vary across developing countries, and depend on their political, social and economic situations. Most importantly, it depends on their degree and level of food self-sufficiency as well as their political will and commitment to ensuring equality of income distribution among the different groups in their population.

In countries where large numbers of people experience food insecurity, and where agriculture is the main component of the economy, accelerating agricultural growth will contribute to food security in two ways. First, growth in agriculture will give people facing chronic food insecurity the opportunity to earn an adequate income. Second, it assures a stable food supply through domestic production. In fact, neglecting agriculture in these cases will jeopardise overall economic growth – and with that the possibility of providing enough work for the growing population and enough food for all (World Bank 2007).

Despite the efforts of governments and of the many bilateral and multilateral aid agencies dealing with food security, there is still news of rising hunger and children dying from malnutrition. Thus, if the world is serious about ending hunger for good, food sovereignty should be given utmost importance in developing countries' national policies and be supported by international development policies dealing with the issue of food insecurity and malnutrition.

Public investments can be complemented by private ones to enhance the resilience of the smallholder farming system, by the provision of the support services that are needed most, such as strengthening agricultural market institutions, and – most importantly – promoting market infrastructure from farm gate to retailer. This involves roads, ports, power, storage facilities, information and communication systems, and marketing channels linking all stages from assembly to processing to purchase and consumption. It is crucial for economic growth and development that farmers are able to access credit and other financial products which can assist them in purchasing the inputs they most need, and to benefit from irrigation systems based on cost effective and appropriate technology. Both research and the development of advisory services should be smallholder focused and geared towards promoting ecologically integrated and sustainable agriculture.

It is also essential to ensure investment in education, health care and sanitation to improve the nutritional standards among all people, and especially among mothers to reduce malnutrition among children in the short run and improve the productivity of the rural labour force in the long run. Due consideration should also be given to the consumption and utilisation of food while formulating food policy. This investment can be complemented by establishing safety nets to protect people against risks and vulnerability, to mitigate the impacts of shocks, and to support people experiencing chronic poverty and food insecurity.

Above all, however, increasing food production must not be achieved at the expense of overexploiting natural resources. Governments, donors and most NGOs can and should play a crucial role in promoting ecologically integrated policies, as well as best practice in soil and water conservation and in protecting biodiversity.

Appendix

GENERAL AGREEMENT ON TARIFFS AND TRADE

The General Agreement on Tariffs and Trade (GATT) was negotiated during the UN Conference on Trade and Employment and was the outcome of the failure of negotiating governments to create the International Trade Organisation (ITO). The GATT was signed in 1947 and lasted until 1993, after which it was replaced by the World Trade Organisation (WTO) in 1995. The original GATT text (1994) is still in effect under the WTO framework, subject to modifications.

GATT AND WTO TRADE ROUNDS

Round name	Date and duration	No. of countries	Subject covered	Achievements
Geneva	April 1947 7 months	23	Tariffs	Signing of GATT, 45,000 tariff concessions affecting US$10 billion of trade
Annecy	April 1949 5 months	13	Tariffs	Countries exchange some 5,000 tariff concessions
Torquay	September 1950 8 months	38	Tariffs	Countries exchange some 8,700 tariff concessions, cutting the 1948 tariff levels by 25%
Geneva II	January 1956 5 months	26	Tariffs, admission of Japan	US$2.5 billion in tariff reduction
Dillon	September 1960 11 months	26	Tariffs	Tariff concessions worth US$4.9 billion of world trade
Kennedy	May 1964 37 months	62	Tariffs, anti-dumping	Tariff concessions worth US$40 billion of world trade
Tokyo	September 1986 87 months	102	Tariffs, non-tariff measures, 'framework' agreements	Tariff reductions worth US$300 billion achieved

continued

Round name	Date and duration	No. of countries	Subject covered	Achievements
Geneva Uruguay Round	October 1986–94	118	Tariffs, non-tariff measures, rules, services, intellectual property, dispute settlement, textiles, agriculture, creation of WTO	The round led to the creation of the WTO, and extended the range of trade negotiations, leading to major reductions in tariffs (about 40%) and agricultural subsidies, and agreement to allow full access for textiles and clothing from developing countries, and an extension of intellectual property rights.
Doha	November 2001–04	123	Tariffs, non-tariff measures, rules, agriculture, labour standards, investment, transparency, patents and so on. Rural development and food security for least-developed and net-food importing developing countries Export credit and export credit guarantees or insurance programmes Tariff rate quotas	Not yet concluded

Source: WTO (2011) Understanding the WTO. (Geneva: WTO). Available at http://wto.org/ accessed 20 November 2012.

Numerical targets for agriculture. The reductions in agricultural subsidies and protection agreed in the Uruguay Round. Only the figures for cutting export subsidies appear in the agreement.

	Developed countries 6 years: 1995–2000 %	Developing countries 9 years: 1995–2004 %
Tariffs		
Average cut for all agricultural products	–36	–24
Minimum cut per product	–15	–10
Domestic support		
Total AMS cuts for sector (base period: 1986–88)	–20	–13
Exports		
Value of subsidies	–36	–24
Subsidised quantities (base period: 1986–90)	–21	–14

Source: WTO (2011) Understanding the WTO (Geneva: WTO). Available at http://wto.org./ accessed 20 November 2012.

Least developed countries do not have to make commitments to reduce tariffs or subsidies.
The base level for tariff cuts was the bound rate before 1 January 1995; or, for unbound tariffs, the actual rate charged in September 1986 when the Uruguay Round began. The other figures were targets used to calculate countries legally binding 'schedules of commitments'.
Without prejudging the outcome, member governments commit themselves to comprehensive negotiations aimed at:

• Market access; various trade restrictions confronting imports.
• Domestic support; subsidies and other programmes including those that raise or guarantee farmgate prices and farmers income.
• Export subsidies; other methods to make export artificially competitive.

Notes

CHAPTER 1

1. Beriberi is caused by vitamin B1 deficiency, and its early symptoms include tiredness, irritability, poor memory, sleeping problems, weight loss and stomach pain. Symptoms of severe deficiency in vitamin B1, known as beriberi, include confusion, pain and weakness in the legs and arms, nerve damage, oedema (fluid under the skin) and irregular heart rate. It can lead to heart failure and death.

   Pellagra is caused by deficiency in vitamin B3 which causes a slowdown in the body's metabolism, making people feel the cold more. Severe deficiency causes pellagra. The name 'pellagra' comes from the Italian for 'rough skin'. Its symptoms are often described as the 'four Ds' – diarrhoea, dermatitis (skin inflammation), dementia and death. Other symptoms include sensitivity to sunlight, aggression, hair loss, oedema, swelling and reddening of the tongue, trouble sleeping, weakness, lack of coordination and heart disease.

2. Haughton and Khander (2009) and IFAD reports on rural poverty (1992; 2001; 2011).

3. Xerophthalmia is a term that usually implies a destructive dryness of the conjunctival epithelium due to dietary vitamin A deficiency – a rare condition in developed countries, but still causing much damage in developing countries. Other forms of dry eye are associated with aging, poor lid closure, scarring from previous injury, or autoimmune diseases such as rheumatoid arthritis, which can all cause chronic conjunctivitis. Radioiodine therapy can also induce xerophthalmia, often transiently, although in some patients late onset or persistent xerophthalmia has been observed (Solans et al. (2001).

4. See Chapter 5 on World Bank descriptions of the three rural worlds: agriculture-based; transforming; and urbanised regions and countries (World Bank 2007).

5. Border price criteria for imports are the world prices at cost, insurance and freight, converted into domestic currency at the official exchange rate. This border price needs to be adjusted in order to bring it into comparison with domestic prices such as retail prices, wholesale prices or farm-gate prices (Ellis 1992: 72–3).

6. See Ellis (1992: 72–3):

   The gap between export parity and import parity prices for such commodities may be very large, meaning that world prices provide no precise guide to appropriate domestic price levels. For example maize imported from the US might have an import parity value of $300 in the centre of Zambia, while maize from the centre of Zambia destined for the USA (assuming such trade were to take place) would have an export parity value of $80. While these countries may represent an extreme in this regard, the same problem exists in varying degrees for a staple grain in roughly self-sufficient supply. Another factor that is relevant here is that quality differences between domestic and world traded grain reduce the effective world price for domestic exports, and thus widen the export parity/import parity.

CHAPTER 2

1. Olivier Rubin (2009: 699–717) points out that 'democracies are not homogenous political entities and there might be countervailing forces in a democracy. These forces could include everything from direct lobbying conducted by outside groups to "log rolling" and "vote trading" from factions within the political system. Famine relief could be further prevented by "pork barrel politics" or the corresponding "not in my backyard" attitude, where locally elected politicians place the interests of their home constituents ahead of the emergency in working for or against initiative depending on the interests of their constituents'.
2. The Indian Famine Codes are the first written statements of famine policy in the modern era (see Hall-Matthews in ÓGráda 2009: 206–8). It was drafted in 1880, guided by the enlightenment principles that the authorities should not interfere with the grain trade or compromise economic activity in other ways, and that relief should not give rise to more permanent dependency. In combating famine, 'it must be laid down as a first principle that the object of State intervention is to save life and that all other considerations should be subordinated to this'. It sets down a procedure to watch for signs of distress in rising prices, and establish 'test works' and soup kitchens. It sought to minimise delays in providing relief, realising that delays cost lives. Numbers applying for relief were monitored, and if they rose rapidly famine was declared. If the famine was extensive, a commissioner was appointed. Moreover, public works, providing employment at low wages on infrastructural projects were central, allied with adequate medical care. According to ÓGráda, the codes 'formed part of a move, however hesitant, toward greater state responsibility'.
3. According to Watts (1983: 100) and Devereux (2000: 6), famine chronologies remain embarrassingly incomplete and often highly ambiguous. Problems exist in obtaining accurate data of fertility births and deaths before and after famine in poor countries.
4. Market clearing equilibrium is a market clearing price of goods or a service at which quantity supplied is equal to quantity demanded – it is also called the equilibrium price. In simple terms, this means that markets tend to move towards prices which balance the quantity supplied and the quantity demanded, such that the market will eventually be cleared of all surpluses and shortages (excess supply and demand). The first version assumes that this process occurs instantaneously (Wikipedia, accessed October 2011).
5. Inter-temporally can be explained as the relative value people assign to two or more payoffs at different points in time (Wikipedia, accessed October 2011).

CHAPTER 3

1. In 2000, 189 nations made a promise to free people from extreme poverty and multiple deprivations. This pledge turned into the eight Millennium Development Goals. For details see The UN Declaration 18 September 2000. Available at http://www.un.org. Accessed 19 November 2012.
2. Professor Marshall Martin, head of the Department of Agricultural Economics at Purdue University in the US.
3. For full scientific analysis of the issue, see Lemaux (2009).

4. Lang and Heasman (2004: 24). Nutrigenomics is the application of a new understanding of genes and how they operate in plants, animals and micro-organisms to help unravel the mechanisms behind which foods and ingredients have an impact on which genes and diseases. This would have been inconceivable without the completion of the mapping of the human genome by US and European scientists. It is another line of research being pursued within the emerging LSIP and it seeks to understand how nutrition, and particularly dietary intake, interacts with the structure and expression of genes and with genetic pre-potential. It relies on novel but unproven impacts, and argues that health can be 'fixed' technically by new combinations of screening on an individualised basis. It thus seeks to improve the beneficial traits of crops for human health.
5. See chapter 4 for detailed discussion on this concept.

CHAPTER 4

1. 'Market imperfection' is a concept which is defined by comparison to the hypothetical ideal of perfect competition. 'Perfect competition' in economics emphasises the neutrality of the price mechanism and its role as the arbiter of all economic decisions. In the perfect state there are many buyers and sellers in a market, for both inputs and outputs. No producer or consumer is able to influence price levels by individual action. There is freely available and accurate information on market prices. There is freedom of entry and exit in any branch of activity, and competition ensures that inefficient producers are forced out of production, while only the most efficient survive. The perfect competition model implies that no coercion, domination, or exercise of economic power, by some economic agents over others, can exist (Ellis 1996: 10).
2. Ellis (1996: 13). The term 'traditional' seems to refer partly to production techniques and partly to psychological factors. 'Subsistence' describes only a partial aspect of the peasant farm household, which is not always the most significant feature for economic analysis. The term 'small farmer' is attractive and used widely because it lacks emotive connotations, but it also lacks theoretical content, since it is not possible to set a farm size limit to the domain of peasant economics.
3. Vanhaute (2008: 40). World-system analysis is one of the strongest tools for analysing the relationships between the global and the local during the process of transformation in any given society. World-systems analysis labels the modern world-system as both an historical and geographical structuring system.
4. Anderson and Masters (2009). The nominal rate of assistance (NRA) is defined as the percentage by which government policies have raised gross returns to farmers above what they would be without the government's intervention. Consumer tax equivalent (CTE) is the percentage that policies have raised prices paid by consumers of agricultural outputs.

   The Relative Rate of Assistance can be defined in percentage terms as: RRA = $100*[(100 + NRAag^t)/(100 + NRAnonag^t)-1]$. RRA is the tradable parts of both the agricultural and non-agricultural sectors. Since the NRA cannot be less than 100 per cent if producers are to earn anything, neither can the RRA. If both sectors are assisted equally, the RRA is zero. This measure is useful in that, if it is below (or above) zero, it provides an internationally comparable indication of the extent to which a country's policy regime has an anti-agricultural or pro-agricultural bias.

CHAPTER 5

1. See Ellis (1992) for full explanations of the four elements of land distribution.
2. Government of the United Republic of Tanzania (1994) *Report of the Presidential Commission of Enquiry into Land Matters*, Vol 1, Dar-es-Salaam: Ministry of Lands, Housing and Urban Development: 247, in Musembi (2007: 1457–78).
3. In 1934, the ejido system was introduced as an important component of the land reform programme in Mexico. The typical procedure for the establishment of an ejido involved the following steps: (1) landless farmers who leased lands from wealthy landlords would petition the federal government for the creation of an ejido in their general area; (2) the federal government would consult with the landlord; (3) the land would be expropriated from the landlords if the government approved the ejido; and (4) an ejido would be established and the original petitioners would be designated as *ejidatarios* with certain cultivation/use rights.

   Ejidatarios did not actually own the land, but were allowed to use their allotted parcels indefinitely as long as they did not fail to use the land for more than two years. They could even pass their rights on to their children. According to the World Bank (2007: 140) the 'Mexico ejido system now includes mediation to protect the property rights of women'. However, this system is under threat from the legislation of 1991, when President Carlos Salinas de Gortari decided to eliminate the constitutional right to ejidos, citing the 'low productivity' of communally owned land. The change was largely a result of the North American Free Trade Agreement (NAFTA).
4. MLAR in South Africa has had some success in terms of transferring land and in not antagonising landowners, but the complexity of the process, its slow pace, and its inability to effectively target the most needy households or the most appropriate land (especially in term of plot size), makes it unlikely that it can ever be a means of large-scale redistribution or poverty alleviation. In practice, the policy of 'willing buyer, willing seller' as implemented in South Africa is little more than a programme of assisted purchase, masquerading as agrarian reform, under which the main beneficiaries are likely to be white landowners and a small minority of better-off black entrepreneurs (see, Lahiff et al. 2007).

CHAPTER 6

1. The World Bank (2007: 290) commented:

   A traditional society in which women do not work outside the home can remain that way for a long time, even as conditions outside the household, such as female wages, are changing. But once women start working, the change can be very rapid, with lots of women coming out of their homes to be active in the labour market. This suggests that there can be payoffs to one-time interventions by governments or non-governmental organisations that assist women's entry into the labour force: once it has started, it will stick as a new self-fulfilling pattern has been established.

2. For details on the costs of migration, see IFAD (2011: 209).

CHAPTER 7

1. As Harper (2003) states:

    The theory of microfinance, if it exists, could be said to be based on the principle of free markets, where resources are allowed to flow to those who can make best use of them. There are as yet very few examples of microfinance institutions that are totally 'sustainable', in that they receive no subsidy at all, in cash or in kind. There are even fewer examples of institutions that pay their original investors any return on their investments. The initial set-up costs, or the equivalent of the 'risk capital' which funds the start-up of commercial firms, are often unknown, and most have been set up by donor organisations that would be most surprised if anyone tried to repay their grants.

2. *Purdah or* pardeh (from Persian: پرده , meaning 'curtain') is the practice of concealing women from men) (www.wikipedia.org 2012).

CHAPTER 8

1. Rijsberman (2004) suggests that it takes one cubic metre of water to produce 1 kg of wheat, 1.2 cubic metres to produce 1 kg of rice, and as much as 13 cubic metres to produce 1 kg of beef, due to the volume of grain fed to beef cattle, alongside large amounts of drinking water. Moreover, McDonald et al. (in Webb et al. 2005) indicate that a cow yielding 10 litres of milk per day under semi-arid conditions needs around 100 litres of water, but to raise that milk yield by one third requires a more than one-third increase in the volume of water available to the animal.
2. The Mekong River is considered one of the most endangered rivers in terms of the risk of drying out. Key threats identified include: overfishing; the building of 149 dams; deforestation and pollution.
3. See UNDP (2006: 195–8) and Webb et al. (2005: 6) for case studies of low-technology solutions in relation to water harvesting and micro-irrigation which produce high human development returns.
4. See http://sri.ciifad.cornell.edu/index.html for details.
5. Ellis (1992: 269) outlined a number of practical solutions to improve water governance.

CHAPTER 9

1. Gender implies the different roles of women and men, including their different responsibilities and tasks in a given culture or location (Moser 1989).
2. 'Reproductive gender role' refers to the bearing and rearing of children and most household work such as cooking, cleaning, and looking after the elderly and the disabled. 'Productive role' refers to both paid and unpaid types of work carried out both within the household (such as small income-generating activities) and outside the home (off-farm paid work) (Moser 1989).
3. Gender equality refers to equal access to the opportunities that allow people to pursue a life of their own choosing and to avoid extreme deprivation in outcomes, highlighting gender equality in rights, resources, and voice (World Bank, FAO and IFAD 2009: 2).

4. Gender division of labour: this refers to the different types of work that men and women do as a consequence of their socialisation, and acceptable patterns of work within a given context (see, Moser 1989; Ellis 1992).

5. For details of Beijing platform for action, see http://www.un.org/womenwatch/daw/beijing/platform/declar.htm. See also details of the three Decades for Women in Development from Mexico, to Copenhagen and Nairobi, to Beijing.

6. The most recent publication by the World Bank, FAO and IFAD (2009), *Gender in Agriculture,* provides some comprehensive lists of indicators that should be used as a guide for governments, development agencies and practitioners in advancing their work towards gender equality in agriculture.

CHAPTER 10

1. WTO (2011), Understanding the WTO (Geneva: WTO). Available at http://wto.org/ accessed 20 November 2012.

2. See Appendix one for historical records of trade rounds and negotiations and outcomes on AoA.

3. The total net Official Development Assistance (ODA) flows from DAC members amounted to US$119.8 billion in 2008 to those developing countries with over 85 per cent of the world's poor, an increase of 10.2 per cent in real terms compared with 2007. This represents 0.3 per cent of members' combined gross national incomes (GNI) in 2008 (OECD 2009).

4. Researchers are predicting that food prices will rise to record highs by 2013, the *New York Times* (8 March 2012) reports. The spike will lead to widespread hunger in 'the most vulnerable populations with an enormous potential for loss of human life'. The research was generated by the New England Complex Systems Institute in September 2011 and has gained credibility by successfully predicting food prices over the past ten months. The key factors leading to rising food prices are the conversion of corn crops to ethanol and speculation on the agricultural futures market.

   'There are two policy decisions we've identified as key drivers,' said Yaneer Bar-Yam, president of the Institute. 'The first is the promotion of ethanol conversion, which provides the U.S. with less than one percent of its energy but has a much larger effect on global food availability'. And the second is the deregulation of commodity markets.

5. A very recent report, *The Future of Food and Farming: Challenges and Choices for Global Sustainability,* published by the United Kingdom Government Office of Science (2011) concludes with a stark warning for both current and future policymakers on the consequences of inaction to mitigate against the challenges to food security, which need to be addressed in ways that promote people's resilience to shocks and future uncertainties.

Bibliography

Abbott, P. and de Battisti, A. B. (2009), 'Recent global food price shocks: causes, consequences and lessons for African governments and donors'. Paper presented at the International Agricultural Trade Research Consortium (IATRC) Analytic Symposium. 'Confronting food price inflation: implications for agricultural trade and policies'. June 21–23 (Seattle, WA: IATRC).

Adams, D. W., Graham, D., and von Pischke, J. D. (1984), *Undermining Rural Development with Cheap Credit* (Boulder, CO: Westview Press).

Adams, D. W., and Canavesi de Sahonero, M. L. (1989), 'Rotating savings and credit associations in Bolivia'. *Savings and Development* 36(2): 351–67.

AMCEN (African Ministerial Conference on the Environment) (2002), 'Framework for the Action Plan for the Environment Initiative of NEPD'. AMCEN 9th session (Kampala: UN Environment Programme).

Alamgir, M. (1980), *Famine in South Asia: Political Economy of Mass Starvation* (Cambridge, MA: Oelgeschlager, Gunn and Hain).

Alamgir, M. (1981), 'An approach towards a theory of famine'. In Robson, J. (ed.) *Famine: Its Causes, Effects and Management* (New York: Gordon and Breach).

Alderman, H., and Haque, T. (2006), 'Countercyclical safety nets for the poor and vulnerable'. *Food Policy* 31(4): 371–83.

Alhassan, H. S. (2009), 'Viewpoint butterflies vs. hydropower: reflections on large dams in contemporary Africa'. *Water Alternatives* 2(1): 141–60.

Altaf, M., Whittington, D., Jamal, H., and Smith, K. (1993), 'Rethinking rural water supply policy in Punjab, Pakistan'. *Water Resources Research* 29(7): 1941–54.

Anderson, K., Martin, W., and van der Mensbrugghe, M. D. (2006), 'Distortions to world trade: impacts on agricultural markets and farm income'. *Review of Agricultural Economics* 28(2): 161–95.

Anderson, K., and Masters, W. A. (2009), 'Sub-Sahara and North Africa'. In Anderson, K. (ed.) *Distortions to Agricultural Incentives: a Global Perspective. 1951–2007* (Washington, DC: World Bank).

Anríquez, G., and Bonomi, G. (2007), 'Long-term farming and rural demographic trends'. *Background Paper* (Washington, DC: World Bank).

Antrobus, P. (2003), 'MDGs – most distracting gimmicks'. *Contextualising the MDGs*. Available at: http://www.dawn.org.fi/global/mdgs.html. Accessed November 2011.

Amin, S. (2003), 'World poverty, pauperization and capital accumulation'. *Monthly Review*, LV, 5(1–9). Available at: http://monthlyreviwe.org/1003amin.htm. Accessed March 2011.

Badiane, O. (2010), *Agricultural and Economic Growth Recovery in Africa in the Context of Global Crises* (Washington, DC: IFPRI).

Baffes, J. (2009), 'Commodities at the crossroads'. *Seminar,* 5 June (Tokyo: World Bank).

Bahatia, R., and Falkenmark, M. (1993), *Water Policies and Agriculture: The State of Food and Agriculture* (Rome: FAO).

Bairoch, P. (1973), 'Agriculture and industrial revolution, 1701–1914'. In Carlos, M. C. (ed.) *The Industrial Revolution – Fontana Economic History of Europe*. Vol. 3 (London: Collins-Fontana).

Ban Ki-moon (2009), 'World financial and economic crisis and its impact on development', 24–26 June. *Speech at UN Conference on World Financial Crisis* (New York: UN).

Bardhan, P., Bowles, S., and Gintis, H. (2000), 'Wealth inequality, wealth constraints and economic performance'. In Atkinson, A., and Bourguignon, F. (eds) *Handbook on Income Distribution*. Edition 1. Vol. 1. Chapter 10: 541–603 (Amsterdam: Elsevier).

Barnum, H. J., and Morse, S. C. (1979), 'A model of agricultural household: theory and evidence'. World Bank Staff *Occasional Paper* 27 (Baltimore, MD: Johns Hopkins University Press).

Bateman, M. (2010), 'Commercialised microfinance: a Wall Street-style calamity for the poor?' *ODI at 50: Advancing Knowledge, Shaping Policy, Inspiring Practice*. Available at: http://blogs.odi.org.uk/blogs/main/archive/2010/08/17/microfinance. Accessed December 2011.

Bazza, M. (2005), 'Best policies and practices for agricultural water management in the Near East region'. In Hamdy, A., and Monti, R. (eds) *Food Security Under Water Scarcity in the Middle East: Problems and Solutions* (Bari: CIHEAM-IAMB).

Becker, G. S. (1981), *A Treatise on the Family* (Cambridge, MA: Harvard University Press).

Becker, L. C. (2000), 'Garden money buys grain: food procurement patterns in a Malian Village'. *Human Ecology* 28(32): 211–50.

Beegle, K. J., Weerdt, D., and Dercon, S. (2008), 'Migration and economic mobility in Tanzania: evidence from a tracking survey'. *Policy Research Working Paper*, WPS 4798 (Washington, DC: World Bank).

Bernstein, H. (1979), 'African peasantries: a theoretical framework. *Journal of Peasant Studies* 6(4): 421–43.

Bernstein, H. (2000), 'The peasantry in global capitalism: who, where and why?' In Panitch, L., and Leys, C. (eds) *Socialist Register 2001: Working Classes Global Realities* (London: Merlin Press).

Bernstein, H. (2003), 'Farewells to the peasantry'. *Transformation* (52): 1–19.

Besley, T. (1994), 'How do market failures justify interventions in rural credit markets?' *The World Bank Research Observer* 9(1) (Washington, DC: World Bank).

Binswanger, H. P. (2007), 'The political implications of alternative models of land reform and compensation'. In van Zyl, J., Kirsten, J., and Binswanger, H. P. (eds) *Agricultural Land Reform in South Africa* (Oxford: University Oxford Press).

Binswanger, H. P., and Deininger, K. (1997), 'Explaining agricultural and agrarian policies in developing countries'. *Journal of Economic Literature* (35): 1951–2005.

Black, J. (26 November 2008), 'Americans on food stamps to exceed 30 million for first time'. *Washington Post, LA Times and Irish Times* (Dublin: Irish Times).

Bne Saad, M. (1987), 'The role of Iraqi farm women in farm, home and family tasks and decisions'. Unpublished *MSc Thesis* (Dublin: UCD).

Bne Saad, M. (1990), 'An analysis of the needs and problems of Iraqi farm women: implications for agricultural extension services'. Unpublished *PhD thesis* (Dublin: UCD).

Bne Saad, M. (2002), 'Food security for the food insecure: new challenges and renewed commitments'. *Position Paper: Sustainable Agriculture*. CSD NGO

Women's Caucus. Available at: http://www.earthsummit2002.org/wcaucus per cent20Position per cent20Papers/agriculture. Accessed January 2011.

Böserup, E. (1983), 'The impact of scarcity and plenty on development'. In Rotberg, R. and Robb, T. (eds) *Hunger and History* (Cambridge: Cambridge University Press).

Bowbrick, P. (1986), 'The causes of famine: a refutation of professor Sen's theory'. *Food Policy* 1(2): 105–24.

Boyce, J. K. (1988), 'Technological and institutional alternatives in Asian rice irrigation'. *Economic and Political Weekly* 26 March.

Bradshaw, D., Laubscher, R., Dorrington, R., Bourne, D. E., and Timaeus, I. M. (2004), 'Unabated rise in number of adult deaths in South Africa'. *South Africa Medical Journal.* 94(4): 278–9.

Brett-Crowther, M. R. (1983), 'Maluorished database'. *Food Policy* 8(1): 91–5.

Briscoe, J. (2003), *The Water Strategy of the World Bank* (Washington, DC: World Bank).

Bryceson, D. (2000), 'Rural Africa at the crossroad: livelihood practices and policies'. *Natural Resources perspective* 52 (London: Overseas Development Institute).

Bush, R. (2007), 'Politics, power and poverty: twenty years of agricultural reform and market liberalisation in Egypt'. *Third World Quarterly* 28(8): 1591–615.

Carney, J. (1993), 'Converting the wetlands, engendering the environment: the intersection of gender with agrarian change in the Gambia'. *Economic Geography* 69(6): 321–48.

Castello, C., Stearns, K., and Christen, R. (1991), 'Exposing interest rates: their true significance for micro entrepreneurs and credit programmes'. *Accion International Discussion Paper* (6).

Cestii, R. (1993), 'Policies for water demand management and pollution control in the industrial and household sectors in the Jabotabek region'. Research. Indonesia case study (Washington, DC: World Bank).

Cestii, R. (1995), 'Strengthening irrigation management in Egypt: A programme for the future, non-agricultural cost recovery study'. *Mimeo* (Cairo: Ministry of Public Works and Water Resources).

Chambers, R. (1989), 'Vulnerability, coping, and policy'. *IDS Bulletin* 20(2): 1–7.

Chen, S. and Ravallion, M. (2007) 'Absolute poverty measures for the developing world, 1981–2004'. *Development Research Group* (Washington, DC: World Bank).

Chizdero, A., Fröhlich-Lassiom, C., Hunguana, H., and Cuevas, C. (1998), *Mozambique Micro Finance Study* (Maputo: University Press).

Collier, P. (2008), 'The politics of hunger: how illusion and greed fan the food crisis'. *Foreign Affairs* 87(6): 61–8.

Collier, P., and Venables, A. J. (2007), 'Rethinking trade preferences: how Africa can diversify its exports'. *Discussion Paper Series.* Development Economics. Available at: http://www.cepr.org/pubs/DP6262.asp. Accessed November 2010.

Conway, G. (1999), *The Doubly Green Revolution* (Harmondsworth: Penguin).

Cotula, L., and Vermeulen, S. (2009), 'Precious soil'. *D+C* 39(9): 331–6.

Cramer, C., and Sender, J. (1999), 'Poverty, wage labour and agricultural change in rural Eastern and Southern Africa'. *Report* (Rome: IFAD).

Cramer, C., Oya, C., and Sender, J. (2008), 'Rural labour markets in sub-Saharan Africa: a new view of poverty, power and policy'. *Policy Brief* 1, November, Centre for Development Policy and Research.

Currey, B. (1981), 'The famine syndrome: its definition for relief and rehabilitation in Bangladesh'. In Robson, J. (ed.) *Famine: Its Causes, Effects and Management* (New York: Gordon and Breach).

Currey, B., and Hugo, G. (1984), *Famine as a Geographical Phenomenon* (Dordrech: Reidel Publishing)

Currey, B., and Hugo, G. (eds) (2003), 'According to need? Needs assessment and decision-making in the humanitarian sector'. *HPG Report* 15 (London: Overseas Development Institute).

Currie, J. (2007), 'Food, feed and fuels: an outlook on the agriculture, livestock and biofuels market'. *Presentation*. Goldman Sachs.

CUTS (Consumer Unity and Trust Society) (1998), 'Trade liberalisation and food security'. *Briefing Paper* 6. July: 1-11. Available at: http://www.cuts-international. org/1991-6.htm. Accessed March 2009.

de Gorter, H., and Swinnen, J. (2002), 'Political economy of agricultural policy'. In Bruce, G., and Rausser, G. (eds) *Handbook of Agricultural Economics* (Amsterdam: Elsevier).

de Grassi, A., and Rosset, P. (2003), 'A new Green Revolution for Africa? Myths and realities of agriculture, technology and development'. Available at: http:www. ocf.berkeley.edu/~ddegrassi/gra.htm. Accessed May 2011.

de Haen H., Stamoulis, K., Shetty, P., and Pingali, P. (2004), 'The world food economy in the twenty-first century: challenges for international co-operation'. In Maxwell, S., and Slater, R. (eds) *Development Policy Review* 21(1–6): 681–96.

de Janvry, A., Gordillo, G., and Platteau, J.-P. (2001), *Access to Land, Rural Poverty, and Public Action*. A study prepared for the World Institute for Development Economic Research for the United Nations University (UNU/WIDER) (Oxford: Oxford University Press).

de Soto, H. (2003), *The Mystery of Capital: Why Capitalism Triumphs in the West and Fails Everywhere Else* (New York: Basic Books).

de Waal, A. (1989), *Famine that Kill: Darfur, Sudan, 1981–1985* (Oxford: Clarendon Press).

Deere, C. D. (2005), 'The feminisation of Agriculture? Economic restructuring in rural Latin America'. *Occasional Paper* 1. Available at: http://www.unrisd.org/ publications/opgp1. Accessed December 2011.

Deere, C. D., and Doss, C. R. (2001), 'Gender and the distribution of wealth in developing countries'. *Research Paper Series* 2006/115 (New York: United Nations University (UNU) World Institute for Development Economic Research (WIDER)).

Deininger, K. W. (2001), 'Making negotiated land reform work: initial experience from Colombia, Brazil and South Africa'. *World Development* 27(4): 651–72.

Devereux, S. (1988) 'Entitlements, availability and famine: a revisionist view of Wollo, 1971–74'. *Food Policy* 13(3): 271–82.

Devereux, S. (1993), *Theories of Famine* (UK: T. J. Press Padstow Ltd).

Devereux, S. (2000), 'Famine in the twentieth century'. *IDS Working Paper* 105 (Brighton: Institute of Development Studies).

Devereux, S. (2001), 'Sen's entitlement approach: critiques and counter critiques'. *Oxford Development Studies* 29(3): 241–63.

Devereux, S. (2005), 'Can minimum wages contribute to poverty reduction in poor countries?' *Journal of International Development* 17(7): 891–912.

Devereux, S. (ed.) (2007), *The New Famines: Why Famines Persist in an Era of Globalisation* (New York: Routledge).

Devereux, S. (2009), 'Why does famine persist in Africa?' *Food Science* (1): 21–35.

Devereux, S., and Maxwell, S. (eds) (2001), *Food Security in Sub-Saharan Africa* (London: ITDG).

Devereux, S., and Tiba, Z. (2007), 'Malawi's first famine, 2001, 2002'. In Devereux, S. (ed.) *The New Famines* (London: Routledge).

Dixon-Mueller, R. (1985), *Women's Work in Third World Agriculture* (Geneva: ILO).

Djurfeldt, G., Hammarskjöld, M., Jirström, M., and Larsson, R. (2003), *The African Food Crisis: Lessons from the Asian Green Revolution* (Wallingford: CABI).

Dolan, C. S., and Sutherland, K. (2002), 'Gender and employment in the Kenya horticulture value chain'. *Discussion Paper* 8 (Norwich: Overseas Development Group).

Donald, G. (ed.) (1976), *Credit for Small Farmers in Developing Countries* (Boulder CO: Westview Press).

Donaldson, G. (1984), 'Food security and the role of the grain trade'. *Reprint Series* 304 (Washington, DC: World Bank).

Doornbosch, R., Steenblik, R. (2007), 'Biofuels: is the cure worse than the disease?' *Round Table on Sustainable Development* (Paris: OECD).

Dyson, T., and ÓGráda, C. (2002), *Famine Demography* (Oxford: Oxford University Press).

Economist (30 January 1943), 'Food for India'. *International* (London: *The Economist*).

Economist (31 March 2001), 'Poverty and property rights: no title'. *International* (London: *The Economist*).

Economist (14 August 2009), 'Microfinance: sub-par but not subprime. Lending to the poor has held up well but it is not as safe from the credit crisis as its champions hoped'. *International* (London: *The Economist*).

Economist (31 October 2009), 'When people got richer, families got smaller, and as families got smaller people got richer'. *International* (London: *Economist*).

Economist (19 November 2009), 'Feeding the world: if words were food, nobody would go hungry'. *International* (London: *Economist*).

Economist (6 January 2011), 'Africa's impressive growth'. *Report* (London: *Economist*).

Economist (4 June 2011), 'The end of AIDS?' *Report* (London: *Economist*).

Economist (18 February 2012), 'Poverty and food: the nutrition puzzle'. *International* (London: *Economist*).

Edkins, J. (2007), 'The criminalization of mass starvations: from natural disaster to crime against humanity'. In Devereux, S. (ed.) *The New Famines: Why Famines Persist in an Era of Globalisation* (New York: Routledge).

Edmonds, E. V., and Pavcnink, N. (2005), 'Child labour in the global economy'. *Journal of Economic Perspectives* 19(1): 191–220.

Eicher C. K., and Staatz J. M. (1990), *Agricultural Development in the Third World* (Baltimore, MD: Johns Hopkins University Press).

Ellis, F. (1992), *Agricultural Policies in Developing Countries* (London: Cambridge University Press).

Ellis, F. (1996), *Peasant Economics: Farm Households and Agrarian Development*. 2nd ed. (Cambridge: Cambridge University Press).

Ellis, F. (2000), *Rural Livelihoods and Diversity in Developing Countries* (London: Oxford University Press).

Emerson, T. (2001), 'Where the beef?' *Newsweek, Special Report*. 26 February. 11–21.

EU (2007), 'Bio-energy pact between Europe and Africa'. Available at: http://www.biopact.com/site/goals.html. Accessed January 2012.

EU Nutrition (January 2010), 'Malnutrition'. Available at http://www.european-nutrition.org/record. Accessed January 2010.

Eugenio, S., Bobenrieth, H., and Brian, D. W. (2009), 'The price crisis of 2001–2008: evidence and implications'. *Symposium, on Value Chain for Oilseeds, Oil and Fats, Grains and Rice: Status and Outlook.* Santiago, Chile. 1–6 November 2009.

Evans, A. (2009), 'The feeding of the nine billion: global food security for the 21st century'. A *Chatham House Report.* Available at: www.chathamhouse.org.uk. Accessed March 2011.

Evenson, R. E. (2010), 'The Green Revolution in developing countries: an economist's assessment'. Available at: www.unpani.un. Accessed October 2010.

Evenson, R. E., and Gollin, D. (2003), *Crop Variety Improvement and its Effect on Productivity: The Impact of International Agricultural Research* (Wallingford: CABI).

Fan, S., and Rao, N. (2003) 'Public spending in developing countries: trends determination and impact'. EPTD *Discussion Paper* 99 (Washington, DC: International Food Policy Research Institute).

FAO (1975), 'World food conference'. Rome 1–16 November 1974. *Document* E/CONF 65(20).

FAO (1983), 'World food security: a reappraisal of the concepts and approaches'. Director-General's *Report* (Rome: FAO).

FAO (1996), *World Food Security: FAO Sixth World Food Survey* (Rome: FAO).

FAO (1997), *Gender and Food Security: Synthesis Report of Regional Documents.* Women in Development Service. Women and Population Division and Sustainable Development Department (Rome: FAO).

FAO (1999), *Agricultural Censuses and Gender Considerations: Concepts and Methodology* (Rome: FAO).

FAO (2001), *The State of Food Insecurity in the World.* Available at: http://www.unsystem.org/scn/Publications/UN_Report.PDF. Accessed October 2010).

FAO (2002), 'Land tenure and rural development'. *Land Tenure Studies.* Economic and Social Development (Rome: FAO).

FAO (2002a), *Factsheet on Feeding the Cities* (Rome: FAO).

FAO (2003), *Trade Reforms and Food Security: Conceptualising the Linkages.* (Rome: FAO).

FAO (2004), 'Incorporating nutrition considerations into development policies and programmes'. *Policy Brief* (Rome: FAO).

FAO (2005a), 'Food security: concepts and measurement'. In *Trade Reforms and Food Security* (Rome: FAO).

FAO (2005b), *Voluntary Guidelines to Support the Progressive Realization of the Right to Adequate Food in the Context of National Food Security* (Rome: FAO).

FAO (2006), 'FAOSTAT'. (Rome: FAO).

FAO (2007a), *Good Governance in Land Tenure and Administration.* Land Tenure Studies (Rome: FAO).

FAO (2007b), *Factors and Constraints Affecting Women's Role in Food Security.* Available at: www.FAO.org. Accessed December 2010.

FAO (2007c), *Gender and Food Security Facts and Figures* (Rome: FAO).

FAO (2008), *State of Food Security in the World* (Rome: FAO).

FAO (2009a), 'How to feed the world in 2050'. Report of high level expert meeting regarding the outlook for food security towards 2050 (Rome: FAO).

FAO (2009b), *Agricultural Reforms and Trade Liberalisation in China and Selected Asian Countries: Lessons of Three Decades* (Bangkok: FAO, Regional Office for Asia and the Pacific).

FAO (2009g), *Agricultural Reforms and Trade Liberalisation in China and Selected Asian Countries: Lessons of Three Decades* (Bangkok: FAO, Regional Office for Asia and the Pacific).

FAO (2010), *The State of Food and Agriculture. Annual Report* (Rome: FAO).

FAO (2011), *The State of Food and Agriculture. Annual Report* (Rome: FAO).

FAO and WHO (1992), 'World declaration on nutrition, plan of action for nutrition'. *International Conference on Nutrition* (Rome: FAO/WHO).

Farrington, J., Holms, R., and Slater, R. (2007), 'Linking social protection and the productive sectors: agricultural productivity can be supported by well-designed social protection programmes'. *ODI Briefing Paper* 28 (London: Overseas Development Institute).

Feder, G. (1985), 'The relation between farm size and farm productivity: the role of family labour supervision, and credit constraints'. *Journal of Development Economics* 18(2): 291–313.

Field, G., and Kanbur, R. (2005), 'Minimum wages and poverty'. *Mimeo* (New York: Cornell University).

Fine, B. (1997), 'Entitlement failure'? *Development and Change* 28(4): 611–47.

Fitzgerald, M. (30 January 2010), 'The new bread basket of the world'. *New Features Article* (Dublin: Irish Times).

Foster, A. D., and Rosenzweig, M. R. (1994), 'A test for moral hazard in the labour market: contractual arrangements, effort, health and calorie consumption'. *Review of Economics and Statistics* 76(2): 211–27.

Frankenberger, T. R. (1985), 'A food consumption perspective to farming systems research'. *Report* prepared for USDA, Office of International Cooperation and Development, Nutrition Economics Group (Washington, DC: US Department of Agriculture).

Frankenberger, T. R. (1996), 'Measuring household livelihood security: an approach for reducing absolute poverty'. *Food Forum* 34. Washington, DC.

Frasier, S., and Bne Saad, M. (2003), 'Microfinance in post-conflict situations: a case study of Mozambique'. *Development Research Briefings* 2 (Dublin: Centre for Development Studies, University College Dublin).

Friedmann, H. (1980), 'Household production and national economy: concepts for the analysis of agrarian formations'. *Journal of Peasant Studies* 7(2).

Fry, M. J. (1982), 'Models of financially repressed developing economies'. *World Development* 10(9): 731–50.

Garenne, M. (2007), 'A typical urban famine: Antananarivo, Madagascar 1981–1986'. In Devereux, S. (ed.) *The New Famines: Why Famines Persist in an Era of Globalisation* (New York: Routledge).

Gazdar, H. (2007), 'Pre-modern, modern and postmodern famine in Iraq'. In Devereux, S. (ed.) *The New Famines: Why Famines Persist in an Era of Globalisation* (New York: Routledge).

George, H. (2006), *Progress and Poverty* (New York: Robert Schalkenbach Foundation).

Ghalib, A. K., and Hailu, D. (2008), 'Banking the unbanked: improving access to financial services'. *Policy Research Brief*. 70071–900. Brasilia, DF, Brazil, UNDP International Poverty Centre.

Global Issues (2012), 'Social, political, economic and environmental issues that affect us all'. Available at: http://globalissues.org/article/768/global-financial-crisis. Accessed February 2012.

Global Water Partnership (2000), 'Integrated water resources management (IWRM)'. *Definition.* Available at: http://www.gwp.org/. Accessed July 2011.

Glynn, J. R. M., Caraël, B., Avert, M., Kahindo, J., Chege, R., Musonda, F., Kaona, A., Buvé, and the study group on the Heterogeneity of HIV Epidemics in African Cities (2001), 'Why do young women have a much higher prevalence of HIV than young men?' *A Study in Kisumu, Kenya and Ndola, Zambia. AIDS* 15(4): S51–S60.

Government Office of Science (2011), *The Future of Food and Farming: Challenges and Choices for Global Sustainability* (London: Government Office of Science).

GRAIN (1997), *Bio-diverse Farming Produces More.* Available at: http://www.grain/seedling/index.cfm?=72. Accessed April 2010.

Gregory, P. G., Ingram, J. S. I., and Brklacich, M. (2005), 'Climate change and food security'. *Journal of Philosophical Transactiosn of the Royal Society B: Biological Sciences* 360(1463): 1981–2194.

Gross, R. (1999), 'Community nutrition: definition and approaches'. In Sadler, M. J., Strain J., Caballero, B. (eds) *Encyclopaedia of Human Nutrition* (London: Academic Press Ltd).

Guardian (8 September, 2007), 'Global food crisis looms as climate change and fuel shortages bite: soaring crop prices and demand for biofuels raise fears of political instability'. *Article* (London: *The Guardian*).

Guardian (26 January 2012), 'Unemployment in the United States of America'. (London: *The Guardian*).

Guillespie, S. (1998), 'Major issues in the control of iron deficiency'. *Report* (Ottawa, New York: MI UNICEF).

Hahn, H. (2000), 'Conceptual framework of food and nutrition security'. *Report* (Germany: GTZ).

Harper, M. (ed.) (2003), *Microfinance, Evolution, Achievements and Challenges* (London, ITDG).

Haughton, J., and Khander, S. (2009), *Poverty + Inequality Handbook* (Washington, DC: World Bank).

Hazell, P., and Wood, S. (2008), 'Drivers of changes in global agriculture'. *Philosophical Transactions of the Royal Society: Biological Science* 36(3): 495–515.

Hayami, Y. (2005), 'An emerging agriculture problem in high performing Asian economies'. *Paper* presented at the 5th Conference of the Asian Society of Agricultural Economists (Presidential Address). August 29. Zahdan, Iran.

Hayami, Y., and Honma, M. (2009), 'Japan, Republic of Korea and Taiwan China'. In Anderson, K. (ed.) *Distortions to Agricultural Incentives: A Global Perspective 1951–2007* (Washington, DC: The World Bank).

Heintz J., Oya C., and Zepeda, E. (2008), 'Towards an employment-centred development strategy for poverty reduction in the Gambia: macroeconomic and labour market aspects'. *Country Study* (New York: International Poverty Centre/UNDP).

Hendrix, S. E. (1996), 'Myths of Property Rights'. Paper presented at the International Conference on Land Tenure Administration. November 11–14. Orlando, FL.

Herman, P., and Kuper, R. (2003), *Food for Thought: Towards a Future for Farming* (London and Sterling, AV: Pluto Press).

Holmén, H. (2006), 'Myths about agriculture, obstacles to solving the African food-crisis'. *The European Journal of Development Research* 18(3): 451–80.

Howe, P., and Devereux, S. (2007), 'Famine scales, towards an instrumental definition of famine'. In Devereux, S. (ed.) *The New Famines: Why Famines Persist in an Era of Globalisation* (New York: Routledge).

Hulme, D., Mosley, P. (1996), *Finance Against Poverty*. Two Volumes (London: Routledge).

Human Genome Project Information (2010), Available at: http://www.orn/.gov/sci/tecresources/human_Genome/elsi/gmfood.shtml. Accessed September 2010.

Hurst, P., Paola T., and Marilee, K. (2005), *Agricultural Workers and their Contribution to Sustainable Agriculture and Rural Development* (Rome: FAO and ILO).

Hussain, I., and Wijerathna, D. (2004), 'Implications of alternate irrigation water charging policies for the poor farmers in developing Asia: a comparative analysis'. *Workshop and Policy Roundtable.* Pro-poor Intervention Strategies in Irrigated Agriculture in Asia. 21–27 August (Colombo: International Water Management Institute).

IFAD (1992), *The State of World Rural Poverty: An Inquiry into its Causes and Consequences* (New York: Oxford University Press).

IFAD (2001), *Rural Poverty Report: The Challenge of Ending Rural Poverty* (New York: Oxford University Press).

IFAD (2003), *Enabling the Rural Poor to Overcome Poverty*, Annual Report (New York: Oxford University Press).

IFAD (2009), 'International day of Rural Women: IFAD pledges to "do something extra" through the MDG3 Torch Campaign'. Available at: http://www.ifad.org. Accessed November 2010.

IFAD (2011), *Rural Poverty Report 2011: New Realities, New Challenges, New Opportunities for Tomorrow's Generation* (Rome: Quintily Print).

IFPRI (1998), 'Fostering global well-being: a new paradigm to revitalize agricultural development'. In Bathrick, D. (ed.) *A 2020 Vision for Food, Agriculture, and the Environment*. Brief 54 (Washington, DC: IFPRI).

IFPRI (2008), 'Sustaining and accelerating Africa's agricultural growth recovery in the context of changing global prices'. *Policy Brief 9.*

IFPRI (2011), *Global Hunger Index: The Challenge of Hunger Taming Price Spikes and Excessive Food Price Volatility* (Washington, DC, Bonn, Dublin: IFPRI).

Iliffe, J. (1979), *A Modern History of Tanganika* (Cambridge: Cambridge University Press).

ILO (1981), 'Women, technology, and the development processes'. In Dauber, R., and Cain, M. L. (eds) *Women and Technology in Developing Countries* (Boulder, Co: Westview).

ILO (2003), 'Decent work in agriculture'. *Symposium on Decent Work in Agriculture.* Organized by the ILO Bureau for Workers Activities, 11–18 September 2003, Geneva.

ILO (2006), *Gender Equality and Decent Work: Selected ILO Conventions and Recommendations Promoting Gender Equality*, Report (Geneva: ILO).

ILO (2011), 'Labour statistics for rural development'. ILO initiative to compile rural labour statistics in the context of national development and decent work (Geneva: ILO Department of Statistics).

Irish Times (8 October 2010), 'Large farmers face limit on subsidies if EU plan adopted'. *Home News* (Dublin: Irish Times).

Jackelen, H. R., and Rhyne, E. (1991), 'Toward a more market oriented approach to credit and savings for the poor'. *Small Enterprises Development* 4(2): 1–20.

Johnson, S., and Rogaly, B. (1997), *Microfinance and Poverty Reduction* (UK and Ireland: Oxfam).

Johnston, D. (1997), 'Migration and poverty in Lesotho: a case study of female farm laborers'. *PhD Thesis*. University of London.

Josling, T. (2009), 'Western Europe'. In Anderson, K. (ed.) *Distortions to Agricultural Incentives: A Global Perspective 1951–2007* (Washington, DC: World Bank).

Kabeer, N. (1988), 'Monitoring poverty as if gender mattered: a methodology for rural Bangladesh'. *Discussion Paper 255* (Brighton: Institute of Development Studies).

Kanbur, R., and Lusting, N. (1999), 'Why is inequality back on the agenda?' *The Annual Conference on Development Economics* (Washington, DC: World Bank).

Kaosa-ard, M., and Rerkasem, B. (2000), 'The growth and sustainability of agriculture in Asia'. In *Rural Asia: Beyond the Green Revolution*. Appendix 3 (Manila: Asian Development Bank).

Kaplinsky, R., McCormick, D., and Morris, M. (2007), 'The impact of China on sub-Saharan Africa'. *Working Paper 291* (Brighton: IDS).

Karl, M. (2009), 'Inseparable: the crucial role of women in food security: whatever happened to the pledges of world leaders to reduce the number of hungry in the world?' *Women in Action*: 1–11.

Keen, D. (1994), *The Benefits of Famine: A Political Economy of Famine and Relief in South Western Sudan, 1981–1989* (Princeton, NJ: Princeton University Press).

Kevane, M. (1996), 'Agrarian structure and agricultural practice: typology and application to western Sudan'. *American Journal of Agricultural Economics* 78(1): 231–45.

Killick, A., Kydd, J., and Pulton, C. (2000), 'The rural poor and the wider economy: the problem of market access'. Thematic paper for IFAD's *Rural Poverty Report 2001: The Challenge of Ending Rural Poverty* (Rome: IFAD).

Kirkpatrick, C. (2006), 'Trade and sustainable development: assessing the impact of WTO negotiations on developing countries'. In Bne Saad, M., and Leen, M. (eds) *Trade, Aid and Development: Essays in Honour of Helen O'Neill* (Dublin: UCD Press).

Koc, M., Macrae, R., Mougeout, L. J. A., and Welsh, J. (2010), 'Introduction: food security is a global concern'. *International Development Research*. Doc(s) 17 of 34, IDRC. Available at: http://www.idrc.ca/en/ev-30581-201-1-Do_TOPIC.html. Accessed June 2010.

Kochar, A. (1997), 'Smoothing consumption by smoothing income: hours of work response to idiosyncratic agricultural shocks in India'. *Review of Economics and Statistics* 81(1): 51–61.

Kracht, U. (ed.) (2005), *Whose Right to Food? Vulnerable Groups and the Hungry Poor* (Rome: FAO).

Krueger, A. M., Schiff, M., and Valdès, A. (1991), *The Political Economy of Agricultural Pricing Policy. Volume 2: Asia* (Baltimore, MD: Johns Hopkins University Press. For the World Bank).

Kumar, B. (1990), 'Ethiopian famines 1971–1985: a case study'. In Drèze, J., and Sen, A. (eds) *The Political Economy of Hunger. Volume 2: Famine Prevention* (Oxford: Clarendon Press).

Lahiff, E., Borras, S. M. Jr., and Kay, C. (2007), 'Market-led agrarian reform: policies, performance and prospects'. *Third World Quarterly* 28(8): 1411–36.

Lang, T., and Heasman, M. (2004), *Food Wars: The Global Battle for Mouths, Minds and Markets* (London: Earthscan).

Lastarria, C. S. (2006), 'Feminisation of agriculture: trends and driving forces'. *Document*. Rimisp-Latin American Centre for Rural development. Available at: http://www.idrc.ca. Accessed November 2010.

Lautze, S., and Maxwell, D. (2007), 'Why do famines persist in the Horn of Africa? Ethiopia, 1999–2003'. In Devereux, S. (ed.) *The New famines: Why Famines Persist in an Era of Globalisation* (New York: Routledge).

Lautze, S., and Raven-Roberts, A. (2004), 'Famine (again) in Ethiopia?' *Humanitarian Exchange Magazine*. Humanitarian Practice Network. Available at: http://www.odihpn.org. Accessed March 2011.

Le Magadoux, A. (1995), *Development Policy and Strategy for the Benefit of Rural Women*. FAO Study (Rome: FAO).

Leathers, H. D., and Foster, P. (eds) (2004), *The World Food Problem: Tackling the Causes of Undernutrition in the Third World*. (UK: Lynne Rienner Publishers).

Ledgerwood, J. (1999), *Sustainable Banking with the Poor: An Institutional and Financial Perspective. Microfinance Handbook* (Washington, DC: World Bank).

Ledgerwood, J., and White, V. (2006), *Transforming Microfinance Institutions: Providing Full Financial Services to the Poor* (Washington, DC: World Bank).

Lemaux, P. G. (2009), 'Genetically engineered plants and foods: a scientist's analysis of the issues (Part II)'. In *The Annual Review of Plant Biology*. Department of Plant and Microbial Biology, University of California. Available at: http://www.annualreviews.org/doi/abs/10.1146/annurev.arplant.043008.092013. Accessed March 2011.

Ligon, E. (2008), 'Notes on the farm-household model'. *Lectures*. 21 October 2008. Available at: http://are.berkeley.edu/courses/ARE251/fall2008/Lectures/farm-household_model.pdf. Accessed July 2011.

Lin, J. (2008), 'Preparing for the next global food price crisis'. *Round Table* (Washington, DC: World Bank).

Lipton, M. (1968), 'The theory of the optimizing peasant'. *Journal of Development Studies* 4(3): 321–51.

Lipton, M. (1969), 'Forward from personism'. *Bulletin* 2(2): 11–18 (Sussex: Institute of Development Studies).

Lipton, M. (1974), 'Towards a Theory of Land Reform'. In Lehmann, D. (ed.) *Agrarian Reform and Agrarian Reformism: Studies in Peru, Chile, China and India* (London: Faber and Faber).

Lipton, M. (2004), 'Approaches to rural poverty alleviation in developing Asia: role of water resources'. Plenary address at the regional Workshop and Policy Roundtable *Pro-poor Intervention Strategies in Irrigated Agriculture in Asia*, 21–27 August 2004 (Colombo: International Water Management Institute). Available at: http://www.sussex.ac.uk/Units/PRU/iwmi_irrigation.pdf. Accessed September 2012.

Lipton, M. (2005), 'The family farm in a globalising world: the role of crop science in alleviating poverty'. *2020 Discussion Papers* 40 (June) (Washington, DC: IFPRI).

Lipton, M., and Lichfield, F. J. M. (2003), 'The effect of irrigation on poverty'. *Water Policy* (5): 411–27.

Lovell, C. J., Batchelor, C. H., Waughray, D. K., Semple, A. J., Mazhangara, E., Mtetwa, G., Mura, M. W., Dube, T., Thompson, D. M., Chilton, P. G., Macdonald, D. M. J., Conyers, D., and Mugweni, O. (1996), 'Small-scale irrigation using collector wells pilot project – Zimbabwe'. *Final Report.* ODA 95/14 (Wallingford: Institute of Hydrology).

MacDonald, N. (2004), 'Genetically modified organisms: the last thing the developing world needs'. *Global Envision.* Available at: http://globalenvision. org/library/6/561. Accessed September 2011.

Mackie, A. B. (1974), 'International dimension of agricultural prices'. *Southern Journal of Agricultural Economics* 11(22): 11–21.

Madeley, J. (2002), *Food for All: The Need for a New Agriculture* (London: Zed Books).

Malthus, T. R. (1872), *An Essay on the Principle of Population.* (London: Murray).

Manji, A. (2006), *The Politics of Land Reform in Africa* (London: Zed Books).

Matin, I., Hulme, D., and Rutherford, S. (1999), 'Financial services for the poor and poorest: deepening understanding to improve provision'. *Finance and Development Working Paper 9.* Institute of Development Policy and Management (IDPM), University of Manchester. Available at: http://www.idpm.man.ac.uk. Accessed July 2010.

Matthews, A. (2006), 'The development Box in the WTO agreement on agriculture'. In Bne Saad, M., and Leen, M. (eds) *Trade, Aid and Development: Essays in Honour of Helen O'Neill* (Dublin: UCD Press).

Maxwell, S. (2001), 'The evolution of thinking about food security'. In Devereux, S. and Maxwell, S. (eds) *Food Security in Sub-Saharan Africa* (London: ITDG).

Maxwell, S., and Frankenberger, T. R. (1992), *Household Food security: Concept, Indicators, Measurements: A Technical Review* (London: UNICEF, IFAD).

Maxwell, S., and Slater, R. (2003), 'Food policy old and new'. In Maxwell, S., and Slater, R. (eds) *Food Policy Old and New* (London: Blackwell Publishing).

Mayer, J. (1975), 'Management of famine relief'. *Science* 188(4188): 571–7.

McKinnon, R. I. (1973), *Money and Capital in Economic Development* (Washington, DC: Brookings Institution).

McMichael, P. (2006), 'Peasant prospects in the neoliberal age'. *New Political Economy* XI(3): 401–18.

McNeill, D. (1998), 'Water as an economic good'. *Natural Resources Forum* 22(4): 251–61.

Mduma, J. K., Wobst, P. (2005), 'Determinants of rural labour market participation in Tanzania'. *African Studies Quarterly.* Available at: http://www.africa.ufl.edu/ asq/v8/v8i2a2.htm. Accessed May 2011.

Meillassoux, C. (1997), *Femmes, Greniers, Capitaux* (Paris: Maspéro).

Mellor, J. W. (1986), 'Agriculture on the road to industrialisation'. In Lewis, J. P., and Kallab, V. (eds) *Development Strategies Reconsidered* (Washington, DC: Overseas Development Council).

Mellor, J. W. (1990), 'Global food balances and food security'. In Eicher, C. K., and Staatz, J. M. (eds) *Agricultural Development in the Third World.* 2nd edition (Baltimore, MD: Johns Hopkins University Press).

Mendola, M. (2007), 'Farm household production theories: a review of "Institutional" and "Behavioural" Responses'. *Asian Development Review* 24(1): 41–68.

Millennium Ecosystem Assessment (2005), *Current State and Trends Assessments* (Washington, DC: Island Press).

Mkodzongi, G. (2010), 'Zimbabwe's land reform is common sense'. *Issue 473.* Available at: http://Pambazuka.org/en/category/features/62917. Accessed January 2012.

Morduch, J. (1995), 'Income smoothing and consumption smoothing'. *Journal of Economic Perspectives* 9(3): 103–14.

Moser, C. (1989), 'Gender planning in the third world: meeting practical and strategic gender needs'. *World Development* 17(11): 1791–1825.

Movik, S., and Mehta, L. (2009), 'Going with the flow? Directions of innovation in the water and sanitation domain'. *Working Papers*. Available at STEPS Centre: http://www.steps-centre.org. Accessed March 2011.

Moyo, S. (2008), *African Land Questions, Agrarian Transitions and the State: Contradictions of Neoliberal Land Reforms* (Dakar: CODESRIA Green Book).

Musembi, C. N. (2007), 'De Soto and land relations in rural Africa: breathing life into dead theories about property rights'. *Third World Quarterly* 28: 1451–78.

Ndulu, B. S. A., O'Connell, R. H., Collier, P., Soludo, C. C., Azam, J. P., Fosu, A. K., Gunning, J. W., and Niinkeu, D. (2008), *The Political Economy of Economic Growth in Africa, 1961–2000* (Cambridge and New York: Cambridge University Press).

Nelson, M., and Maredia, M. K. (2007), 'International agricultural research as a source of environmental impacts: challenges and possibilities'. *Journal of Environmental Assessment Policy and Management* 9(1): 101–19.

New York Times (8 March 2012), 'Spikes in food prices predicted for 2013'. *Article* (New York: *The New York Times*).

Ngom, P., and Clark, S. (2003), *Adult Mortality in the Era of HIV/AIDS: Sub-Saharan Africa* (New York: Population Division, United Nations).

Nuffield Trust (2004), 'Nutrigenomics'. *Seminar*. 5 February 2004 (London: Nuffield Trust).

Nutrigenomics (2010), 'Nutrition genomics'. Center of Excellence for Nutritional Genomics (CENG). *Research* (Davis: the University of California). Available at Nutrigenomics.ucdavis.edu. Accessed March 2011.

OECD (2001), *Agricultural Policies in OECD Countries: Monitoring and Evaluation* (Paris: OECD).

OECD (2006), 'Agricultural market impacts of future growth in the production of biofuels'. Avaiable at: http://www.oecd.org/dataoecd/58/62/36074135.pdf. Accessed March 2012.

OECD (2009), 'Development aid at its highest level ever in 2008', *News Release* 31 March 2009. Available at: http:/www.oecd.org/documentprint /0,3455,en_2649 _42458595_1_1_1_1_1,00.html. Accessed March 2012.

ÓGráda, C. (2009), *Famine: A Short History* (Princeton and Oxford: Princeton University Press).

Oshaug, A. (1985), 'The composite concept of food security: introducing nutritional considerations into rural development programmes with focus on agriculture'. *Report No. 1: A Theoretical Contribution* (Oslo: Institute for Nutrition Research, University of Oslo).

Osmani, S. R. (2003), 'Exploring the employment nexus: topics in employment and poverty'. *Monograph* (Geneva: International Labour Office).

Osmani, S. R. (2006), 'Exploring the employment nexus: the analytics of pro-poor growth'. In Islam, R. (ed.) *Fighting Poverty: The Development–Employment Link*. ILO (London: Lynne Rienner).

Otsuka, K., and Quisumbing, A. R. (2001), 'Land rights and natural resources management in the transition to individual ownership: case studies from Ghana and Indonesia'. In de Janvry, A., Platteau, J. P., Gordillo, G., and Sadpulet, E.

(eds) *Access to Land, Rural Poverty and Public Action* (New York: Oxford University Press).

Pachauri, R. K., and Reisinger, A. (eds) (2007), *Climate Change 2007: Synthesis Report*. (Geneva: IPCC).

Payne, G. (2002), *Land, Rights and Innovation: Improving Tenure Security for the Urban Poor* (London: ITDG).

Perry, C. J., Rock, M., and Seckler, D. (1997), 'Water as an economic good: a solution, or a problem?' *Research Report* 14 (Colombo: International Water Management Institute).

Pinckney, T. C., and Kimuyu, P. K. (1999), 'Land tenure reform in East Africa: good, bad or unimportant?' *Journal of African Economics* 3(1): 1–26.

Política Y Gobierno (2010), 'More harm than good? The two faces of genetically modified agriculture'. *Universal Knowledge at Wharton*. Available at: http://www.universia.net/GM/. Accessed September 2010.

Pretty, J. (2002), *Agriculture* (London: Earthscan).

Pringle, P. (2003), *Food Inc. Mendel to Monsanto: The Promises and Perils of the Biotech Harvest* (New York: Simon and Schuster).

Puri, S., and Arnold, G. (2002), 'Challenges to management of transboundary aquifers: the ISARM programme'. *Second International Conference on Sustainable Management of Transboundary Waters in Europe*. 21–24 April 2002, Miedzyzdroje, Poland. Available at: www.unece.org/env/water/meetings/conf2/3-transboundaryaquifers_puri.pdf. Accessed May 2006.

Ranck, J. (1997), 'Women at the centre: Grameen Bank borrowers after one decade'. *The Journal of Developing Area* 31(2): 31.

Rangasami, A. (1985), 'Failure of exchange entitlements' theory of famine: a response'. *Economic and Political Weekly* XX(20): 21.

Rangasami, A. (1993), 'The masking of famine: the role of the bureaucracy'. In Floud, J., and Rangasami, A. (eds) *Famine and Society* (New Delhi: Indian Law Institute).

Ravallion, M. (1987a), 'Famines and economies'. *Policy Research Working Paper* 1693 (Washington, DC: World Bank).

Ravallion, M. (1987b), *Markets and Famines* (Oxford: Clarendon).

Reardon, T. (1998), 'Rural non-farm income in developing countries'. Paper prepared for FAO. Available at: http://siteresources.worldbank.org/DEC/Resources/ruralNonfarmIncomeinDevegCountries.pdf. Accessed July 2011.

Remenyi, J. (1997), 'Microfinance: a panacea for poverty?' *Development Research Briefings* 2 (Dublin: CDS UCD).

Remenyi, J. (2000), 'Transition into poverty: the Mongolian experience, 1981–95'. In Holger, H., and Boxill, I. (eds) *The End of the 'Asian Model'*? (Amsterdam: John Benjamins).

Remenyi, J. (2006), 'Globalising credit: prospects for microfinance institutions and non-governmental development organisations' strategic alliances'. In Bne Saad, M., and Leen, M. (eds) *Trade, Aid and Development: Essays in Honour of Helen O'Neill* (Dublin: UCD Press).

Remenyi, J., and Quinons, B. (2000), *Microfinance and Poverty Alleviation* (London: Pinter).

Reutlinger, S. (1982), 'Policies for food security in food importing developing countries'. In Chisholm, A. H., and Tyers, R. (eds) *Food Security: Theory, Policy and Perspectives from Asia and the Pacific Rim* (Massachusetts: Lexington Books).

Reutlinger, S. (1985), 'Policy options for food security'. *Discussion Paper*. Report ARU 44, Agriculture and Rural Development Department, Research Unit (Washington, DC: World Bank).

Reutlinger, S., and Knapp, K. (1980), 'Food security in food deficit countries'. *World Bank Staff Working Paper* 393 (Washington, DC: World Bank).

Rijsberman, F. (2004), 'The Water Challenge'. *Copenhagen Consensus Challenge Paper*. Environmental Assessment Institute. Available at: www.copenhagenconsensnsus.com. Accessed November 2011.

Roberston, J. (1979), *The Sane Alternative* (St Paul, MN: River Basin Publishing).

Robinson, M. (2001), *The Microfinance Revolution* (Washington, DC: World Bank).

Rosegrant, M. W., Paisner, S., and Witcover, J. (2001), *2020 Global Food Outlook: Trends, Alternatives, and Choices* (Washington, DC: International Food Policy Research).

Rosegrant, M. W., and Cline, S. A. (2003), 'Global food security: challenges and policies'. *Science* 302(12): 1911–19.

Rubin, O. (2009), 'The merit of democracy in famine protection: fact or fallacy?' *European Journal of Development Research* 21(5): 691–717.

Sachs, J. (2005), *The End of Poverty: How We Can Make it Happen in Our Lifetime* (UK: Penguin Books).

Sadoff, C. W., and David, G. (2002), 'Beyond the river: the benefits of cooperation on international rivers'. *Water Policy* 4(5): 381–403.

Sarap, K. (1990), 'Factors affecting small farmers' access to institutional credit in rural Orissa, India'. *Development and Change* 21(2): 281–307.

Save the Children (2002), 'Food security: freedom from hunger and the fear of starvation'. *Research Report*. Available at: http://www.savethechildren.org/food-security.shtml. Accessed August 2011.

Scanlan, S. (2004), 'Women, food security, and development in less-industrialised societies: contributions and challenges for the new century'. *World Development* 32(11): 1801–29.

Schultz, T. W. (1953), *The Economic Organisation of Agriculture* (New York: McGraw-Hill).

Schultz, T. W. (1964), *Transforming Traditional Agriculture* (New Haven: Yale University Press).

Schultz, T. W. (1978), *Distortions of Agricultural Incentives* (Bloomington: Indiana University Press).

Sebastian, K. (2007), 'GIS/spatial analysis contribution to 2008 WDR: technical notes on data and methodologies'. *Background Paper* for World Bank Report 2007.

Sen, A. (1981), *Poverty and Famine: An Essay on Entitlement and Deprivation* (Oxford: Clarendon Press).

Sen, A. (1982), 'The food problem: theory and policy'. *Third World Quarterly* 4(3): 447–59.

Sen, A. (1985), 'Points on food, cash and entitlements'. *Mimeo* (Oxford: Oxford University Press).

Sen, A. (1999), *Democracy as Freedom* (Oxford: Oxford University Press).

Sen, A., and Derzey, J. (1995), *The Political Economy of Hunger* (Oxford: Oxford University Press).

Shaw, J. (2007), *World Food Security: A History Since 1945* (New York: Palgrave Macmillan).

Shaw, E. S. (1973), *Financial Deepening in Economic Development* (New York: Oxford University Press).

Siamwalla, A., and Valdes, A. (1980), 'Food insecurity in developing countries'. *Food Policy* 5(4): 251–72.

Simon, J. (1996), *The Ultimate Resource II: People, Materials, and Environment* (Oxford: Princeton University Press).

Sitorus, S. (2009), 'Space, scale and territorialisation in integrated water resources management: the case of Indonesia'. *Unpublished PhD thesis* (Norwich: University of East Anglia).

Smith, J., and Wallerstein, I. (1992), *Creating and Transforming Households: The Constraints of the World Economy* (Cambridge: Cambridge University Press).

Smith, L., and Haddad, L. (1999), 'Expanding child malnutrition in developing countries: a cross country analysis'. *Discussion Paper* 60 (Washington, DC: IFPRI).

Solans, R., Bosch, J. A., and Galofre, P. (2001), 'Salivary and lacrimal gland dysfunction (sicca syndrome) after radioiodine therapy'. Journal of Nuclear Medicine (5): 738–43.

Steinberg, M., Johnson, M. S., Schierhout, G., and Ndewa, D. (2002), 'Hitting home: how households cope with the impact of the HIV/AIDS epidemic'. *A Survey of Households Affected by HIV/AIDS in South Africa* (Menlo Park, CA: The Henry Kaiser Family Foundation).

Stern, N. (2007), *The Economics of Climate Change: The Stern Review* (Cambridge: Cambridge University Press).

Stevens, R., and Jabara, C. L. (1988), *Agricultural Development Principles: Economic Theory and Empirical Evidence* (London: Johns Hopkins University Press).

Taylor, J. E., and Adelman, I. (2003), 'Agricultural household models: genesis, evolution and extensions'. *Review of Economics of the Household* 1(1): 31–58.

Timmer, C. P. (2005), 'Agriculture and pro-poor growth: an Asian perspective'. *Working Paper* 63. Centre for Global Development.

Todd, H. (1996), *Women at the Centre: Grameen Bank Borrowers after One Decade.* (Boulder, CO: Westview Press).

Toulmin, C. (14 March 2005), 'The new tragedy of the commons'. *New Statesman.*

Tovar, L. G., Cruz, MAG., Schwentesius, R., and Nelson, E. (1987) 'Towards sustainable development'. Chapter. 2 in *Our Common Future.* World Commission on the Environment (Oxford: Oxford University Press).

Trostle, R. (2008), *Global Agricultural Supply and Demand: Factors Contributing to the Recent Increase in Food Commodity Prices* (Washington, DC: US Department of Agriculture Economic Research Service).

UN (1975), *Report of the World Food Conference.* Rome 5–16 November 1974, Document E/CONF. 62/20.

UN (1993), 'Declaration and programme of action'. *World Conference on Human Rights.* 14–25 June 1993 (Vienna: UN Human Right Commission).

UN (1995), 'Beijing declaration and platform for action'. *Policy Document.* Fourth World Conference on Women. Available at: http://www.un.org/womenwatch/daw/Beijing/platform/. Accessed November 2011.

UN (1997), *Mainstreaming the Gender Perspective into All Policies and Programmes in the United Nations.* Report of the Secretary-General (New York: UN).

UN (2007), *World Urbanisation Prospects: The 2007 Revision Population Database.* Available at: http://esa.un.org/unup. Accessed August 2011.

UN (2010), *The World's Women 2010.* Report of the United Nations Department of Economic and Social Affairs (New York: Oxford University Press).

UN (2011), *Progress of the World's Women 2011–2012: In Pursuit of Justice*. UN Women Entity for Gender Equality and the Empowerment of Women. Available at: http://progress.unwomen.org. Accessed September 2011.

UN Habitat (2001), *The State of the World's Cities 2001* (Nairobi: UN Habitat).

UNDP (2006), *Beyond Scarcity: Power, Poverty and Global Water Crisis*. *Human Development Report* (New York: Oxford University Press).

UNEP and AMCEN (2002), *Africa Environment Outlook: Past, Present and Future Perspectives*. United National Environment Programme and African Ministerial Conference on the Environment. 6 August 2002.

UNICEF (2007), *State of the World's Children* (Paris: UNICEF).

Ureta, M. (2002), 'Rural labour markets in Nicaragua'. Background paper for World Bank Report 25115-NI: *Nicaragua: Promoting Competitiveness and Stimulating Broad-based Growth in Agriculture* (Washington, DC: World Bank).

USAID (1992), *Policy Determination: Definition of Food Security*. 13 April 1992. (Washington, DC: USAID).

USAID (2006), *Household Food Security Access Scale for Measurement of Food Access: Indicator Guide, Version 2, Food and Nutrition Technical Assistance*. (Washington, DC: USAID).

US Department of Energy (2010), GM products: benefits and controversies. *Human Genome Project Information*. Available at: http://www.genomweb.com/newsletter/informatics. Accessed September 2011.

Valdé, A., Foster, W., Anríquez, G., Azzarri, C., Covarrubias, K., Davis, B., DiGiuseppe, S., Essam, T., Hertz, T., de la, A. P., Quiñones, E., Stamoulis, K., Winters, P., and Zezza, A. (2008), 'A profile of the rural poor'. *Background Paper* for the IFAD Poverty Report 2011.

Vanhaute, E. (2008), 'The end of peasantries? Rethinking the role of peasantries'. *World Historical View. Review*. xxxi(39): 59.

Visvader, H., and Burton, I. (1974), *Natural Hazards and Hazard Policy in Canada and the US* (New York: Oxford University Press).

von Braun, J. (2003), 'Agricultural economics and distributional effects'. *Agricultural Economics* 32(1): 1–20.

von Braun, J., Gultai, A., and Orden, D. (2004), 'Making agricultural Trade liberalization work for the poor'. *Address* delivered by von Braun, Director, IFPRI at the WTO Public Symposium 'Multilateralism at a Crossroads'. Geneva, 25 May 2004.

von Braun, J., and Kennedy, E. (1994), *Agricultural Commercialisation, Economic Development, and Nutrition* (Baltimore, MD: Johns Hopkins University Press. For IFPRI).

von Braun, J., Teklu, T., and Webb, P. (1999), *Famine in Africa: Causes, Responses, and Prevention* (Baltimore, MD: Johns Hopkins University Press).

Walker, P. (1989), *Famine Early Warning Systems: Victims and Destitution* (London: Earthscan).

Walker, T., and Jodha, N. (1986), 'How small farmers adapt to risk'. In Hazell, P., Pomareda, C., and Valdez, A. (eds) *Crop Insurance for Agricultural Development* (Baltimore, MD: Johns Hopkins University Press).

Warriner, D. (1969), *Land Reform in Principle and Practice* (Oxford: Clarendon Press).

Warner, J., Wester, P., and Bolding, J. A. (2008), 'Going with the flow: river basins as the natural units for water management. *Water Policy* 10 (Supplement 2): 121–38.

Watkins, K. (1991), 'Agriculture and food security in the GATT Uruguay Round'. *Review of African Political Economy* 18(50): 31–50.

Watts, M. (1983), *Silent Violence: Food, Famine and Peasantry in Northern Nigeria* (Berkeley: University of California Press).

Webb, P., Gerald, J., and Friedman, D. R. (2005), 'Water and food security in developing countries: major challenges for the 21st Century'. *Discussion Paper 6.* Food Policy and Applied Nutrition Programme (Boston, MA: Tufts University).

Wegner, L. (2006), 'Microfinance: how bankers could buy back their soul'. *Policy Insights* 31 (Paris: OECD Development Centre).

WFP (World Food Programme) (2009), *World Food Programme Annual Report: Review of 2008* (Rome: WFP).

Whitehead, A. (2008), 'The gendered impacts of liberalisation policies on African agricultural economics and rural livelihoods'. In Razavi, S. (ed.) *The Gender Impacts of Liberalisation: Towards Embedded Liberalism?* (New York: Routledge).

Whittington, D., Lauria, D., and Mu, X. (1991), 'A study of water vending and willingness to pay for water in Onitsha, Nigeria'. *World Development* 19(2/3): 171–98.

WHO (2002), 'Diet, nutrition and the prevention of chronic diseases'. *Technical Report* 916 (Geneva: WHO).

WHO (2009), *World Health Organisation Report* (Geneva: WHO).

Wiggins, E. S., and Deshingkar, P. (2007), 'Rural employment and migration: in search of decent work, new thinking on rural employment is needed to create more and better rural jobs'. *Briefing Paper* (London: ODI).

Wiggins, E. S., and Hazell, P. B. R. (2008), 'Access to rural non-farm employment and enterprise development'. Background paper for the IFAD *Rural Poverty Report* 2011.

Wikipedia (2012a), *The Global Financial Crisis.* www.wikipedia.org.

Wikipedia (2012b), *Purdah: definition.* www.wikipedia.org.

Wild, L., and Mepham, D. (2006), *The New Sinosphere: China in Africa.* (UK: Institute for Public Policy Research).

Windfuhr, M., and Jonsén, J. (2005), *Food Sovereignty: Towards Democracy in Localised Food Systems* (Warwickshire: ITDG Publishing).

Wolf, E. R. (1966), *Peasants* (Englewood Cliffs, NJ: Prentice-Hall).

World Bank (1974), *Land Reform* (Washington, DC: World Bank).

World Bank (1975), 'Agricultural credit'. *Sector Policy Paper* (Washington, DC: World Bank).

World Bank (1985), 'Ensuring food security in the developing world: issues and options'. Reutlinger, S., Jack, van H., and Pellekaan, H. (eds) (Washington DC: World Bank).

World Bank (1986), *Poverty and Hunger: Issues and Options for Food Security in Developing Countries* (Washington, DC: World Bank).

World Bank (1989), *World Development Report 1989: Financial Systems and Development* (New York: Oxford University Press).

World Bank (1992), *Development and Environment: World Development Report* (Washington, DC: World Bank).

World Bank (1993), *Poverty Reduction Handbook* (Washington, DC: World Bank).

World Bank (2001), *Engendering Development through Gender Equality in Rights, Resources, and Voice* (Washington, DC: World Bank).

World Bank (2003), *Rural Poverty Alleviation in Brazil: Toward an Integrated Strategy* (Washington, DC: World Bank).

World Bank (2005), 'Pakistan water economy: running dry', *Report* 34081-PK. South Asia Region, Agriculture and Rural Development Unit (Washington, DC: World Bank).

World Bank (2007), *World Development Report 2007–2008: Agriculture for Development* (Washington, DC: World Bank).

World Bank (2008), *Double Jeopardy: Responding to High Food and Fuel Prices.* G8 Hakkaido-Tokyo Summit (Japan: World Bank).

World Bank (2010), *World Development Indicators* (Washington, DC: World Bank).

World Bank, FAO and IFAD (2009), *Gender in Agriculture: Source Book* (Washington, DC: World Bank).

World Bank and the World Conservation Union (IUCN) (2000) *Dams and Development: A New Framework for Decision-Making.* The Report of the World Commission on Dams (London: Earthscan).

World Resources Institute (2003), *World Resources 2001–2004*, (Washington, DC: World Resources Institute).

Yaron, J. (1994), 'What makes rural finance institutions successful?' *The World Bank Research Observer* 9(1) (Washington, DC: World Bank).

Yaron, J., Benjamin, M. P. Jr., and Piprek, G. L. (2007), 'Rural finance: issues, design, and best practices, environmentally and socially sustainable development'. *Monographs.* No. 14. Available at: http//www.worldbank.org/infoshop. Accessed July 2011.

Yunus, M. (2009), *Banker to the Poor: Micro-lending and the Battle Against World Poverty.* Available at: http://www.grameen-info.org/bank/WhatisMicrocredit. htm. Accessed March 2012.

Zimmerman, F., and Carter, M. R. (2003), 'Asset smoothing, consumption smoothing and dynamic persistence of inequality under risk and subsistence constraints'. *Journal of Development Economics* 71(2): 231–60.

Index

Compiled by Sue Carlton

Page numbers followed by 'n' refer to the notes